HERMANN HUNGER / REGINE PRUZSINSZKY (EDS.)

MESOPOTAMIAN DARK AGE REVISITED

ÖSTERREICHISCHE AKADEMIE DER WISSENSCHAFTEN
DENKSCHRIFTEN DER GESAMTAKADEMIE, BAND XXXII

Contributions to the Chronology of the Eastern Mediterranean

Edited by Manfred Bietak
and Hermann Hunger

Volume VI

VERLAG DER ÖSTERREICHISCHEN AKADEMIE DER WISSENSCHAFTEN
WIEN 2004

ÖSTERREICHISCHE AKADEMIE DER WISSENSCHAFTEN
DENKSCHRIFTEN DER GESAMTAKADEMIE, BAND XXXII

MESOPOTAMIAN DARK AGE REVISITED

Proceedings of an International Conference of SCIEM 2000
(Vienna 8th–9th November 2002)

Edited
by

HERMANN HUNGER and REGINE PRUZSINSZKY

VERLAG DER ÖSTERREICHISCHEN AKADEMIE DER WISSENSCHAFTEN
WIEN 2004

Vorgelegt von w. M. HERMANN HUNGER in der Sitzung am 8. Oktober 2003

Spezialforschungsbereich SCIEM 2000
„Die Synchronisierung der Hochkulturen im östlichen Mittelmeerraum
im 2. Jahrtausend v. Chr."
der Österreichischen Akademie der Wissenschaften
beim Fonds zur Förderung der wissenschaftlichen Forschung

Special Research Programme SCIEM 2000
"The Synchronisation of Civilisations in the Eastern Mediterranean
in the Second Millennium B.C."
of the Austrian Academy of Sciences
at the Austrian Science Fund

British Library Cataloguing in Publication data.
A Catalogue record of this book is available from the British Library.

Umschlagbild: Dominique Collon, Išar-Lim, in: MARI, Annales de Recherches Interdisciplinaires 5,
Éditions Recherche sur les Civilisations, Paris 1987, Abbildung auf Seite 148.

Die verwendete Papiersorte ist aus chlorfrei gebleichtem Zellstoff hergestellt,
frei von säurebildenden Bestandteilen und alterungsbeständig.

ISBN 3-7001-3278-6

Grafik, Satz, Layout: Angela Schwab
Umschlagentwurf: Hannes Weinberger
Druck: Druckerei Ferdinand Berger & Söhne GesmbH, Horn
Printed and bound in Austria

Contents

Preface

Within the scope of the Austrian special research programme SCIEM 2000 ("Synchronisation of the Civilisations in the Eastern Mediterranean in the 2nd Millennium BC") a small conference with the title "Mesopotamian Dark Age Revisited" took place on the 8th and 9th of November 2002, which was organised by the project 1405 "Chronological Data in Mesopotamia".

SCIEM 2000's projected and primary goal is to synchronise chronologies for the 2nd millennium of the regions in the Eastern Mediterranean and to create a definite chronological framework for its history. The project "Chronological Data in Mesopotamia" focuses on information mainly deriving from written sources dealing with historical events and rulers of Mesopotamia and its surrounding areas, namely Syria, Anatolia, the Levant and Elam. By establishing reliable connections between these regions, correlating all data relevant for relative and absolute chronology and synchronising the known "facts" it is hoped to offer new insights and results in respect to chronological issues.

The aim of this conference was to bring together various colleagues specialized in chronology and to discuss (new) sources, research results presented and their compatibility with the recently proposed "New Chronology" by Gasche *et al.* 1998[1] by taking a closer look at the so-called "Dark Age" (period starting after the fall of the Babylon I Dynasty). Being aware of the numerous problems and shortcomings of the textual evidence in this respect, we still wanted to try to approach a reconstruction of chronology of the 2nd mill. BC by defining the "Dark Age" once again. In the course of this the material's overall importance for the process of historical and chronological reconstruction was presented and discussed.

Our main objective in this workshop was to evaluate sources from Mesopotamia and its so-called peripheral areas shortly before, during and slightly after the "Dark Age" and to possibly overcome and define this period of darkness by chronological means. We tried to lay an emphasis on the documentation and history of the regions adjacent to core Mesopotamia, i.e. Anatolia and Syria, concentrating mainly on philological evidence, since synchronisms disclose contacts and links are important to refine absolute chronology.

It is hoped that the conference has helped disclose valuable new links, interconnections and results concerning the understanding of Mesopotamian chronology, also judged from the angle of "peripheral areas" within Ancient Near Eastern Studies. We believe to have collected seven valuable contributions covering different aspects for chronological research in this volume, which may clearly show the abundant work still to be done in order to find reliable answers to chronological questions.

We should like to thank the Austrian Academy of Sciences for sponsoring this conference. For organisational help we thank Angela Schwab.

The Editors

---

[1] Gasche, H. *et al.* 1998, *Dating the Fall of Babylon, A Reappraisal of Second-Millennium Chronology (A Joint Ghent-Chicago-Harvard Project)*, Mesopotamian History and Environment Series II Memoirs IV 4, Ghent.

The Geography of the Slave Trade and Northern Mesopotamia in the Late Old Babylonian Period

*Frans van Koppen**

Prolegomena

The sources available for a study of the history of the later Old Babylonian period easily lend themselves to misunderstanding.[1] The historian is confronted with the disorderly remnants of a large number of contemporaneous archives, but is short of helpful texts of a narrative character. Historical research has therefore primarily focused on the corpus of year name formulae appearing in these texts, but interpretations of this corpus as signs of economic decline, limited state resources and weak performance in foreign policy are still more popular than the analysis as a body of programmatic statements aimed at communicating particular qualities of kingship. Archival texts have been used profitably to study various aspects of the state's economic and social institutions, but much work remains to be done in editing and analysing these terse and sometimes deceptive sources.

Yet, an informed political history of the late Old Babylonian state would be most useful in clarifying much of the "Mesopotamian Dark Age", but remains, in view of the present state of documentation, an unachievable goal. Nonetheless, the late Old Babylonian archival sources, deriving from a limited number of cities in the core area of the Babylonian state,[2] should play a role in discussions of this topic. Obviously, these sources are too early to inform us of events that took place after the fall of the First Dynasty of Babylon. They are neither useful as tools to establish absolute dating. In contrast, their value lies in the fact that they are the most substantial corpus of cuneiform texts from the last century before the fall of Babylon, the period when records from other regions of Mesopotamia are scarce and historical developments remain obscure. Even though archival sources mainly deal with matters of local interest, their data can sometimes be used to observe events far beyond Babylonia's borders. These observations can be linked with the exact internal chronology of the First Dynasty of Babylon and have potential relevance for matters of synchronization of cultures in the larger area of Mesopotamia and beyond.[3]

In this article we will therefore concentrate on one particular type of document that makes explicit reference to areas outside of the Baby-

* University of Leiden

[1] Abbreviations: Ad = Ammiditana, Ae = Abiešuh, Aṣ = Ammiṣaduqa, Sd = Samsuditana, Si = Samsuiluna. Text editions are cited according to the list of abbreviations in the *Chicago Assyrian Dictionary* 14 (R), Chicago, 1999. Numbers refer to the list of slave sale contracts in the appendix. I would like to thank the following institutions and persons for their help in realizing this study: the Trustees of the British Museum for permission to refer to unpublished material in their collection; Prof. B. Salje and Dr. J. Marzahn of the Vorderasiatisches Museum for the possibility to examine Old Babylonian material in the Homsy collections, where the relevant tablet VAT 718 (appendix no. 40) was identified; Prof. F. Joannès for information about the unpublished texts from Ḫarradum (KD numbers); Prof. K.A. Kitchen for comments. This study was undertaken as part of a PhD research project financed by a grant of the Nederlands Organization for Scientific Research (NWO).

[2] An exhaustive catalogue of sources published up to then is found in Pientka 1998.

[3] This contribution will make no case for any of the various proposals for the absolute date of the Ur III – Babylon I block of time. The merit of Gasche *et al.* 1998 and the following polemics is that they have effectively shown that none of the instruments applied up to now to assign absolute dates to the fall of Babylon is adequate. Until better tools are available, chronology must be based primarily on historical considerations and will for that reason remain inexact. I agree with Gasche *et al.* 1998 that archaeological arguments support a lower date than the conventional Middle Chronology, but take note of the reservations of Kühne 1999: 203 note 1 and Beckman 2000 that an Ultra-low Chronology is problematic in the light of Hittite evidence. Textual evidence about early Kassite rule over Babylon also disagrees with the Ultra-low Chronology; the correction proposed by Gasche *et al.* 1998: 88 fails to convince.

lonian state: the slave sale contract. In order to establish the value of these statements, the slave sale contract as a legal instrument and developments of law and custom concerning slavery in the course of the Old Babylonian period will be discussed first. An examination of slave trade practice and the prices of slaves will be necessary to determine whether patterns in our sample of geographical indications are significant. Finally, the implications of these data for the detection and dating of political structures outside of Babylonia will be discussed. The early history of the Mittani state and the role of a Kassite polity to the Northwest of the Babylonian core territory will then be our main concern.

Slave sale contracts

The sale of slaves was a universal phenomenon in the ancient Near East and is attested throughout the Old Babylonian period in the form of a corpus of contracts recording the acquisition of slaves. It is well known that the wording of slave sale contracts issued under Babylonian law changed over time. This can be best observed in those from Sippir, where the phrasing of contracts dating to the reign of Abiešuh and later greatly differs from that of earlier specimens. The differences between earlier and later contracts can be illustrated with the following examples:

CT 48 28 (Si 9)	TCL 1 147 (Ae h)
"One slave woman by the name of PN,	"One slave woman by the name of PN,
a carpet knotter,	an imported Subarean woman from the city of Qaṭṭarā,
from SELLER	from SELLER, the owner of the slave woman,
BUYER has bought.	BUYER has bought (...).
For her full price BUYER paid x silver.	For her full price BUYER paid x silver,
(The slave) was passed over the *bukānum*.	and placed x silver as SI.BI-payment.
His (SELLER's) heart is satisfied; the transaction is completed; they (SELLER and BUYER) swore by Šamaš, Aja, Marduk and king Samsuiluna that nobody will ever bring claim against the other."	Three days (for) investigation, one month (for) epilepsy; SELLER will be responsible for claims on her (the slave) in accordance with the royal regulation."
(Witnesses and date.)	(Witnesses and date.)
(Seal impression of SELLER.)	(Seal impression of SELLER.)

These differences were brought about by a number of independent developments. One of them is the disappearance of the *bukānum*-clause and the inclusion of a remark about the payment of an additional fee (the SI.BI-clause), which can be observed in sale contracts for all categories of objects. Another is the emergence of separate contract clauses for movable and immovable property in Northern Babylonian sale contracts. But two traits are typical for slave sale contracts only: late Old Babylonian specimens give a specific description of the sale object, and they contain a unique warranty clause.

This clause contains three separate elements. The first two fix terms for the seller's warranty against hidden defects of the slave. These defects bear upon the slave's health and status: the seller guarantees against epilepsy and against the outcome of an "investigation".[4] The third stipulates the seller's liability to answer claims on the slave.

Although these three elements always appear together, they presumably originate from different sources. Warranty against eviction was an accepted feature of common law and is stipulated in earlier sale contracts from southern cities and from Dilbat.[5] The laws of Hammurabi (¶ 279) prescribe it with regard to the sale of slaves. It is a standard element of late Old Babylonian sale contracts for movable property, where its inclusion can be traced back to a royal regulation that specified warranty for eviction of various objects of sale.[6] Guarantee against epilepsy was also traditional and recurs in the laws of Hammurabi (¶ 278) and elsewhere.[7] Guarantee against "investi-

[4] For this translation of *tebʾītum* see STOL 1993: 134–135.
[5] WILCKE 1975–76: 260.
[6] VEENHOF 1997–2000: 69–71.
[7] STOL 1993: 132–141.

gation", however, first appears in the reign of Abiešuh and must be interpreted as a legal innovation. The incorporation of these last two elements in the contract formula presumably goes back to another royal decree that stipulated requirements for the sale of slaves and concerned both traditional (epilepsy) as well as new ("investigation") liabilities.

The introduction of liability for the outcome of an "investigation" into the contract's phrasing must be linked with the simultaneous appearance of a statement concerning the origin of the slave. Both innovations indicate new regulations regarding the admissibility of countrymen as slaves.

The creation of slaves

It is well known that a number of mechanisms could turn freeborn individuals into slaves in ancient Mesopotamia. The head of a household was authorized to sell off his dependants and, under certain restrictions, the members of his family. He himself could be enslaved as a measure of punishment and could be forced into servitude as a result of insolvency for debts or in order to escape from famine. These forms of servitude could develop into full slavery. Foreigners, finally, when taken as prisoners of war or kidnapped or when sold by foreign merchants could enter Mesopotamian society as slaves.

The legal status of slaves varied according to the mechanisms that had brought them into this position. One can distinguish between chattel-slaves and debt-slaves: while both categories were characterized by the loss of personal freedom and submission to their master, only the first category could be freely traded as a commodity. When a debtor assigned property to his creditor as security for the debt, he could do so by handing over individuals who fell under his authority, like members of his family or his slaves. When the debtor defaulted, the creditor retained the pledge or was entitled to take over property of the debtor, including members of his family or other dependants. As debt-slaves they obeyed the creditor and worked for him, but the creditor could in general not sell them, since he did not hold full title: they retained the traditional right of redemption with a price amounting to the sum of the original debt. Nevertheless, the right of redemption was in real terms probably limited or else the creditor could acquire full ownership of his debt-slaves by transferring their full value to the debtor. Sale of the slave and ceding full title to the buyer were then possible.[8]

Thus enslavement of countrymen under conditions of economic hardship, in particular forfeiture for a debt, was legally possible, but was at the same time perceived as social abuse. Mesopotamian legal systems contained various laws and measures of social justice to repair this disorder, and it was, according to royal ideology, especially the duty of kings to defend the weak. The efforts of the kings of Babylon to control debt-slavery manifest themselves in various royal statements with legal purpose: while the laws of Hammurabi prescribe liberation of debt-slaves after serving the creditor for three years, and thus prevent debt-slavery to develop into a permanent condition,[9] the royal equity-decrees stipulate remission of consumptive credits and the repair of their negative consequences, such as loss of property or freedom of distressed debtors.[10]

Restrictions on slave alienation

Our knowledge about other royal measures intended to control slavery is sparse, but the development of slave sale terminology indicates that another legal innovation aimed at prohibiting sale of former freeborn citizens was implemented in the reign of Samsuiluna or his successor Abiešuh.

[8] Westbrook 1995: 1660–1662.

[9] CH ¶ 117 with Westbrook 1995: 1656–1657.

[10] The preserved texts of these equity-decrees only contain a paragraph about the release of debt-slaves from specific cities and countries (Kraus 1984: 180 ¶ 20), but it is clear that these texts only contain a selection of measures covered by the equity act. For example, the preserved texts do not discuss the effect of the act on real property sold under force of a debt, whereas restitution of such property is abundantly documented. There is therefore every reason to assume that the act of equity was intended to effectuate a nation-wide release of debt-slaves. This paragraph of the traditional text of the equity-decree was already incorporated in the exemplar published in the eighth year of Samsuiluna (Hallo 1995), and it must probably be interpreted as a fossilized text from an even earlier date. The enumerated toponyms are all known to have been integrated into the kingdom of Babylon during the fourth decade of Hammurabi's reign. It seems therefore likely that the text was originally proclaimed by this king as a social measure for the newly incorporated territories.

All slave sale contracts from this time on specify that the object sold belonged to one of the following categories:

1. House-born slaves from Babylon.[11]
2. Foreigners identified as members of particular ethnic groups or as natives of some foreign place.

Since almost all contracts[12] state that the slave in question belonged to one of these categories, we conclude that from the reign of Abiešuh onwards the sale of slaves was only then legally possible if they fell into these groups. As the seller's assertion was evidently not sufficient to ascertain the slave's background, a term of two or three days was stipulated for "investigation". This refers to some type of inquiry, presumably involving the local authorities, meant to verify the seller's statement about the status of the slave. The seller's warranty indicates that the outcome of this procedure could invalidate the sale. This implies that sale of other categories of slaves, such as freeborn citizens who had become enslaved through indebtedness or other reasons, was not permitted.

This new legal device was probably implemented by order of the king, but the historical background of such an act remains obscure.[13] Even its precise moment of introduction cannot yet be ascertained: the warranty against "investigation" and the distinctive description of the origin of the slave are present in the earliest examples of the typical late slave sale contract first attested in Abiešuh's reign. The corpus of slave sale contracts from the final decades of Samsuiluna's reign is limited, and so far no specimen to exhibit all features typical for the late contract type has come to light. But it is certainly relevant that in sale contracts from the third decade of his reign the typical description of the slave as either a house-born slave from Babylon or a foreigner first appears.

The following are the five latest slave sale contracts from Samsuiluna's reign:[14]

		description of object	*contract formula*
Si 24	CT 48 60	1 sag-ìr tur lú-su-bir$_4$^{ki} / *am-mu-wa* mu-ni	"old type"
Si 27	MHET 2/3 444	1 sag-géme *a*-x-*i* x x / *qá-du* dumu-munus-*ša*	"mixed type"
Si 27	BIN 2 80	1 sag-géme uru *ši-mu-ru-um*^{ki}	[...]
Si 28	BM 22513	1 sag-ìr ^{d}utu-[...] / sag-ìr *e*-[*la-am-tim*]	"old type"
Si 30	VAS 29 5	1 sag-géme *i-na-qá-bi-ša-ab-lu-uṭ* mu-ni / *wi-li-id* é *ša* ká-dingir-ra^{ki}	[...]

[11] For this concept see KRAUS 1984: 280–283 and HALLO 1995: 87–88.

[12] Two examples of late Old Babylonian slave sale contracts without a description of the origin of the slave are presently known (BM 16495 and VAS 16 207). Remarkably enough, for both sales we also have slightly later contracts where a statement about the origin of the slave is included (see commentary to nos. 13 and 17 in the appendix). This suggests that the production of a new sale contract was necessary to prevent an annulment of the sale. The information about the background of the slave in the new contract might then be fictitious.

[13] A couple of references have been collected in the literature. Most telling is a letter of Samsuiluna to an administrator containing a tersely formulated official ban on the acquisition of citizens of Idamaraṣ and Arrapḫa as slaves from Sutean merchants (AbB 3 1 with KLENGEL 1977: 67, KRAUS 1984: 72–74 and HALLO 1995: 86–87). This message was apparently not intended as a reply to an earlier question of the addressee, so that it can be interpreted as the publication of a royal directive. The same king describes in a royal inscription the release of civil and military prisoners from Ešnunna and Idamaraṣ (RIME 4.3.7.8 with KLENGEL 1977: 66–67). Finally, an undated legal record, probably from the same time, deals with the matter of the illegal enslavement of a citizen of Idamaraṣ. As she is a freeborn woman (dumu-munus *a-wi-lim*), her detainment by a man from Mutiabal is unlawful and must be remedied "in accordance with the (royal) regulation" (AbB 6 80 with CHARPIN 1987: 43–44, WESTBROOK 1995: 1642 and VEENHOF 1997–2000: 62). While these references bear witness to Samsuiluna's efforts to restrict the sale of citizens of specific countries for political purposes, the relation between these measures and the introduction of a new check on all slave sales merits further investigation.

[14] The slave sale contract BDHP 46 is traditionally assigned to Si 33, but as it does not exhibit any of the typical later features, its fragmentary date formula must be interpreted as an earlier year name of Samsuiluna.

Only one of these contracts, MHET 2/3 444, seems to lack information about the origin of the slave, but it exhibits a number of other traits typical for later contracts:[15] it combines the old clause "the transaction is completed, his heart is satisfied" with the provision that the seller "will forever be responsible for claims on her (*i.e.* the slave woman)" and does not include an oath formula. Furthermore, the text contains a remark about the payment of a SI.BI-fee.[16] This shows that in Sippir during the third decade of Samsuiluna's rule, contracts formulated according to the conventional pattern (CT 48 60 and BM 22513) were issued simultaneously with at least one example of a "mixed" type, where warranty for eviction (but yet without reference to the royal decree) is already mentioned.[17] As the clauses of other contracts are broken and no slave sale contracts from his fourth decade of rule have yet come to light, details about this reform are still lacking. But it seems nonetheless likely that the inclusion of information about the origin of the slave in the sale contract indicates that the slave trade had become restricted already in the second half of Samsuiluna's reign. Shortly afterwards, either in his final decade or in the early years of his successor, a royal directive was given out to formalize these restrictions by introducing the instrument of "investigation". About the same time another decree giving rules for warranty for eviction was issued, and these rulings shaped the typical wording of slave sale contracts for the rest of the Old Babylonian period.

Thus the post-Samsuiluna slave sale differs in one aspect fundamentally from earlier practice: while the seller traditionally guarantees title and quality (*i.e.* health) of the slave, the seller now also guarantees the slave's status. As a result of this, the slave sale contract came to serve two purposes: it was a tool to provide evidence for title as well as for the status of the slave. The role of the contract as evidence for title is traditional: for this purpose the seller handed over older title deeds concerning the property to the buyer, and the history of the seller's acquisition of ownership could be described when necessary. This principle is well known for real estate transactions, and the sale of slaves operated similarly: older title deeds for the same slave were kept by the new owner,[18] and the sale contract sometimes details how the seller acquired title.[19] The role of the sale contract as evidence for the slave's status, however, is new and provides us with important information about the concept of nationality and the geography of slave trade in the later Old Babylonian period.

NATIVES AND FOREIGNERS

The restriction on slave trade is of importance for the question of the geographic extent of the Babylonian state, or, more precisely, the question which population groups were protected against the sale as slaves by Babylonian law. The area in question can be roughly described as the traditional territory of the Babylonian state before the expansion accomplished in Hammurabi's

---

15 The sale clauses of MHET 2/3 444 read as follows (collated): $^{1-2}$ object ^{3} ki ^{d}utu-*ša-ta-ka-lim* $^{4-5}$ buyer ^{6} ⸢*i*⸣-*n*[*a*] ḫar [kù-babbar]-*ša* ^{7} [in]-ši-[in-s]a$_{10}$ ^{8} [šá]m-til-l[a-ni-š]è ^{9} [o] ma-na [o gín] kù-babbar na$_{4}$ ^{d}utu ^{10} [*ù* o] gín kù-babbar SI.BI ^{11} [ì]- ⸢lá-e⸣ ^{12} [inim]-bi al-til ^{13} [šà-g]a-a-ni al-du$_{10}$ ^{14} [u$_{4}$]-kúr-šè *a-na ba-aq-ri-ša* ^{15} [*i*]*z-za-az*.

16 This is the earliest attestation of the SI.BI-clause known so far; the next occurs in a contract for the transfer of a house plot from Si 31 (VAS 22 4), see WILCKE 1990: 297.

17 The clause in CT 8 43c, a slave sale from Hammurabi's 18th year, should not be interpreted as an (abnormal) early attestation for the statement of the seller's warranty (thus WILCKE 1975–76: 257 note 9 and 262), as it probably stipulates warranty provided by another person than the seller (as in the Hammurabi-time house sale contract RA 85 43 no. 12).

18 See no. 16: two sale contracts for the same slave are known, the first documenting the sale of the slave woman from A to B (YOS 13 39), the second witnessing the sale of the slave from C to the final owner Uṣriya (VAS 7 50). At least one more sale contract, for the transfer of the slave woman from B to C, is missing to complete this "chain of transmission". Both documents were found in the archive of the last buyer Uṣriya (for which see STOL 1973: 225). See also the commentary to no. 13 in the appendix.

19 For example in VAS 22 19 (date broken, reign of Sd), the sale contract for "one slave woman, a suckling child [by the name of ...], a house-born slave of Babylon, daughter of the slave woman Atkal-ana-[...], part of the dowry of Lamass[ānī?], the daughter of Ana-pāni-Na[bium-nadi]," sold by the two brothers (see CHARPIN 1985: 272). The mother of this slave girl was part of the dowry of a woman whose inheritance had been passed on to the sellers (was she their mother?).

fourth decade, in combination with the adjacent territories then incorporated.[20] It has been observed that much of this area was no longer subject to Babylonian rule after the first decade of Samsuiluna's reign,[21] but if the paucity of mention of slaves from these territories in later sale contracts is significant, then this suggests that their inhabitants were as a rule still treated as Babylonian citizens.

The occurrence of slaves from the Diyala region forms a special case: slaves from Ešnunna and other cities in the "land of Ešnunna" are solely attested in the first decade of Ammiṣaduqa. Ešnunna was normally not considered as foreign territory and the admission of persons from Ešnunna as slaves was most likely brought about by special circumstances at that time.[22]

Native house-born slaves are exclusively labelled as "house-born slave from Babylon":[23] the absence of other city names in this combination would imply that the name of the city is used to refer to the territory it controlled. This seems to be earliest attestation for the use of the name of the capital city in the sense of "Babylonia".[24]

Suḫûm, the area located along the Middle-Euphrates, was under Babylonian control from the last third of the reign of Samsuiluna onwards.[25] Slaves from Suḫûm are described as "house-born slave from Suḫûm", but also as natives of a "town in the pasture land of Suḫûm". The first term suggests that trade in slaves from Suḫûm was likewise restricted to innate slaves only, but the second shows that other slaves from Suḫûm could also be sold. Thus this area seems to have taken up an intermediate position between Babylonian domain and foreign country.

In the description of foreign slaves a number of general labels are used that are most often combined with the name of an actual city. These general labels in effect partition the geographic horizon of Mesopotamia into distinct zones: "Between-river" designates the area east of the Euphrates bend, including the Habur basin; to its eastern side arches Šubartum over the region at the northern course of the Tigris and east of this river; southeast of Šubartum lies Elam. Šubartum[26] and Elam[27] are traditional appellations for Mesopotamia's neighbours and function as ethnic terms, labelling persons as well as land. "Between-river", or "Land of the region between" (*birīt nārim*, *māt birītim*), seems to be a new name first attested in these contracts. It only functions as a geographic name and never serves to describe persons.[28]

Other cities, however, are not combined with a general label. Some of them, like Ḫaḫḫum and Ursum, are old and important trading centres to the Northwest of Mesopotamia. Perhaps these cities were not perceived as part of some bigger ethno-linguistic entity from a Babylonian point of view.

Acquisition orders for slaves also detail the origin of foreign slaves, but these descriptions differ from those found in sale contracts: one finds orders to buy "splendid Subarean slaves from Between-river"[29] or "Subarean slaves of splendid ... from Between-river",[30] each combining Šubartum and "Between-river" – categories

---

[20] These are the territories listed in the text of the equity decree (KRAUS 1984: 180 ¶ 20) that presumably goes back to the last decade of Hammurabi's reign (see footnote 10).

[21] CHARPIN 1987: 41–44.

[22] A slave from Dūr-Mankisayû was sold in Aṣ 16 (no. 36). If this place can be linked with Mankisum, then it would also be located within the territory traditionally taken to be part of the Babylonian realm. This isolated incident cannot yet be explained.

[23] VAS 29 5 (Si 30), YOS 13 248 (Ae u), VAS 29 3 (Ad 8?), YOS 13 5 (date broken, reign of Ad), BM 80420 (broken year of Aṣ) (uncertain: ^{1} 1 sag-géme tur-r[a] ^{2} ^{munus}*id*?-x-*a-gu*-[o m]u-ni ^{3} *wi-li-id* é *ša* [...]) YOS 13 409 (date broken, prb. reign of Aṣ), VAS 22 19 (date broken, reign of Sd).

[24] Thus WILCKE 1975–76: 271 note 26. KRAUS 1984: 281 objects to this conclusion and refers to a "house born slave woman from Dilbat" in TCL 1 133 (Si 11), but this text antedates the slave trade reform. A "house born slave woman from Sippir" appears in DK 105 (date broken, reign of Aṣ), but the phrasing of this sale contract deviates from the typical late Old Babylonian type.

[25] JOANNÈS 1992.

[26] STEINKELLER 1998, MICHALOWSKI 1999 and GUICHARD 2002: 134–137.

[27] POTTS 1999: 1–4.

[28] FINKELSTEIN 1962.

[29] CT 48 66 (Ad 22): sag-ìr su-bir$_{4}$^{ki} *nam-ru-*<*tim*> / [*bi-ri-i*]*t* íd.

[30] VAS 22 49 (date broken, reign of Sd): sag-ìr su-bir$_{4}$^{ki} / x NI-BI-*i nam-ru-tim* / *bi-ri-it na-ri* according to the excavation photograph (PEDERSÉN 1998: 338), excluding the restoration [*ša p*]*í-i nam-ru-tim* (CHARPIN 1985: 271) or [*gu-t*]*i*!-*i nam-ru-tim* (WILCKE 1990: 299) proposed on the basis of the copy.

that are strictly distinguished in slave sale contracts. In this combination, Šubartum is used in a more general sense of "northern foreigner", while "Between-river" points to a specific area. Another acquisition order stipulates the delivery of "splendid Gutean slaves",[31] a lable not attested elsewhere in our corpus. It is not clear whether at that time Gutium was still in use as the name of a specific Zagros polity, but it seems that the term was commonly used in a broad sense as denoting "mountain dweller" or the like. It was applied to people serving as mercenaries and especially as bodyguards throughout the Near East in Old Babylonian times,[32] and perhaps in this case the acquisition of men with the appropriate physique to serve as bodyguard was required.

Slave trade routes

In Figure 1 the toponyms attested as the place of origin of foreign slaves that can be located with some precision are put on the map (for locations

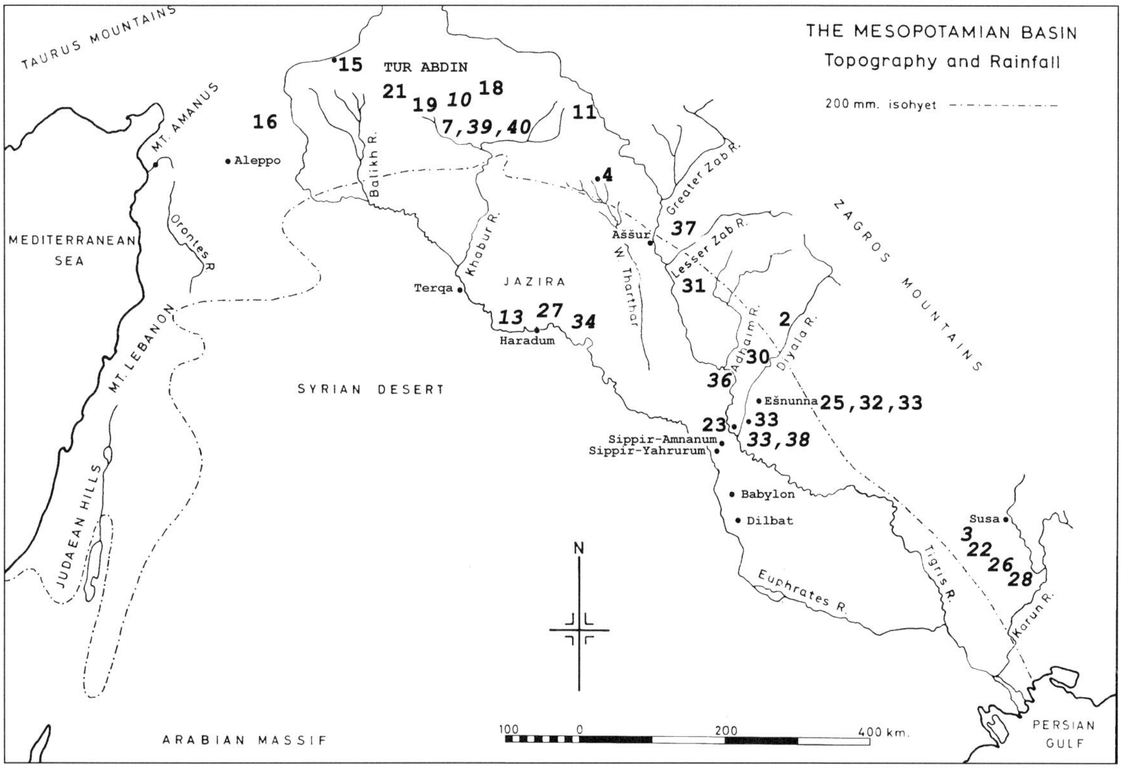

Figure 1 Origin of foreign slaves from Samsuiluna until Samsuditana

Si 27	2	Šimurrum	Ad 21	19	Ašlakkā	Aṣ 8	32	Ešnunna
Si 28	3	Elam	Ad 37	21	Talḫayum	[Aṣ 5–10]	33	Nērebtum, Ešnunna and Aškuzum
Ae h	4	Qaṭṭarā	Ad 37	22	Elam			
Ae m	7	"Between-river"	Aṣ 2	23	Zarilulu	Aṣ 10	34	Suḫûm
Ad 1	10	Idamaraṣ	Aṣ 3	25	Ešnunna	Aṣ 16	36	Dūr-Mankisayû
Ad 1	11	Mardaman	Aṣ 3	26	Ālum-ša-Sîn-išme	Aṣ 17	37	Karanā
Ad 3	13	Suḫûm	Aṣ 3	27	Suḫûm	[Aṣ]	38	Kudla[...]?
Ad 4	15	Ḫaḫḫum	Aṣ 4	28	Elam	Sd 11	39	"Between-river"
Ad 7	16	Ursum	Aṣ 6	30	Arramu	Sd 12	40	"Between-river"
Ad 20	18	Šinaḫ	Aṣ 6	31	Ašuḫ and Lubda			

Confirmed or probable locations are indicated with a dot, approximate locations without. Digits in italics serve to indicate the region where the place can be located. Map adapted from D. Oates, *Studies in the ancient history of Northern Iraq*, London, 1968, fig. 1.

---

[31] Meissner BAP 4 (Aṣ 10): sag-ìr-meš *gu-ti-i*^{ki} / *nam-ru-tim*.

[32] Eidem and Læssøe 2001: 31–32 and Eidem 1996: 80.

see the discussion in the appendix). Two early attestations, from the reign of Samsuiluna, can be located to the East or Southeast of Mesopotamia, and the identified suppliers from the reign of Abiešuh are positioned in the North. Then this picture reveals an important shift of direction: up to the end of the reign of Ammiditana, slaves were mainly imported from regions to the North and Northwest of Mesopotamia, while later most slaves came from regions to the East and Southeast of Mesopotamia.

It must be noted that this impression is based on limited evidence: some place names are broken while others are obscure or unattested elsewhere. Moreover, the corpus of slave sale contracts constitutes a limited sample resulting from random finds and is unevenly distributed over time: the lack of data from the reign of Samsuditana is particularly unfortunate. Nevertheless, the shift that can be observed in the period around the beginning of the reign of Ammiṣaduqa is supported by adequate evidence and seems to be significant. The reappearance of northern slaves in the reign of Samsuditana is also noteworthy.

To appreciate the historical implications of this shift, the trading system that supplied slaves for the Babylonian market must be briefly discussed.[33] Foreign slaves were imported by foreign as well as Babylonian traders. The sale contracts fail to specify whether the seller was the trader who had imported the slave, or perhaps a middleman or a slave owner selling his property, but it is evident that foreign traders played an important role: some of them came from Aššur,[34] and also Suteans were prominent slave traders.[35] There is some evidence for slave markets: the slaves of nos. 30 and 31 were sold just three days apart, probably to the same buyer and certainly at the same place.[36] One of the sellers is an Assyrian who presumably acted as an import trader; the other bears a Babylonian name. Both their merchandise originates from the east Tigris region. All this suggests some kind of a slave fair where merchants from the same caravan sold their stock.

Agents sent abroad also obtained foreign slaves. There is substantial evidence for trading expeditions organised to buy foreign slaves and funded by wealthy Babylonian officials and the palace.[37] Some of these references belong to a type of commercial loans so far attested during Samsuditana's reign only: middlemen made silver of wealthy money lenders available to fund trade enterprises along the Euphrates.[38] Although in many instances the objective of such undertakings is not expressed, it is clear that slave acquisition was one of their primary goals.[39]

Finally, another source of foreign slaves were soldiers selling their share of the booty after a military campaign. Evidence for this practice from Babylonian sources is slim, but its importance should not be underestimated.[40] There is

[33] For a general discussion see Leemans 1960: 110–112 and Leemans 1968: 181–185.

[34] Judging by the names of the sellers of nos. 12 and 30.

[35] Joannès 1997: 408, 411 and De Graef 1999a: 21–22, 25.

[36] The texts share at least four witnesses: YOS 13 35: rev. 1'–3' = YOS 13 89: 28–30. Seal B on YOS 13 35 reappears on YOS 13 89, where it is marked as the seal of Gimillum, being the fifth witness Gimil-Marduk, whose name can thus be restored in the broken lines of YOS 13 35. The name of the buyer in YOS 13 35 is broken, but he might have been identical with the buyer in YOS 13 89. Other texts belonging to this buyer, Amurrum-nāṣir son of Nabium-nāṣir, are discussed by Wilcke 1982: 468–471.

[37] Stol 2002: 748–750.

[38] References in Pientka 1998: 309–310.

[39] Explicit in VAS 22 49 (with Pedersén 1998: 338)(date broken, reign of Sd) and JNES 21 75b (Sd 13). Another objective was the acquisition of *i-ṭ[i-im]*, according to AoF 11 102 no. 11 (date broken, reign of Sd), which can be restored with the help of Van Lerberghe 1995: 391 no. 1 (Sd 11), VAS 29 62 (Sd 14) and VAS 22 55 (Sd 26/27). The meaning of the word *i*-DI(*-im*) in these texts is ambiguous, but new exemplars show that loans with the purpose of buying this product were common in the days of Samsuditana. This suggests that the commodity is "bitumen", rather than "bracelets" as proposed by Charpin 1985: 272 (see also Wilcke 1990: 300 and Pientka 1998: 287 note 39). Bitumen was extracted in the area of Hit in Lower Suḫûm (Michel 2001).

[40] The slave woman from Ursum in no. 16 came into possession of her last owner together with at least one other contract for a previous sale (see footnote 18). The seller in this earlier contract held a military title and is known from contemporary texts (for Sîn-nādin-šumi PA.PA son of Sîn-išmeanni see van Koppen 2002: 162–163). It is possible that he imported this slave woman when returning home, especially as another military commander who was associated with him is known to have done business in Naḫur, a city in the Habur basin, from where he brought slaves to Babylonia (AbB 11 158 with van Koppen 2002: 164–165 note 27).

also evidence that the palace occasionally disposed of slaves; this can presumably be explained as the selling off of war booty in excess of the palace's needs.[41]

Much less is known about the foreign suppliers of slaves. Obviously, social and legal systems aimed at protecting citizens against kidnapping and forced recruitment as slaves were also in force in the supplier states. The letters from Tell Leilan, for example, clearly show that local authorities were strongly interested in remedying incidents of that sort.[42] This policy included populations of allied countries, and letters from Mari speak of measures aimed at suppressing the trade in citizens from vassal states, arguing that it constituted a violation of and threat to the existing treaties.[43] Nonetheless, the prominence of the topic of slave piracy in the Tell Leilan correspondence, mostly dating to a period of political instability, clearly shows how this practice flourished under conditions of social and political turmoil.

The importance of legal slave export, on the other hand, cannot easily be determined with the help of these letters, as they are largely devoted to matters of political interest. Yet from the Mari sources we know of an episode of slaves sold abroad with the consent of a local ruler,[44] and hence we should also assume the presence of a regular export market of slaves in the supplier states.

Slave prices

The fluctuation in slave prices during the Old Babylonian period shows a sweeping curve, with a major increase of prices setting in after the early years of Samsuiluna until the highest level was reached in Abiešuh's reign. Thereafter, prices dropped steadily, again reaching a very low level in the first decade of Ammiṣaduqa's reign.[45] Price levels reflect, among other factors, supply, and it has for example been argued that a sudden drop in slave prices in Hammurabi's final years must be correlated with an increased influx of war captives.[46] Assuming that demand remained steady, the sharp price-rise in Samsuiluna's later years then indicates diminished supply, presumably due to the recently introduced restrictions on slave trade. Prices stayed at a very high level throughout the reign of Abiešuh, but the gradual reduction that followed indicates that supply increased again. Increased supply can perhaps be taken as a sign that the slave sale restrictions relaxed over time,[47] and certainly indicates that new markets were opened. This was the case early in the reign of Ammiṣaduqa, when low slave prices coincided with supply of slaves from the land of Ešnunna (attested in the years Aṣ 2-8, with two instances of broken dates) and Elam (attested in the years Ad 37-Aṣ 4). These slaves were sold at prices far below those paid for slaves in preceding decades. The development of slave prices under Samsuditana's rule is insufficiently documented.

The downward adjustment of slave prices from the reign of Abiešuh onwards can be followed with the data in Figure 2, where prices of native house-born slaves, slaves from Suḫûm and foreign slaves are listed separately.[48] Foreigners are divided in: "northerners", *i.e.* slaves from Šubartum and Between-river, and "easterners" from Ešnunna and Elam. A third category comprises foreign slaves designated with the name of

---

[41] TIM 7 45 (Aṣ 3). The place of origin of these slave women is not clear (gú? íd-ma-ra-da^{ki}; Stol 2002: 750 tentatively interprets this as Idamaraṣ). The low slave prices and the unusual occurrence of slaves from the land of Ešnunna in the time when this text was written must probably be explained as the effects of warfare.

[42] Eidem 2000: 261 and Eidem 1996: 82 with note 17 on page 85.

[43] See ARMT 14 51 (Durand 2000: 226–228 no. 1054) and ARMT 14 79 (Durand 2000: 229–230 no. 1056).

[44] ARMT 27 117, where a royal official commissioned to buy slaves in Idamaraṣ pays money to king Šubram of Susā, one of the states of Idamaraṣ (*cf. e.g.* ARMT 9 298: 6 and Durand 1988b: 109 A.1610^{+}: 5, A.1212: 6). Did the king supply slaves himself, or was it necessary to pay for the cooperation of a local sovereign in order to gain access to the market?

[45] Farber 1978: 12–14. New data comply with this trend. Note, however, that the price given by Farber for male slaves at the apex of the curve, 110 shekels, is certainly too high, for the high prices from the reign of Abiešuh and early in the reign of Ammiditana all concern female "northern" slaves. They were more expensive than their male counterparts, in sharp contrast to the prices for house-born slaves. Furthermore, CT 45 44 does not record a price of 107 shekels for one male (so Farber 1978: 42), but gives the price of two slaves, both presumably female.

[46] Farber 1978: 14.

[47] See footnote 12 above.

[48] The reign of Samsuiluna is excluded, as statements of prices in the five latest known slave sale contracts from his reign (discussed above) are all broken except in BM 22513 (Si 28), where a Elamite slave costs 25 shekels of silver. An Elamite slave woman sold in the same year costs 35 shekels (TLB 1 216).

House-born slaves	Slaves from Suḫûm	"Northerners" (Between-river and Šubartum)	Identified by city and other geographic names	"Easterners" (Ešnunna and Elam)	Without ethnic or geographic specification
Ae u (a) ♀ 43		Ae h (4) ♀ 72 Ae m (7) ♀ 84 Ae m (i) ♀ 84,9	[Ae] (5) ♀ 75 (Ae) (6) ♂ 70		Ae 3 (o) ♀ 60(+)
Ad x (b) ♂ 60 [Ad] (c) ♂ 50	Ad 2 (13) ♀ 13	Ad 1 (10) ♀ 65 Ad 4 (14) ♀ 64 Ad 13 (17) ♀ 21 (j) Ad 20 (18) ♀ 57 Ad 21 (19) ♀ 54 Ad 37 (21) ♂ 12	Ad 2 (12) ♀ 53,5 Ad 4 (15) ♀ 25 (l) Ad 7 (16) ♀ 36>51 (m) Ad 25 (20) ? 20(+)		
[Aṣ] (d) ♀ 3 (e) Aṣ x (f) ♀ 5	Aṣ 3 (27) ♀ 4 Aṣ 10 (34) ♀ 5(+)	Aṣ 6 (31) ♀ 28 Aṣ 6 (31) ♀ 30	Aṣ 2 (24) ♀ 3 Aṣ 3 (n) ♀ 3,9 Aṣ 4 (29) ♀ 4 Aṣ 16 (36) ♂ 16	Aṣ 2 (23) ♀ 3(+) Aṣ 3 (25) ♀ 5,3 Aṣ 3 (26) ♀ 4,5 Aṣ 4 (28) ♀' 9(+) Aṣ 8 (32) ♀ 8	Aṣ 6 (p) ♀ 3,8 Aṣ 11 (q) ♀ 5,3 Aṣ 12 (r) ♂ 10 Aṣ 13 (s) ♂ 10 Aṣ 15 (t) ♀ 10 Aṣ 17 (u) ♀ 13
[Sd] (g) ♀ 16 (h)		Sd 12 (40) ♂ 20/40 Sd 13 (k) ♂ 20			

Figure 2 Slave prices from Abiešuh until Samsuditana

Slave prices (excluding SI.BI-fees) in shekels of silver; x(+) indicates that the figure is partly damaged, different readings of a broken figure are separated as x/y. Numbers between brackets refer to texts in the appendix, letters to the following remarks:
(a) YOS 13 248; (b) VAS 29 3; (c) YOS 13 5; (d) YOS 13 409; (e) old woman; (f) BM 80420 (see footnote 23 above); (g) VAS 22 19; (h) suckling child; probably under special circumstances, see footnote 19 above; (i) BM 12951, munus-su-bir$_4$; (j) suspiciously cheap, see footnote 12 above; (k) JNES 21 75b, sag-ìr su-bir^{ki}; (l) young girl; (m) the value of the same slave increased between two sale transactions; (n) TIM 7 45 (see footnote 41 above); (o) CT 48 47, a "splendid" slave woman (sag-géme *na-wi-ir-tim*), presumably from the North; (p) TIM 7 46 with TIM 7 47; (q) TIM 7 48 with TIM 7 50; (r) TIM 7 49; (s) BM 97250; (t) Van Lerberghe OB Texts (= OLA 21) 58, a female ox driver (sag-géme šà-gu$_4$); (u) TCL 1 170.

a city or country, but without a general label. Prices in this third category follow prices of "northern" and "eastern" slaves in the reigns of Abiešuh-Ammiditana and Ammiṣaduqa, respectively. According to these data, "northern" slaves were the most expensive kind while Babylonian house-born slaves were somewhat cheaper. Slaves from Suḫûm, in contrast, were always the most affordable category; only when "eastern" supply had become available were slaves from Ešnunna and Elam sold for prices comparable to those for slaves from Suḫûm.

While the common reduction of prices can be safely explained with increased supply, the table also shows that demand did not always follow supply: Subarean slaves were still significantly more expensive than other categories in the early years of Ammiṣaduqa when slaves were bought cheaply.[49] "Northern" slaves, from Šubartum and Between-river, were evidently the most popular category of slaves. Thus it is of interest to note how the place of origin of these priced slaves changed over time: from the Habur basin and the upper course of Euphrates and Tigris in the reigns of Abiešuh and Ammiditana to the foothills of the Zagros east of the Tigris in the reign of Ammiṣaduqa. Not a single slave from Northern Mesopotamia is found in sale contracts from the reign of Ammiṣaduqa; they first reappear after the first decade of Samsuditana.

Thus the development of prices and the information about slave origins allow to draw the following conclusions: Import was limited during the reigns of Abiešuh and Ammiditana, when foreign slaves primarily came from Northern Mesopotamia and were sold by foreign traders or bought by Babylonian merchants abroad. Some trade, moreover, took place as a result of Babylonian military presence in the North.[50] The abrupt appearance of slaves from Ešnunna and Elam in the early years of Ammiṣaduqa, some of them sold by the palace, must be ascribed to particular circumstances, but data to determine the nature of this situation is lacking. Probably it is an indication of another episode of military conflict between Babylon and Ešnunna.[51] The abrupt lack of supply from Northern Mesopotamia at the same time suggests developments in that region or elsewhere that effectively reduced the export of slaves. An alternative source for popular Subarean slaves was then found in the area at the foothills of the Zagros. After an interruption of about 30 years slaves from Northern Mesopotamia are again documented in the second decade of Samsuditana's reign. The number of sale contracts from this period is limited, but the prominence of slave trade enterprises along the Euphrates in the second and third decade of his reign confirms that the northern markets for slaves were open again.

Historical implications

The question to be addressed in the framework of a study of synchronization of cultures in the period of the "Mesopotamian Dark Age" is whether the change of direction in slave trade can be used to draw conclusions about social conditions and the development of political structures in the slave supplying territories outside of Mesopotamia. In this context, the early history of the Mittani state is pertinent.[52] This important political entity can be well observed in the 15th century B.C., but its formative and early stages are still obscure in the absence of pertinent historical sources. While some scholars assume the existence of the Mittani state in Northern Mesopotamia before the end of the Old Babylonian period,[53] others suppose the establishment of Mittani power first to have taken place after this event.[54]

---

49 Based on the price in no. 31; the prices in nos. 30 and 37 are broken.

50 See footnote 40 above.

51 See footnote 41 above. Conflicts with Ešnunna are reported during the reigns of Samsuiluna (Charpin 1998) and Abiešuh (Pientka 1998: 263). Later, in the time of Samsuditana, relations with Ešnunna were apparently peaceful (Pientka 1998: 296 with VAS 29 66 [Sd 13]), though occasional hostility is mentioned (AbB 12 182 with Pientka 1998: 263–264). There is no evidence in the Old Babylonian sources that the lower Diyala region was ever the theatre of conflict between the Babylonian army and Kassites coming from the Diyala region (*pace* Pientka 1998: 262 with note 33).

52 The term Mittani is anachronistic in reference to the Old Babylonian period, as it is first attested in the early 15th century B.C. (Klinger 1988: 28–29 and Wilhelm 1993–97: 287–290), but will be used here as I argue that Old Babylonian Ḫanigalbat is the same state as Mittani of the 15th century B.C.

53 Thus *e.g.* Astour 1972 and Klinger 1988.

54 Thus *e.g.* Oates, Oates and McDonald 1997: 145 and Salvini 1998: 310.

The best information is still to be found in the accounts of the military exploits of the Old Hittite kings who confronted the "Hurrian enemy" or the "enemy of the country of Ḫanigalbat" in the course of their expansion into Syria.[55] Their ruler is referred to as the "king of the Hurrian troops",[56] a title that may be indicative of the ethnic and military character of the ruler's legitimacy.[57]

Another source of information about Mittani's power in its early existence is the statue inscription of Idrimi, ruler of Mukiš and Alalaḫ, who concluded a treaty with Parattarna, "king of the Hurrian troops", and mentions the alliance of his forefathers with earlier Hurrian kings. Idrimi must be dated sometimes in the 15th century B.C., but it is not clear how much time separates him from the fall of Aleppo. If we assume that this was a lengthy period of time, then his predecessors, who accepted Hurrian supremacy, would be dated to the period after Muršili's I conquest of Aleppo,[58] an event that took place shortly before his campaign against Babylon. Alternatively, Idrimi may have ruled directly after this event, thus dating his ancestors to the obscure period of undetermined length in Aleppo's history from Hattušili's campaign against Alalaḫ to the fall of Aleppo.[59] The question of the relative date of Idrimi's reign is important for the historical role of Mittani, for its dominance over Aleppo either took place after the end of the Old Babylonian period, or it was contemporary with (part of) the reign of Samsuditana.

The rise of Mittani, or any other political structure in the area, was shaped by long-term trends that can to some extent be recognized with the help of earlier textual material. Recent studies have emphasized the relevance of data from Shemshara, Mari and Tell Leilan to understand later socio-political developments in Northern Mesopotamia. The type of inter-Zagros conflicts reinforced by Mesopotamian intervention and leading to resettlement of mountain population groups in the plains that is so vividly illustrated by the Shemshara and Mari sources[60] may serve as an example for the outcome of the Zagros campaigns in Hammurabi's last years.[61] There is extensive evidence for the presence of Zagros deportees in the Babylonian alluvium,[62] and it is among them that one should look for the kernel of the Kassite groups who manifested their military power in Samsuiluna's eighth year.[63] Early in Samsuiluna's third decade, the sources from Tell Leilan bear witness to the decisive role of large armies of mercenaries in resolving inter-state conflicts in Northern Mesopotamia.[64] This seems to be a relatively new phenomenon and may be explained in part as the manifestation of uprooted people from the Zagros and elsewhere.

With the destruction of Tell Leilan in Samsuiluna's 22nd year, historical sources for Northern Mesopotamia become scarce. Babylon and Aleppo presumably continued to hold authority over their areas of influence. Babylon tried to control the Euphrates route and was sometimes able to extend its power up to Terqa, but the eastern extent of the Aleppine dominion remains unclear. Political conditions in the Habur basin are essentially undocumented, but the Babylonian slave sale records show that conditions facilitating slave export persisted throughout the reign of Abiešuh up to (at least) the early third decade of the reign of Ammiditana, suggesting that the state of political fragmentation marked by occasional social and political disruptions, that characterized the final years documented in the Tell Leilan sources, continued for a period of about 70 years. The disappearance of slave export in the following period would then suggest that conditions impeding such trade prevailed for the next 30 to 40 years. This might be taken as an indication that some kind of unified political structure

---

55 References collected by Wilhelm 1993–97: 292.

56 In Hittite and Syrian sources, see Wilhelm 1993–97: 292 and Kühne 1999: 208 with note 34.

57 Kühne 1999: 209.

58 Thus *e.g.* Kühne 1999: 211.

59 Thus van Soldt 2000. Mittanian influence on Aleppo in the time of Ḫattušili I is suggested by the Aleppo treaty, see Klinger 1988, who interprets the mention of submission of Idrimi's predecessors to the king of the Hurrians to refer to the same events as described in the Aleppo treaty.

60 Eidem and Læssøe 2001.

61 The main source of information about these campaigns are Hammurabi's year name formulae studied by Stol 1976: 33–42; some of the geographic names in a relevant *tamītum*-text (Stol 1976: 42) are quoted in Frayne 1997: 254 and 259.

62 Charpin 1992: 213–217.

63 See Stol 1976: 44–45, but note that the event commemorated in Samsuiluna's 9th year name might have taken place in the preceding year, see De Smet 1990: 4–6.

64 Eidem 1991: 120–131, Eidem 1996, Dercksen and Donbaz 1997–2000.

had taken form that effectively managed to impose social order in the region.

This power is occasionally mentioned: some attestations date to the reign of Ammiṣaduqa and are therefore contemporary with the low in slave export,[65] another to the reign of Samsuditana.[66] All mention "Ḫanigalbatean troops", showing that the name was then commonly used to designate members of a specific ethnic group.[67] Its non-appearance in the rich ethnic terminology used in texts from Mari and elsewhere can safely be taken to indicate that it was a neologism, of unclear etymological meaning,[68] first introduced at an unknown point in time after the reign of Hammurabi. In the 15th century B.C., this term designated the core area of the Mittani state in the Habur basin,[69] and it was presumably used in the very same sense already in the days of Ammiṣaduqa.

One should, however, bear in mind that this explanation might easily fail to take other factors into account. It is perhaps more than coincidence that, during the time that sales of Northern Mesopotamian slaves are not documented, evidence for hostility against the Babylonian state is abundant. Reports on enemy threat against the territory of Sippir-Yaḫrurum are dated to Ammiṣaduqa's 15th year,[70] and in his 18th year the city of Sippir-Amnānum was destroyed.[71] The chronological distribution of texts from the city of Dilbat suggests that one or more record keeping institutions in that city came to an abrupt and probably violent end later that year.[72] The abandonment of the fortress town of Ḫarradum on the Middle Euphrates in the second half of the year Aṣ 18 shows that Babylonian control of Suḫûm weakened at the same time.[73] It remains unclear who was responsible for all this, but there may be a link with the hostile troops of Samḫarû and Bimatû mentioned in the reports from three years before. Little is known of these groups, but the second is attested much earlier as the name of a Kassite military unit in Babylonian service.[74] The loca-

[65] Quoted in GELB 1968: 97: "An unpublished Old Babylonian text dated to Ammi-ṣaduqa (circa 1600 B.C.), the knowledge of which I owe to the kindness of Mr. Douglas Kennedy of the Centre National de Recherches de Paris, deals with the issue of beer to the *tu-ur-gu-ma-an-ni ša* éren *ḫa-bi-in-gal-ba-ti-i* 'the dragomans of the Ḫanigalbatian soldiers/workers'." Gelb fails to point out where this tablet was kept and its present whereabouts are unknown to me (see also GRONEBERG 1980: 90 and CHARPIN 1997: 190). A personnel register, probably also from the reign of Ammiṣaduqa, mentions the person *ib-ba-tum* éren *ḫa-bi-in-ga-al-ba-at* (BM 96955 iii 9).

[66] CTN 4 63 i 35: [éren] *ḫa-ni-gal-ba-ti-i*, a Neo-Assyrian manuscript of a *tamītum* from the reign of Samsuditana, see CHARPIN 1997: 190.

[67] Its use in Old Babylonian texts suggests that the appearance of lú-kúr kur *ḫa-ni-kal-bat* in the Akkadian version of the "Deeds of Ḫattušili", where the Hittite version has LÚ-KÚR *ŠA* URU *ḫur-ri*, is not necessarily the result of later revision, see ASTOUR 1992: 4 note 12. See HOUWINK TEN CATE 1983 for the argument that the prototype of these texts was written in Akkadian.

[68] ASTOUR 1972: 105 and KÜHNE 1999: 205 connect Ḫanigalbat with the name Ḫanû, but this seems doubtful in consideration of the form Ḫabingalbat attested during the reign of Ammiṣaduqa and in later sources (BRINKMAN 1964: 36–37 and NASHEF 1982: 117–118).

[69] For a definition see KÜHNE 1999: 205–206.

[70] References in PIENTKA 1998: 260–262.

[71] Archaeologically well observed and exactly dated by the excavation of the house of Ur-Utu: the last dated text was written on Aṣ 18-5-26 (TANRET 2001: 458) and botanical finds suggest that the house burned down in the summer season (GASCHE 1989: 105). The archives of Sippir-Amnānum residents excavated in the late 19th century and preserved in the British Museum and elsewhere all cease in this year or before. These sources not only allow to put the *terminus post quem* for the destruction of Sippir-Amnānum one week forward (BM 80978, Aṣ 18-6-4), but, more importantly, show that the violence that destroyed Ur-Utu's house affected a large part of the city. Sippir-Amnānum is rarely mentioned thereafter (for example in CT 48 37 of Sd 1); although a later year name of Ammiṣaduqa ("17+d") refers to repairs of the temples of Sippir-Yaḫrurum and Sippir-Amnānum, the latter city apparently did not return to its former importance.

[72] The organisations that generated the late Old Babylonian records customarily assigned to Dilbat remain to be described, but the prominence of ration lists and other texts with short-term value from the years Aṣ 17 and 18, in combination with the absence of documents from later years that unequivocally belong to the same archive, suggests that at least one of them was terminated sometimes in the second half of Aṣ 18. The area of Dilbat was already threatened by the activities of an unidentified enemy in the preceding year, see KOSHURNIKOV 1993: 176 and PIENTKA 1998: 267.

[73] JOANNÈS 1992: 34–35. The *terminus post quem* for the desertion of Ḫarradum is Aṣ 18-6-20 (KD 31).

[74] VAN LERBERGHE 1995: 384–385; see also the remarks of DE GRAEF 1999a: 10–12. Note that BE 6/2 136 dates to Ae 3.

tion of the destroyed cities suggests that the direction of attack followed the Euphrates as far down as the area of Dilbat, and it might be relevant that somewhere upstream this river the famous "Kassite houses" were situated.[75]

These "Kassite houses" were the seat of a semi-independent Kassite polity located somewhere to the Northwest of the core area of the Babylonian state.[76] Its recognition allows for a consistent answer to a number of separate questions: it permits a plausible explanation for the presence of Kassite elements in an otherwise autonomous Hana culture;[77] it accounts for a military force able to inflict sudden destruction far into the Babylonian heartland; it gives a satisfactory explanation for the later career of the name Samḫarû;[78] and, finally, it is consistent with the genealogy of later rulers of Suḫûm.[79] The Kassite rulers normally recognized the supremacy of Babylon, but could on occasion turn against it.[80] This is illustrated by the events of the reign of Ammiṣaduqa. The motive for this aggression is still unknown, and it cannot be excluded that the Kassites operated in alliance with some other power. Nonetheless, Ammiṣaduqa was able to ward off this invasion,[81] and continued to rule for three more years. Relations with the Kassites were again pacified in the early reign of Samsudi-

---

[75] This expression does not designate military camps located in the surrounding of major Babylonian cities and cannot be compared with fortified settlements in the countryside (thus PIENTKA 1998: 258 with literature), but is used in a specific geographic sense. It is a place that can be reached from Babylon passing through Sippir (VAN LERBERGHE 1995: 392 no. 2), a place of departure for people with important information for the king (AbB 7 47) and the destination for trading missions (VAN LERBERGHE 1995: 391 no. 1). This last reference is revealing when compared with similar loans for other destinations (such as VAS 22 37 and VAS 29 66); its objective, getting bitumen, points to a destination near Hit on the Euphrates, see footnote 39 above. A similar, if not the same, institution are the "houses" in combination with the name of a leader; they designate both place (AbB 6 24) as well as relationship (BE 6/2 136) in accordance with the various meanings of the word "house".

[76] Babylonian evidence agrees with the theory originally proposed by SMITH 1940: 17–25, largely ignored since the critical remarks of LANDSBERGER 1954: 66–67 but recently revived by PODANY 2002: 43–51, for the existence of a Kassite state at least from the reign of Abiešuh onwards (see the text published by VAN LERBERGHE 1995: 392 no. 2 and another quoted by VAN LERBERGHE 1995: 383 note 8); its precise location (north of Terqa, according to PODANY 2002: 50) remains to be identified.

[77] PODANY 2002: 50–51.

[78] The name Samḫarû has been linked with Egyptian *Sngr*, Šanḫara in Hittite and Amarna texts and, much later, Biblical Šinʿār (ZADOK 1984). In Egypt, *Sngr* is used as the name of the Kassite kingdom of Babylon. It is mentioned for the first time in the annals of Tuthmosis III and then became a common element in geographical lists from the 18th and 19th dynasty (GARDINER 1947: I 209*–212*). In the geographical lists of Ramses II at Amarah West, *Sngr* (no. 4) appears together with Babylon, its capital city (*Bbr*, no. 89), the city of Uruk (*ʾIrk*, no. 88) and perhaps even the Kassites (*Ksy*, no. 29) (KITCHEN 1996: 74–75 and 1999: 126–129). In the Amarna letters and Hittite texts, Šanḫara is used in the same sense as the name of the Kassite kingdom of Babylon (DEL MONTE and TISCHLER 1978: 344 and BELMONTE 2001: 263–264), but there is one famous passage in a Hittite ritual where Šanḫara appears alongside Aššur, Babylon, Egypt and many other countries (KUB 15 34 i 57: KUR URU *aš-šur* KUR URU KÁ-DINGIR-RA KUR URU *ša-an-ḫa-ra* KUR URU *mi-iṣ-ri*, see GARDINER 1947: I 212* and II 323–324). This passage seems to reveal another tradition, where Šanḫara is distinguished from Babylon.

The prominence of this name outside of Mesopotamia implies that the Samḫarû must have played a far more important role than the few Babylonian attestations, all found in letters referring to their hostile activities in Ammiṣaduqa's 15th year (AbB 1 2, 7 47 and 10 150), would suggest. This is best explained by assuming that the Kassite polity on or near the Middle Euphrates was (also) known by the name Samḫarû. After the Kassites had seized power in Babylon, the name also came to signify the Kassite kingdom in Babylon. This later meaning of the name seems in particular to have taken root in the Levant, and was adopted by the Egyptians, while the Kassite rulers themselves, and most other participants in the international correspondence in Akkadian language, preferred the name Karduniaš to refer to this kingdom. The tradition of KUB 15 34, that separates Šanḫara from Babylon, might be an anachronistic reflection of the situation in the late Old Babylonian period.

[79] Who traced their ancestry back to a "son" of Hammurabi with a Kassite name (RIMB 2 S.0.1002.1: 3–4; S.0.1002.2: 3–4 etc.).

[80] Military settlement at the northern fringes of the Babylonian state (DE GRAEF 2002) evidently served as a defence measure against Kassite and other aggression coming from the North.

[81] The question whether Ammiṣaduqa's inscription from Nippur (RIME 4.3.10.1), dealing with the defeat of an unknown enemy, refers to this accomplishment merits further study.

tana, when strong Babylonian presence in Suḫûm[82] and Terqa[83] is once more documented. The role of the Kassites in the conflict between the Hittites and Babylon at the end of Samsuditana's reign remains to be established.[84]

Any explanation for the failing import of slaves from Northern Mesopotamia during the reign of Ammiṣaduqa must take at least these two political structures into account.[85] Kassite hostility presumably restricted Euphrates traffic, but this alone is insufficient to explain the trend, as the open character of the Mesopotamian landscape offered ample opportunity for mobile traders to operate over alternative routes. The absence of northern slaves can for that reason be interpreted as an indication for the presence of a strong power in Northern Mesopotamia. This allows us to propose that a unified Hurrian polity, of unknown dimensions[86] and known by the name of Ḫanigalbat, had come into existence in the Habur basin at least 50 years before the end of the Old Babylonian period. The later description of its ruler as the "king of the Hurrian troops" in Hittite texts and elsewhere indicates that outsiders noticed the importance of military power for the cohesion of this state, and its beginning was in all probability linked with the class of mercenary forces that is attested in sources from Tell Leilan, written approximately 133 years before the end of the Old Babylonian period. Between these two moments, we must imagine a course of events that included the acquisition of civil power by their leaders, followed by a process of gradual political unification, but none of this is so far documented by contemporary texts.[87]

The subsequent resumption of northern slave trade, starting approximately 20 years before the fall of Babylon, was then the combined effect of two factors: in the first place, increased instability in Northern Mesopotamia, presumably caused by external pressure on the Mittani state; and, in the second place, the pacification of the Kassites and the re-establishment of Babylonian military presence as far north as Terqa. While the first can obviously be ascribed to Hittite expansion into Syria, it cannot be excluded that Babylonian activities in that area contributed to the same effect. Babylon and Hatti were obviously interested in controlling the very same territories, and examples of coalitions serving common interests,[88] but ending in one partner defeating the other are plentiful in Mesopotamian history. The history of the fall of Babylon still remains to be written.

---

[82] MOHAMMAD 2002.

[83] Texts from Terqa are dated with year names of Ammiṣaduqa and Samsuditana (ROUAULT 1992: 253–254). Identification of the pertinent year names is obviously vital for a better understanding of Ammiṣaduqa's conflict with the Kassites. Samsuditana's grip on the Euphrates route is confirmed by the prominence of Euphrates trading enterprises in his reign, see above with footnotes 38–39.

[84] The name [KU]R URU *ša-an-ḫa-ra* in KUB 26 74 i 10, dealing with Muršili's campaigns in Syria (DEL MONTE and TISCHLER 1978: 344 and KEMPINSKI 1983: 53), is not necessarily the name used for Babylon in a late manuscript, but might in fact refer to the Kassite polity. In other historical texts concerning the Hittite campaign against Babylon, its name invariably appears as (URU) KÁ-DINGIR-RA(ki) (DEL MONTE and TISCHLER 1978: 186 and KEMPINSKI 1983: 50, 53–54).

[85] Obviously, one must reckon with other larger political units that have so far left no traces in our record. The state of a ruler with the Amorite name Yaʾusa that temporarily included Terqa, perhaps in the time of Abiešuh or Ammiditana (based on the prosopographic data given in ROUAULT 1992: 251–253, but see the remarks by PODANY 2002: 42–43), can serve as an example.

[86] Absence of reference to such a state in records from Tikunani, located in the area of Bismil (CHARPIN 2000), cannot be used to disprove the existence of a Habur-based Hurrian state (*pace* SALVINI 1998: 310).

[87] It still remains to be decided whether the Indo-European royal names and military terminology that can be observed from the 15th century onwards (KLINGER 1988: 27–29 and WILHELM 1993–97: 292–293) are original or secondary traits of the Ḫanigalbat/Mittani state.

[88] Hittite diplomatic contact with Babylon is revealed by a letter of a merchant from Babylon in the time of Samsuditana, who describes how the Hittites address him about their business deals in the "palace gate" (VAS 22 85 with KLENGEL 1979: 86–87). This indicates that the merchant did business with Hittite emissaries, who combined commerce with their diplomatic or military missions to the Babylonian court.

APPENDIX

Foreign slave sales in the later Old Babylonian period

1	Si 24	CT 48 60	1 sag-ìr lú-su-bir$_4^{ki}$ / *am-mu-wa* mu-ni
2	Si 27	BIN 2 80	1 sag-géme uru *ši-mu-ru-um*^{ki}
3	Si 28	BM 22513	1 sag-ìr ^{d}utu-[... mu-ni] / sag-ìr *e-[la-am-tim]*
4	Ae h	TCL 1 147	1 sag-géme *ma-am-ma* m[u-ni] / munus-su-bir$_4^{ki}$ *wa-ri-it-tum* / uru *qá-ṭa-ra*^{ki}
5	[Ae?]	VAS 29 7	1 sag-géme *wa-ri-[it]-tum* / uru *ša-ḫa-aḫ-ḫu-*⌜*um*⌝ / [^{I}o]-x-*en-na-tum* m[u-ni]
6	(ca. Ae)	VAS 9 146	1 lú tur *ši-ni-bu* / uru^{ki} *ša-ḫa-aḫ-ḫu* / *wa-ri-it-tum* x-*še-tum*
7	Ae m	CT 8 27a	1 sag-géme *ì-lí*-x x x mu-ni / *qá-du* dumu-gaba-*ša* / šà *ma-at bi-ri-tim*
8	Ae B	AoF 11 100 no. 9	1 sag-géme munus-su-bir$_4^{ki}$ x x / ^{I}*me-a-tum* mu-ni / *a-lum* AN-*ba-pa*^{ki}
9	[Ae / Ad]	VAS 9 219	1 sag-ìr [... mu-ni] / uru$^{?}$ *bi-te-eš-*[...]
10	Ad 1	VAS 18 15	1 sag-géme *al-li-ḫa-ba-ar* mu-ni / šà *ma-at i-da-ma-ra-aṣ* / *bi-ri-it* íd
11	Ad 1	VAS 29 6	1 sag-ìr su-bir$_4$ *ì-lí*-[o (o)] mu-ni / uru^{ki} *mar-da-ma*⌜^{ki}⌝
12	Ad 2	CT 45 44	1 [sag-gé]me *ku-te-e* mu-ni / [uru^{ki} (o)] x-*šu-u*[*l*$^{?ki}$] [1 sag-géme] ^{d}utu-[o mu]-ni / uru^{ki} [o o] x x x [o]
13	Ad 2-3	BM 16495 BM 80359 BM 16946	1 sag-géme *be-el-ti-la-ma-sí* 1 sag-géme *be-el-ti-la-ma-sí* / *wi-li-id* é *ša su-ḫu-um*^{ki} 1 *be-e*[*l-ti-la-ma-sí*] / *i-l*[*i-id* é *ša su-ḫu-um*^{ki}]
14	Ad 4	CT 33 41	1 sag-géme *um-mi-*^{d}*ḫe-pé-et* mu-ni / munus-su-bir$_4^{ki}$ uru *ta-ad-ni*
15	Ad 4	CT 45 45	1 munus-tur-r[a] / munus *ḫa-aḫ-ḫ*[*u-u*]*m*[^{ki}]
16	Ad 7	YOS 13 39 VAS 7 50	1 sag-géme *i-na*-é-úl-[maš]-x mu-ni / munus *ur-su*^{ki} 1 sag-géme *i-na*-é-ul-maš-*ba-na-at* mu-ni / uru *úr-su-um*^{ki}
17	Ad 13	VAS 16 207, YOS 13 253	1 sag-géme *a-bi-du-ri* mu-ni 1 sag-géme *a-bi-du-ri* mu-ni / su-bir$_4^{ki}$
18	Ad 20	VAS 7 53	1 sag-géme *su-ul-gi* mu-ni / uru *ši-na-aḫ*^{ki} *ma-at bi-ri-tim*^{ki}
19	Ad 21	YOS 13 246	1 sag-ìr su-bir$_4^{ki}$ *a-ga-ab*-x / uru *aš-la-ak-ka*^{ki} *bi-ri-it* íd
20	Ad 25	Di 1191	1 sag-[...]-AN mu-ni [...]-x-*la-da*$^{?ki}$
21	Ad 37	TCL 1 156	1 sag-ìr dingir-*ma*-x-[o mu-ni] / uru^{ki} *ta-al-ḫu-ú* [*bi-ri-it* íd]
22	Ad 37	Di 1163	"esclave Marduk-rimanni" uru^{ki} elam-ma
23	Aṣ 2	BM 97134	1 sag-géme ^{d}suen-*na-da* mu-ni / uru *za-ri-lu-lu*^{ki} èš-nun-na^{ki}
24	Aṣ 2	Di 1956	1 *e*-[...] mu$^{?}$-[ni$^{?}$] / uru^{ki} [...]-*a-bi*
25	Aṣ 3	BM 92606	1 sag-géme géme-*ku-bi* mu-ni / uru áš-nun-na^{ki}
26	Aṣ 3	MEISSNER BAP 3	1 sag-géme ^{munus}*na-ru-ub-tum* mu-ni / elam-ma uru–*ša*–^{d}suen-*iš-me*^{ki}
27	Aṣ 3	Di 1412	1 sag-géme *um-mi-*^{íd}buranun$^{?}$ *wilid* é *ša* x-x-*ḫu*^{ki}
28	Aṣ 4	Di 2074	"esclave Inbuša" *ša* elam-ma x x
29	Aṣ 4	BM 87243	1 sag-géme ^{d}iškur-*du-um-qí* [mu-ni] / uru ⌜*ka*⌝-*al-le-e*^{ki}
30	Aṣ 6	YOS 13 35	1 sag-géme *ta-ga-ša* mu-ni / uru *ar-ra-mu*^{ki} / *ma-a-at* su-bir$_4^{ki}$
31	Aṣ 6	YOS 13 89	1 sag-géme *a-ba-šu-ša* mu-ni / uru *a-šu-uḫ*^{ki} / 1 sag-géme *pa-ḫa-ia* mu-ni / uru *lu-ub-da*^{ki} / *ma-a-at* su-bir$_4^{ki}$
32	Aṣ 8	YOS 13 408	1 sag-géme *be-el-ta-ni* mu-[ni] / uru^{ki} áš-nun-na^{ki}
33	[Aṣ 5-10]	YOS 13 199	[1 sag-géme ...]-x-[... mu-ni] / [uru / šà *ma-at*] áš-nun-na[^{ki}] / [1] sag-g[éme ^{d}*š*]*a*$^{!}$-*la*$^{!}$-*um-mi* m[u-ni] / uru [*ne*]-*re-eb-tum*^{ki} / šà *ma-at* áš-nun-na[^{ki}] / [1 sag]-géme x-*ḫu-um-mu-da*-x mu-[ni] / [(...)] uru$^{?}$ *áš-ku-z*[*u-um*^{ki}]
34	Aṣ 10	CTMMA 1 54	1 sag-géme *a-ḫa-ta-ni* mu-[ni] / uru *na-me-e su-ḫi-*⌜*im*^{ki}⌝
35	Aṣ 11	YOS 13 382	1 sag-géme ^{munus}*ši-nu-nu-tum* mu-ni / munus-su-bir$_4^{ki}$ / uru *ar-ra-aḫ-ru*^{ki}
36	Aṣ 16	RA 73 79	1 sag-ìr mi-*lí*-^{d}nu-mu[š$^{?}$-da$^{?}$ mu-n]i-im / uru bàd-*ma-an-ki-sa-ia-*[*a*$^{?}$]-*ú*^{ki}
37	Aṣ 17	BM 17212	1 sag-géme su-bir$_4^{ki}$ / ^{munus}*ši-du-ri* mu-ni / [ur]u *ka-ra-na-a*^{ki}
38	[Aṣ?]	SZLECHTER TJA pl. 26	1 sag-ìr i-x-[...] / uru^{ki} *ku-ud-la-*[...] / *ma-a-at* áš-nun-[na^{ki}]
39	Sd 11	JNES 21 75a	1 sag-géme *ḫa-ši-ia* mu-ni / uru *ta-da-an-ne*^{ki} / šà *m*[*a-a*]*t bi-ri-ti*
40	Sd 12	VAT 718	1 sag-ìr [...] / *bi-ri-it* íd

Remarks on the texts

3: The second line is indented, the next two lines contain the name of the seller (ìr PN / ki PN). Restored with the help of TLB 1 216, a legal settlement from the same year concerning the price of an Elamite slave woman (sag-géme elam-ma^{ki}).

5: This reference is assigned to the reign of Abiešuh because of the adjective *wārittum*, which appears elsewhere in nos. 4 (Ae h) and 6, and the high price of the slave woman.

6: The reading of the last word of the third line is unclear.[89] This text was written outside of the territory of the Babylonian state, as it does not conform to Babylonian sale clauses. Its late Old Babylonian date, already suspected by HARRIS 1975: 339 note 51, is proven by the appearance of the same place name in our no. 5. This implies that the year name in this text is the second year of Ḫam[...],[90] a king of an unknown polity who ruled at the time of Abiešuh (*cf.* the adjective *wārittum* and the high price). This tablet was found in Sippir-Yaḫrurum and was presumably brought there as proof of title when this slave was sold to an inhabitant of that city.

7: Collation of line 3 in FINKELSTEIN 1962: 74 note 10.

9: For the date of this text see PIENTKA 1998: 505 *sub* no. 611.

10: The name might also be read as *iz-zi-te-ḫa-ba-ar*, see KLENGEL 1977: 63 with note 2 and DE GRAEF 1999b: 5 note 4.

13: Partial copy of BM 80359 in Figure 3. The information from three sale contracts concerning the same slave girl, Beltī-lamassī, is presented in the table below.

The earliest contract does not contain a statement about her origin, but she is labelled as a "house-born slave woman from Suḫûm" in the two later contracts. These three texts were kept by the last buyer of this slave, probably the *nadītum*-devotee of text C. A possible scenario to explain the composition of this file is as follows: The last buyer acquired the original sale contract for the acquisition of the slave by the seller (text A), a fictitious sale contract written for the benefit of the seller to serve as proof of the lawful background of the slave (text B), and the sale contract for the acquisition of the slave by the buyer (text C). Bēl-lītim-Marduk (= Bēlī-lītim) was probably the real seller in the final transaction, but might have preferred to remain disconnected with this fraudulent act by having his accomplices act as sellers.[91] See footnote 12 above.

16: Last sale contract and sale contract for an earlier transfer, see footnote 18 above.

17: Two contracts are available concerning this sale, one, VAS 16 207, without description of the origin of the slave, and another, YOS 13 253,

	Text A BM 16495 (Ad 2-9-15)	Text B BM 80359 (Ad 3-3-3)	Text C BM 16946 (Ad 3-3-[..])
object	1 sag-géme *be-el-ti-la-ma-sí*	1 sag-géme *be-el-ti-la-ma-sí* / *wi-li-id* é *ša su-ḫu-um*^{ki}	1 *be-e*[*l-ti-la-ma-sí*] /*i-l*[*i-id* é *ša su-ḫu-um*^{ki}]
seller	*ia-áš-ku-ri be-li-ša* (+ seal)	*i-din-*^{d}*da-gan ù mu-ta-ra-mu be-li-ša* (+ seals)	*i-din-*[^{d}*da-gan ù mu-ta-ra-mu*] dumu-[meš ...] *be-li-ša* (+ seals)
intermediary	*i-din-nu* lú *na-ag-ga-ri* (no seal)	*ba-li-ṭa* dumu *mu-ti-ia-da-du* (+ seal)	*ba-li-ṭa* dumu *mu-ti-ia-da-du* (+ seal)
buyer	*be-lí-li-tim* dumu *na-ka-rum*	*be-el-li-tim-*^{d}marduk dumu *na-ka-rum*	[...] lukur-^{d}utu dumu-munus [...]
price	13 gín + igi-6-gál SI.BI	13 gín + igi-4-gál SI.BI	13 gín + igi-4-gál SI.BI

Three contracts concerning the same slave girl (appendix no. 13)

[89] *CAD* E 100a and *CAD* A/2 269a propose *e-li-*[*tum*].

[90] VAS 9 146: 20–22: mu *ḫa-am-ti*$^{?}$(-) / x-e / mu-gi-bi-il. This formula clearly imitates late Old Babylonian practice, where mu-gibil$_{(4)}$ year names are particularly prominent.

[91] I intend to publish these texts and discuss the underlying scenario in more detail elsewhere.

referring to the same slave, seller and buyer and dated some days later. The second contract identifies the slave as a foreigner and adds the name of an intermediary absent from the first sale contract. See footnote 12 above.

20: For Di 1191 see DE GRAEF 1999b: 3 and 5.

22: For Di 1163 see DE GRAEF 1999a: 17.

23: Partial copy of BM 97134 in Figure 3.

24: For Di 1956 see DE GRAEF 1999b: 3 and 6.

25: Partial copy of BM 92606 in Figure 3.

26: Partial copy of BM 92551 (= Meissner BAP 3) in Figure 3.

27: For Di 1412 see DE GRAEF 1999b: 3 and 6. Probably to be read as *wilid* é *ša Suḫû*[ki] (cf. no. 13).

28: For Di 2074 see DE GRAEF 1999b: 3 and 6.

29: Partial copy of BM 87243 in Figure 3.

33: For the date of the text see PIENTKA 1998: 433 *sub* no. 266. Šala-ummī is attested as a slave name (AbB 1 27: 10, 16, 23; 28: 16).

37: Copy of BM 17212 in Figure 3.

38: The text can be approximately dated by means of the name of the scribe, who was active from Ad 23 until Sd 12, see PIENTKA 1998: 342 *sub* no. 87.

The descriptions of the slaves can be sorted in the following groups:

"Between-river":	Ašlakkā (19), māt Idamaraṣ (10), Šinaḫ (18), Tadanne (39), Talḫayû (21), without specification (7, 40).
Šubartum:	Anzupa? (8), Arraḫru (35), Arramu (30), Ašuḫ (31), Karanā (37), Lubda (31), Mardaman (11), Qaṭṭarā (4), Tadni (14), without specification (1, 17).
Elam:	Ālum-ša-Sîn-išme (26), "town in Elam" (22), without specification (3), unclear (28).
(Country of) Ešnunna:	Aškuzum (33), Ešnunna (25, 32, 33?), Kudla[...]? (38), Nērebtum (33), Zarilulu (23).
Suḫûm:	"house-born slave of Suḫûm" (13, 27), "town in the pasture land of Suḫûm" (34).
City names only:	Dūr-Mankisayû (36), Ḫaḫḫum (15), Kallē (29), Šaḫaḫḫum (5, 6), Šimurrum (2), Ursum (16), unclear (9, 12, 20, 24).

Location of the toponyms

2. Šimurrum was presumably situated on the Sirwan river, one of the source rivers of the Diyala (Frayne 1997).

4. Qaṭṭarā has been identified with Tell Rimah (CHARPIN and DURAND 1987 and EIDEM 1989).

5 and 6. The location of Šaḫaḫḫum, to be kept apart from Ḫaḫḫum (*pace* LEEMANS 1960: 73, 110–111 and GRONEBERG 1980: 85), is unknown.

8. *ālum* AN-*ba-pa*[ki] or, probably better, *ālum an-zu-pa*[ki] seems to be unattested elsewhere.[92] KLENGEL 1984: 99 read in line 3 *a-lum* [d]ba-Ú[?ki], which is also unknown.

9. This example is problematic. HARRIS 1975: 340 assumes that line 2 gives the name of the slave (*iš-bi-te-eš-*[*šu-ub*]). This is problematic because this name is not attested elsewhere (based on SCHWEMER 2001). Furthermore, hybrid names with Teššub are rare in all periods (SCHWEMER 2001: 474). The absence of a personal determinative suggests that this line originally contained a description of the slave and that his name was mentioned in the first line. If so, then the second line presumably contains a toponym which, however, seems to be unattested so far.

10. Northern Idamaraṣ (in contrast to the east Tigris land by the same name) designates the land and states at the foothills of the Ṭur-ʿAbdin (GUICHARD 2002: 142–143).

11. Mardaman cannot be identified with modern Mardin nor be located in northern Syria, but

[92] The element *anz-* is attested as an element of personal names from Nuzi (FINCKE 1993: 23). Compare perhaps the rare Hittite toponym Anzipa (DEL MONTE and TISCHLER 1978: 25 and DEL MONTE 1992: 8)?

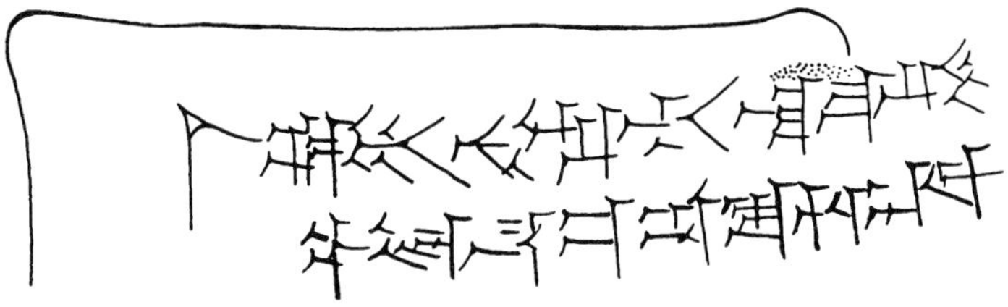

No. 13 BM 80359:1–2

No. 23 BM 97134:1–2

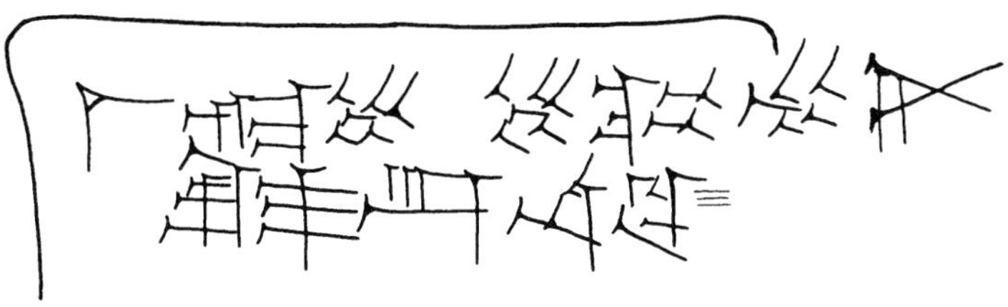

No. 25 BM 92606:1–2

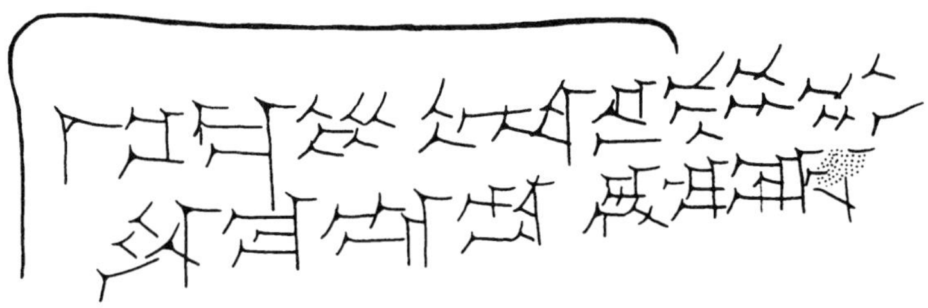

No. 26 BM 92551:1–2
(=Meissner BAP 3)

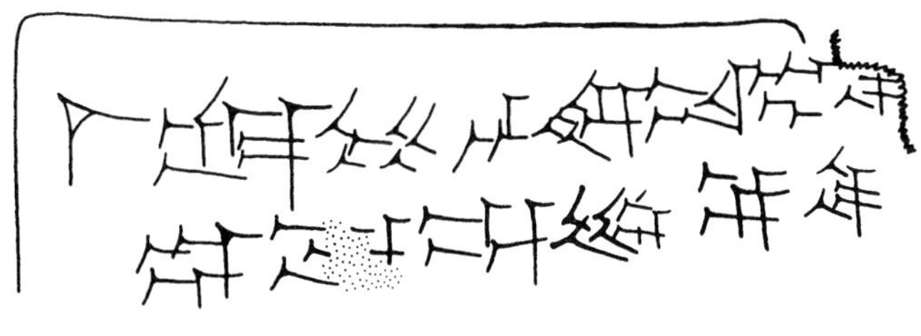

No. 29 BM 87143:1–2

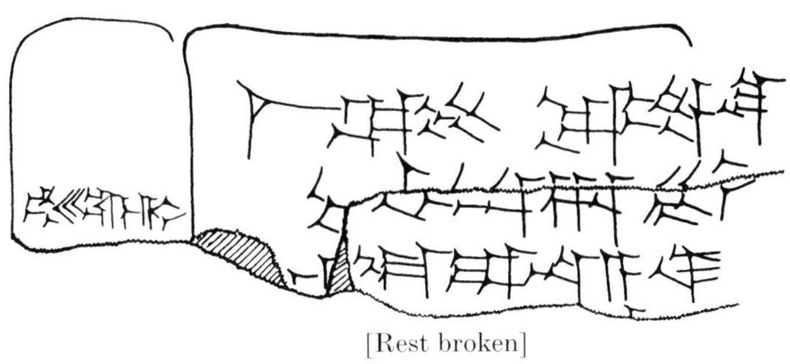

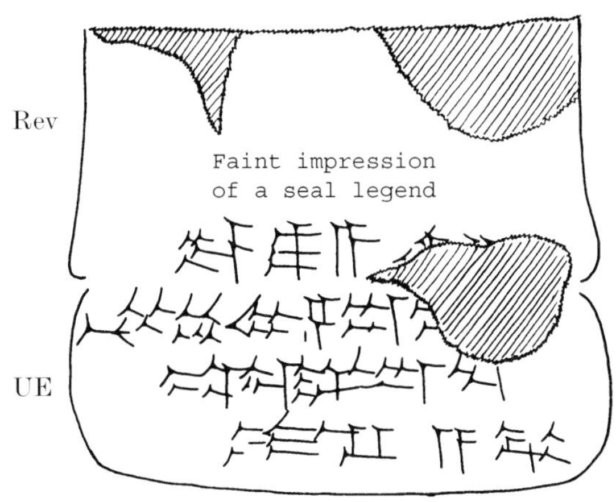

No. 37 BM 17212
(h × w × th = 2,8 × 4,6 × 2,6 cm)

Figure 3 Copies, reproduced at 150%

should be sought in northeasterly Mesopotamia (DURAND 1988a: 294). In Ur III, Old Assyrian and Mari sources it is associated with Ḫaburā (later Ḫaburātum), which must have been located in its vicinity. The name of the latter city has been linked with the Little Habur, a tributary of the Tigris on its eastern side near the Iraqi-Syrian border. For this reason these cities are sometimes located on the left river bank (JOANNÈS and ZIEGLER 1995 and ZIEGLER 2002: 267), but their relations with polities west of the Tigris and their appearance in Old Assyrian texts concerning the westbound trade route (MICHEL 1993: 175) favours a location on the right bank of the Tigris. They were made up by a Hurrian speaking population (DURAND 1988a: 294).

Mardaman and Ḫaburā joined the uprising of Simanum against the alliance of the ruler of Simanum with the royal house of Ur, but king Šū-Sîn suppressed this rebellion and deported their population (RIME 3/2.1.4.1 iii 26-iv 46; 3/2.1.4.3 vi 8–18). Mardaman and Ḫaburātum again come into focus in the time of the Mari archive. Samsī-Addu managed late in his reign to incorporate them in his realm (DURAND 1990: 274–275). Later, their rulers maintained diplomatic contacts with Zimri-Lim (BIROT 1989 and KUPPER 1994). In this time the city of Mardaman again suffered defeat: rulers from the Sindjar region and the Turukkeans from across the Tigris took control of the city and deported its population to the extent that the city was deemed uninhabited (ARMT 26 128 and ARMT 28 156 with DURAND 1988a: 245, 294). Nevertheless, the city seems to have continued to exist, as its deity Šuwala of Mardaman appears in literary texts from Ḫattuša (HAAS 1994: 389).

14. This is the only attestation of the place name Tadni.[93] WILCKE 1975–76: 271 note 29 and MICHALOWSKI 1986: 170 argued that it is identical with Tadanne, the place of origin of a slave sold 65 years later (according to no. 39), but apart from the likeness of both names there is no indication that they can actually be linked.

15. According to LIVERANI 1988 the city of Ḫaḫḫum, an important station on the route from Aššur to Kaneš, is to be identified with the ruins of Lidar Hüyük, ca. 10 km north of Samsat on the eastern bank of the Euphrates. He argues that the violent destruction of the Middle Bronze level 8 can be associated with the destruction of the town by Ḫattušili I. NASHEF 1991: 47 prefers a position west of the Euphrates.

16. Ursum, another important Syrian trading centre (KLENGEL 1989), is most likely to be found in the area of Gaziantep, cf. NASHEF 1991: 130 and DURAND 1998: 76.

18 and 19. The cities of Šinaḫ[94] and Ašlakkā can be fairly accurately located with the help of the sources from Mari. Šinaḫ is often mentioned together with Urkeš during the reign of Zimri-Lim and the cities were probably neighbours. The identification of Tell Mozan with ancient Urkeš allows to locate Šinaḫ in the same area, at the foothills of the Ṭur-ᶜAbdin west of Qamišliye. Both cities were controlled by the kings of Ašnakkum, a city presumably situated to the south, somewhere near the centre of the Habur basin (GUICHARD 2002: 137–138). Ašlakkā was Ašnakkum's permanent rival for local supremacy and cannot have been too far removed (DURAND 1997: 423). It was presumably located somewhere in the northwesterly part of the Habur basin, close to the mountain ranges in the North (JOANNÈS 1996: 345 and DURAND 2000: 462).

During the reign of Zimri-Lim, these polities found themselves under the control of Mari. While they usually acknowledged Mari's supremacy, the city of Ašlakkā was several times objective of military action and at least once part of its population was deported to Mari (ZIEGLER 1999). Just as Urkeš and, presumably, Šinaḫ were centres of a Hurrian-speaking population, the onomastics of the deportees from Ašlakkā reveal that part of its population also bore Hurrian names (MARELLO 1994: 124–125).

21. Talḫû appears as Talḫayum in Mari texts, the capital of Yapṭurum that was situated between the upper course of the Habur and the Tektek Dağ (DURAND 1988b: 112 and JOANNÈS 1996: 344 note 99, 346). Restoring *bīrit nārim* is based on the appearance of this general term in nos. 18 and 19, both located east of Talḫayûm.

---

[93] For the other reference cited in GRONEBERG 1980: 232 see MICHALOWSKI 1986.

[94] The dubious attestation for the "quay of Šinaḫ" in CT 4 26c: 7 (thus GRONEBERG 1980: 222) can be excluded with the help of its parallel CT 8 11a: 5.

23. Zarilulu can be identified with Tell ed-Dhiba'i on the basis of epigraphic finds made there (ABDULLAH 1967 and GRONEBERG 1980: 261).

26. This place name recurs in PBS 8/1 68 (Rīm-Sîn I year 30), a record of expenditure of a lamb for the purpose of extispicy concerning the "safety" of uru-^{d}suen-*iš-me*-⌜*ni*^{ki}⌝ from the É-tùr-nam-en-na stable in Nippur. This might imply that it was a border town of Rīm-Sîn's state, presumably somewhere in eastern direction.

29. The reading of this name is clear, but the town of Kallē seems to be unknown elsewhere.

30. At least two places by the name of Arramu / Arame are attested in cuneiform records. *Ar-ra-mu* is mentioned in Ebla records and must be located in the vicinity of that city; *A-ra-me* is attested in a year name of the Old Akkadian king Narām-Sîn, in an Ur III record and perhaps in the Harmal geographical list (where the form *a-ra-mi-il*^{ki} appears). Arame evidently lay east of the Tigris, and FRAYNE 1997: 263 situated it on the Diyala River near the point where the river breaks through the Jebel Hamrin.

FINKELSTEIN 1955: 2 (and STEINKELLER 1998: 94 note 67) proposed to link Arramu of no. 30 with this eastern toponym. ARCHI and BIGA 1982: 318 linked the Old Babylonian attestation for Arramu found in our no. 30 with Arramu in the Ebla sources. A third suggestion was made by JOANNÈS 1988: 245, who proposed a connection with the city of Aram(m)anum (*a-ra-ma-ni-ma*^{ki}), located somewhere between the kingdom of Atamrum based in Andarig and Allaḫad, cities located south of the Sinjar, and the kingdom of Išme-Dagan based in Ekallātum on the Tigris (ZIEGLER 2002: 256–257).

Given that nos. 30 and 31 belong together (see above), the place of origin of the slaves sold in no. 31 makes a case that Arramu in no. 30 is to be located to the east of the Tigris. Hence Finkelstein was right in identifying it with the city of Arame on the Diyala, while the city of Aram(m)anum is best kept apart.

31. The position of Lubda is roughly known thanks to its role in political history. It is well attested in Nuzi records and seems to have been situated at or near the southern frontier of the kingdom of Arrapḫa. Then it became subject to Babylonia, but was later disputed over between Assyrian and Babylonian rulers. Hence it was most likely situated in the area between the Lower Zab in the north and the Jebel Hamrin in the south, but its precise location remains unclear (NASHEF 1982: 179; FADHIL 1983: 105–126; FINCKE 1993: 166–168). The cities of Ašuḫ and Lubda occur as a pair in no. 31 and in Nuzi texts (FINKELSTEIN 1955: 1–2 and FADHIL 1983: 66, 108) and were probably located close to each other.

33. Nērebtum is certainly Ishchali (CHARPIN 1999: 179). The wall of Aškuzum was built by Sîn-abušu, a ruler who controlled several cities in the lower Diyala region, such as Šaduppûm (Tell Harmal) and Nērebtum (WU 1994: 47–51). Aškuzum should therefore be located in the same area.

35. Arraḫru is still unattested elsewhere (FINKELSTEIN 1955: 3).

36. The city Dūr-Mankisayû is otherwise unknown. The meaning of the name ("fortress of the inhabitants of Mankisum") might imply that it lay in proximity to Mankisum, a city with a strategic role located east of the Tigris somewhere between Samarra and Baghdad (ZIEGLER 2002: 246–247), but this is far from certain.

37. Although past opinions differed (*e.g.* FADHIL 1983: 92–101), it is now clear that there were at least two towns by the name of Karanā: one closely connected with Qaṭṭarā (Tell Rimah) but whose precise location remains uncertain (JOANNÈS 1996: 351), the other situated somewhere east of the Tigris in the general area of Nuzi (FINCKE 1993: 132–133). The eastern Karanā is preferred here, since other Subareans sold during Ammiṣaduqa's reign come from the east Tigris region.

38. The geographic name as copied is otherwise unknown. WILCKE 1975–76: 271 considers an emendation uru^{ki} *ša*$^{!}$-*ad*$^{!}$-[*la-aš*^{ki}].

39. This toponym occurs only once. FINKELSTEIN 1962: 77–78 combines it with Old Assyrian Dadania (and Hittite Tataniya?) that was presumably located in northern Syria (in the area of Zalpa, cf. NASHEF 1991: 33–34), but this is not necessarily correct. The label *birīt nārim* allows locating this city east of the Euphrates or in the Habur basin.

Bibliography

ABDULLAH, A.K.

1967 The paramount god and the old name of Al-Dhibaʾi, *Sumer* 23, 189–192.

ARCHI, A., and BIGA, M.G.

1982 *Testi amministrativi di vario contenuto (archivo L.2769: TM.75.G.3000–4101)*, *Archivi Reali di Ebla Testi* III, Rome: Missione archeologica Italiana in Syria.

ASTOUR, M.C.

1972 Ḫattušiliš, Ḫalab, and Ḫanigalbat, *JNES* 31, 102–109.

1992 The North Mesopotamian kingdom of Ilānṣurā, 1–33, in: YOUNG, G.D., *Mari in retrospect: fifty years of Mari and Mari studies*, Winona Lake: Eisenbrauns.

BECKMAN, G.

2000 Hittite chronology, *Akkadica* 119–120, 19–32.

BELMONTE, J.A.

2001 *Die Orts- und Gewässernamen der Texte aus Syrien im 2. Jt. v. Chr.*, RGTC 12/2, Wiesbaden: Ludwig Reichert.

BIROT, M.

1989 La lettre de Zimri-Lim à Tiš-Ulme, 21–25, in: LEBEAU, M., and TALON P. (eds.), *Reflets des deux fleuves. Volume de mélanges offerts à André Finet*, Akkadica Supplementum 6, Leuven: Peeters.

BRINKMAN, J.A.

1964 Merodach-Baladan II, 6–53, in: BIGGS, R.D., and BRINKMAN, J.A. (eds.), *Studies presented to A. Leo Oppenheim, June 7, 1964*, Chicago: Oriental Institute.

CHARPIN, D.

1985 Un quartier de Babylone et ses habitants sous les successeurs d'Hammurabi, *BiOr* 42, 265–278.

1987 Les décrets royaux à l'époque paléo-babylonienne, à propos d'un ouvrage récent, *AfO* 34, 36–44.

1992 Immigrés, réfugiés et déportés en Babylonie sous Hammurabi et ses successeurs, 207–218, in: CHARPIN, D., and JOANNÈS, F. (eds.), *La circulation des biens, des personnes et des idées dans le Proche-Orient ancien. Actes de la XXXVIIIe Rencontre Assyriologique Internationale (Paris, 8–10 juillet 1991)*, Paris: ERC.

1997 Review of *CTN* 4, *RA* 91, 188–190.

1998 Iluni, roi d'Ešnunna, *NABU* 1998/29.

1999 Review of *OIP* 98, *RA* 93, 178–180.

2000 Tigunânum et l'horizon géographique des archives de Mari, *NABU* 2000/58.

CHARPIN, D., and DURAND, J.-M.

1987 Le nom antique de Tell Rimāh, *RA* 81, 125–146.

DE GRAEF, K.

1999a Les étrangers dans les textes paléobabyloniens tardifs de Sippar (Abi-ešuḫ – Samsuditana), 1ière partie: Sur les inconnus "connus": Cassites, Elamites, Sutéens, Suḫéens, Gutéens et Subaréens, *Akkadica* 111, 1–48.

1999b Les étrangers dans les textes paléobabyloniens tardifs de Sippar (Abi-ešuḫ – Samsuditana), 2ième partie: Sur les inconnus "connus": des personnes spécifiées comme provenant de telle ville ou de telle region spécifique, *Akkadica* 112, 1–17.

2002 An account of the redistribution of land to soldiers in late Old Babylonian Sippar-Amnānum, *JESHO* 45, 141–178.

DERCKSEN, J.G., and DONBAZ, V.

1997–2000 Merchants in distress. An Old Assyrian text mentioning *habbātu*, *JEOL* 35–36, 103–110.

DE SMET, W.A.J.

1990 "Kashshû" in Old-Babylonian documents, *Akkadica* 68, 1–19.

DURAND, J.-M.

1988a *Archives Épistolaires de Mari* I/1, *Archives Royales de Mari* XXVI, Paris: ERC.

1988b Les anciens de Talhayûm, *RA* 82, 97–113.

1990 Documents pour l'histoire du Royaume de Haute-Mesopotamie II, *MARI* 6, 271–301.

1997 *Documents épistolaires du palais de Mari* I, LAPO 16, Paris: Cerf.

1998 *Documents épistolaires du palais de Mari* II, LAPO 17, Paris: Cerf.

2000 *Documents épistolaires du palais de Mari* III, LAPO 18, Paris: Cerf.

EIDEM, J.

1989 Some remarks on the Iltani archive from Tell al Rimah, *Iraq* 51, 67–78.

1991 The Tell Leilan archives 1987, *RA* 85, 109–135.

1996 North Syrian social structure in the MB Period. New evidence from Tell Leilan, 77–85, in: ISMAIL, F. (ed.), *Proceedings of the International Symposium on Syria and the ancient Near East 3000–300 B.C. University of Aleppo 17–20 October 1992 in association with the University "La Sapienza" of Rome*, Aleppo: Aleppo University Publications.

2000 Northern Jezira in the 18th Century BC. Aspects of geo-political patterns, 255–264, in: ROUAULT, O., and WÄFLER, M. (eds.), *La Djéziré et l'Euphrate syriens de la protohistoire à la fin de IIe millénaire av. J.-C. Tendances dans l'interprétation historique des données nouvelles*, Subartu 7, Turnhout: Brepols Publishers.

EIDEM, J., and LÆSSØE, J.

2001 *The Shemshara Archives 1: The Letters*, Kongelige Danske Videnskabernes Selskab Historisk-filosofiske Skrifter 23, Copenhagen.

FADHIL, A.

1983 *Studien zur Topographie und Prosopographie der Provinzstädte des Königreichs Arrapḫe*, Baghdader

Forschungen 6, Mainz am Rhein: Philipp von Zabern.

FARBER, H.

1978 A price and wage study for Northern Babylonia during the Old Babylonian period, *JESHO* 21, 1–51.

FINCKE, J.

1993 *Die Orts- und Gewässernamen der Nuzi-Texte*, RGTC 10, Wiesbaden: Ludwig Reichert.

FINKELSTEIN, J.J.

1955 Subartu and Subarians in Old Babylonian sources, *JCS* 9, 1–7.

1962 "Mesopotamia", *JNES* 21, 73–92.

FRAYNE, D.R.

1997 On the location of Simurrum, 243–269, in: YOUNG, G.D., CHAVALAS, M.W., AVERBECK, R.E. (eds.), *Crossing boundaries and linking horizons. Studies in honor of Michael C. Astour on his 80th birthday*, Bethesda: CDL.

GARDINER, A.H.

1947 *Ancient Egyptian onomastica, Text, vols.* I–II, Oxford: Oxford University Press.

GASCHE, H.

1989 *La Babylonie au 17e siècle avant notre ère: approche archéologique, problèmes et perspectives*, MHEM I, Ghent: University of Ghent.

GASCHE, H., ARMSTRONG, J.A., COLE, S.W., and GURZADYAN, V.G.

1998 *Dating the fall of Babylon. A reappraisal of second-millennium chronology (a joint Ghent-Chicago-Harvard project)*, MHEM IV, Ghent: University of Ghent, Chicago: Oriental Institute.

GELB, I.J.

1968 The word for dragoman in the Ancient Near East, *Glossa* 2, 93–104.

GRONEBERG, B.

1980 *Die Orts- und Gewässernamen der altbabylonischen Zeit*, RGTC 3, Wiesbaden: Ludwig Reichert.

GUICHARD, M.

2002 Le Šubartum occidental à l'avènement de Zimrî-Lîm, 119–168, in: CHARPIN, D., and DURAND, J.-M. (eds.), *Florilegium marianum VI. Recueil d'études à la mémoire d'André Parrot*, Mémoires de N.A.B.U. 7, Paris: SEPOA.

HAAS, V.

1994 *Geschichte der hethitischen Religion*, Handbuch der Orientalistik I/15, Leiden: Brill.

HALLO, W.W.

1995 Slave release in the Biblical world in light of a new text, 79–93, in: ZEVIT, Z., GITIN, S., and SOKOLOFF, M. (eds.), *Solving riddles and untying knots: biblical, epigraphic and Semitic studies in honor of Jonas C. Greenfield*, Winona Lake: Eisenbrauns.

HARRIS, R.

1975 *Ancient Sippar. A demographic study of an Old-Babylonian city (1894–1595 B.C.)*. PIHANS 36. Istanbul: Nederlands Historisch-Archaeologisch Instituut.

HOUWINK TEN CATE, PH.H.J.

1983 The history of warfare according to Hittite sources: the annals of Hattusilis I, *Anatolica* 10, 91–109.

JOANNÈS, F.

1988 *Deuxième partie*, 233–355, in: CHARPIN, D., JOANNÈS, F., LACKENBACHER, S., and LAFONT, B., *Archives Épistolaires de Mari* I/2, *Archives Royales de Mari* XXVI, Paris: ERC.

1992 Histoire de Harâdum à l'époque paléo-babylonienne, 30–36, in: KEPINSKI-LECOMTE, C. (ed.), *Haradum I. Une ville nouvelle sur le Moyen-Euphrate (XVIIIe–XVIIe siècles av. J.-C.)*, Paris: ERC.

1996 Routes et voies de communication dans les archives de Mari, 323–361, in: DURAND, J.-M. (ed.), *Amurru 1, Mari, Ébla et les Hourrites: dix ans de travaux. Première partie. Actes du colloque international (Paris, mai 1993)*, Paris: ERC.

1997 Palmyre et les routes du désert au début du deuxième millénaire av. J.-C., *MARI* 8, 393–415.

JOANNÈS, F., and ZIEGLER, N.

1995 Une attestation de Kumme à l'époque de Samsî-Addu et un Turukkéen de renom à Shemshâra, *NABU* 1995/19.

KEMPINSKI, A.

1983 *Syrien und Palästina (Kanaan) in der letzten Phase der Mittelbronze IIB-Zeit (1650–1570 v. Chr.)*, Ägypten und Altes Testament 4, Wiesbaden: Harrassowitz.

KITCHEN, K.A.

1996 *Ramesside inscriptions translated & annotated. Translations, vol.* II, *Ramesses II, royal inscriptions*, Oxford: Blackwell.

1999 *Ramesside inscriptions translated & annotated. Notes and comments, vol.* II, *Ramesses II, royal inscriptions*, Oxford: Blackwell.

KLENGEL, H.

1977 Sklaven aus Idamaraz, *AoF* 5, 63–69.

1979 Die Hethiter und Babylon, *ArOr* 47, 83–90.

1984 Altbabylonische Texte aus Babylon. Eine Nachlese zu VS 22, *AoF* 11, 92–109.

1989 Syrischer Handel und die Texte aus Kültepe / Kaniš, 263–268, in: EMRE, K., HROUDA, B., MELLINK, M., and ÖZGÜÇ, N. (eds.), *Tahsin Özgüç'e Armağan. Anatolia and the Ancient Near East. Studies in Honor of Tahsin Özgüç*, Ankara: [Türk Tarih Kurumu Basimevi].

KLINGER, J.

1988 Überlegungen zu den Anfängen des Mittani-Staates, 27–42, in: HAAS, V. (ed.), *Hurriter und Hurritisch*, Konstanzer Altorientalische Symposien II, Xenia 21, Konstanz: Universitätsverlag.

van Koppen, F.

2002 Redeeming a father's seal, 147–176, in: Wunsch, C. (ed.), *Mining the archives. Festschrift for Christopher Walker on the occasion of his 60th birthday*, Babylonische Archive 1, Dresden: ISLET.

Koshurnikov, S.G.

1993 Old Babylonian officers' ranks in Northern Babylonia, 175–182, in: Zabłocka, J., and Zawadzki, S. (eds.), *Šulmu IV. Everyday life in ancient Near East. Papers presented at the International Conference Poznań 19–22 September, 1989*, Poznań Adam Mickiewicz University Press.

Kraus, F.R.

1984 *Königliche Verfügungen in altbabylonischer Zeit*, Studia et documenta ad iura orientis antiqui pertinentia 11, Leiden: Brill.

Kühne, C.

1999 Imperial Mittani: an attempt at historical reconstruction, 203–221, in: Owen, D.I., and Wilhelm, G., *Nuzi at seventy-five*, SCCNH 10, Bethesda: CDL.

Kupper, J.-R.

1994 Une contribution à l'histoire du verre dans le Proche-Orient, 265–270, in: Gasche, H., Tanret, M., Janssen, C., and Degraeve, A. (eds.), *Cinquante-deux reflexions sur le Proche-Orient ancien offertes en hommage à Léon De Meyer*, Mesopotamian History and Environment Occasional Publications II, Leuven: Peeters.

Landsberger, B.

1954 Assyrische Königsliste und "Dunkles Zeitalter", *JCS* 8, 31–45, 47–73, 106–133.

Leemans, W.F.

1960 *Foreign trade in the Old Babylonian period as revealed by texts from Southern Mesopotamia*, Studia et documenta ad iura orientis antiqui pertinentia 6, Leiden: Brill.

1968 Old Babylonian letters and economic history. A review article with a digression on foreign trade, *JESHO* 11, 171–226.

Liverani, M.

1988 The Fire of Ḫaḫḫum, *OrAnt* 27, 165–172.

Marello, P.

1994 Esclaves et reines, 115–129 in: Charpin, D., and Durand, J.-M. (eds.), *Florilegium marianum II. Recueil d'études à la mémoire de Maurice Birot*, Mémoires de N.A.B.U. 3, Paris: SEPOA.

Michalowski, P.

1986 An early Old Babylonian loan document, *JCS* 38, 167–171.

1999 Sumer dreams of Subartu: politics and the geographical imagination, 305–315 in: Van Lerberghe, K., and Voet, G. (eds.), *Languages and cultures in contact. At the crossroads of civilizations in the Syro-Mesopotamian realm. Proceedings of the 42th RAI*, OLA 96, Leuven: Peeters.

Michel, C.

1993 Review of Nashef 1991, *WO* 24, 173–176.

2001 Bitume, 134–135 in: Joannès, F. (ed.), *Dictionnaire de la civilisation mésopotamienne*, Paris: Robert Laffont.

Mohammad, A.K.

2002 Texts from Šišīn, *Akkadica* 123, 1–10.

del Monte, G.

1992 *Die Orts- und Gewässernamen der hethitischen Texte Supplement*, RGTC 6/2, Wiesbaden: Ludwig Reichert.

del Monte, G., and Tischler, J.

1978 *Die Orts- und Gewässernamen der hethitischen Texte*, RGTC 6, Wiesbaden: Ludwig Reichert.

Nashef, K.

1982 *Die Orts- und Gewässernamen der mittelbabylonischen und mittelassyrischen Zeit*, RGTC 5, Wiesbaden: Ludwig Reichert.

1991 *Die Orts- und Gewässernamen der altassyrischen Zeit*, RGTC 4, Wiesbaden: Ludwig Reichert.

Oates, D., Oates, J., and McDonald, H.

1997 *Excavations at Tell Brak. Vol. 1: The Mitanni and Old Babylonian periods*, London: British School of Archaeology in Iraq.

Pedersén, O.

1998 Zu den altbabylonischen Archiven aus Babylon, *AoF* 25: 328–338.

Pientka, R.

1998 *Die spätaltbabylonische Zeit. Abiešuh bis Ammiditana. Quellen, Jahresdaten, Geschichte*, Imgula 2, Münster: Rhema.

Podany, A.H.

2002 *The land of Hana. Kings, chronology, and scribal tradition*, Bethesda: CDL.

Potts, D.T.

1999 *The archaeology of Elam. Formation and transformation of an ancient Iranian state*, Cambridge: Cambridge University Press.

Rouault, O.

1992 Cultures locales et influences extérieures: le cas de Terqa, *SMEA* 30, 247–256.

Salvini, M.

1998 Un royaume hourrite en Mésopotamie du Nord à l'époque de Ḫattušili I, 305–311 in: Lebeau, M. (ed.), *About Subartu. Studies devoted to Upper Mesopotamia. Vol. 1 – Landscape, archaeology, settlement*, Subartu 4/1, Turnhout: Brepols.

Schwemer, D.

2001 *Die Wettergottgestalten Mesopotamiens und Nordsyriens im Zeitalter der Keilschriftkulturen. Materialien und Studien nach den schriftlichen Quellen*, Wiesbaden: Harrassowitz.

Smith, S.

1940 *Alalakh and chronology*, London: Luzac.

van Soldt, W.

2000 Syrian chronology in the Old and early Middle Babylonian periods, *Akkadica* 119–120, 103–116.

Steinkeller, P.

1998 The historical background of Urkesh and the Hurrian beginnings in Northern Mesopotamia, 75–98, in: Buccellati, G., and Kelly-Buccellati, M. (eds.), *Urkesh / Mozan studies 3. Urkesh and the Hurrians. Studies in honor of Lloyd Cotzen*, Bibliotheca Mesopotamica 26, Malibu: Undena Publications.

Stol, M.

1973 Review of *YOS* 13, *JCS* 25, 215–233.

1976 *Studies in Old Babylonian history*, PIHANS 40. Istanbul: Nederlands Historisch-Archaeologisch Instituut.

1993 *Epilepsy in Babylonia*, Cuneiform Monographs 2, Groningen: Styx.

2002 Personen um den König in altbabylonischer Zeit, 735–758, in: Loretz, O., Metzer, K.A., and Schaudig, H. (eds.), *Ex Mesopotamia et Syria lux. Festschrift für Manfried Dietrich zu seinem 65. Geburtstag*, AOAT 281, Münster: Ugarit Verlag.

Tanret, M.

2001 As years went by in Sippar-Amnānum..., 455–466, in: Abusch, T., Beaulieu, P.-A., Huehnergard, J., Machinist, P., and Steinkeller, P. (eds.), *Proceedings of the XLVe Rencontre Assyriologique Internationale, Part I, Harvard University, Historiography in the cuneiform world*, Bethesda; CDL.

Van Lerberghe, K.

1995 Kassites and Old Babylonian society. A reappraisal, 379–393, in: Van Lerberghe, K., and Schoors, A. (eds.), *Immigration and Emigration within the ancient Near East. Festschrift E. Lipiński*, OLA 65, Louvain: Peeters.

Veenhof, K.R.

1997–2000 The relation between royal decrees and 'law codes' of the Old Babylonian period, *JEOL* 35–36, 49–83.

Westbrook, R.

1995 Slave and master in ancient Near Eastern law, *Chicago-Kent Law Review* 70, 1631–1676.

Wilcke, C.

1975–76 Zu den spät-altbabylonischen Kaufverträgen aus Nordbabylonien, *WO* 8, 254–285.

1982 Zwei spät-altbabylonische Kaufverträge aus Kiš. Mit zwei Exkursen. A: *nudunnûm* und *nīšītum*; B: Quasi-Hüllentafeln und *kanīkāt / ṭuppāt ummatim*, 426–483, in: van Driel, G., Krispijn, Th.J.H., Stol, M., and Veenhof, K.R. (eds.), *Zikir Šumim. Assyriological studies presented to F.R. Kraus on the occasion of his seventieth birthday*. Leiden: Brill.

1990 Review of VAS 22, *ZA* 80, 297–306.

Wilhelm, G.

1993–97 Mittan(n)i, Mitanni, Maitani. A. Historisch, *RlA* 8, 286–296.

Wu, Y.

1994 *A political history of Eshnunna, Mari and Assyria during the early Old Babylonian period (from the end of Ur III to the death of Šamši-Adad)*, Journal of Ancient Civilizations Supplement 1, Changchun: IHAC.

Zadok, R.

1984 The Origin of the Name Shinar, *ZA* 74, 240–244.

Ziegler, N.

1999 Le harem du vaincu, *RA* 93, 1–26.

2002 Le royaume d'Ekallâtum et son horizon géopolitique, 211–274, in: Charpin, D., and Durand, J.-M. (eds.), *Florilegium marianum VI. Recueil d'études à la mémoire d'André Parrot*, Mémoires de N.A.B.U. 7, Paris: SEPOA.

Abbreviations

AfO	*Archiv für Orientforschung*
AOAT	*Alter Orient und Altes Testament*
AoF	*Altorientalische Forschungen*
ArOr	*Archiv Orientální*
BiOr	*Bibliotheca Orientalis*
JCS	*Journal of Cuneiform Studies*
JEOL	*Jaarbericht van het Vooraziatisch-Egyptisch Genootschap Ex Oriente Lux*
JESHO	*Journal of the Economic and Social History of the Orient*
JNES	*Journal of Near Eastern Studies*
LAPO	*Littératures Anciennes du Proche-Orient*
MARI	*Mari. Annales de Recherches Interdisciplinaires.*
MHEM	*Mesopotamian History and Environment Series II Memoirs*
NABU	*Nouvelles Assyriologiques Brèves et Utilitaires*
OLA	*Orientalia Lovaniensia Analecta*
OrAnt	*Oriens Antiquus*
PIHANS	*Publications de l'Institut Historique-Archéologique Néerlandais de Stamboul*
RA	*Revue d'Assyriologie et d'archéologie orientale*
RGTC	*Répertoire Géographique des Textes Cuneiformes*
RlA	*Reallexikon der Assyriologie und Vorderasiatischen Archäologie*
SCCNH	*Studies on the Civilization and Culture of Nuzi and the Hurrians*
SMEA	*Studi Miceni ed Egeo-Anatolici*
WO	*Die Welt des Orients*
ZA	*Zeitschrift für Assyriologie und Vorderasiatischen Archäologie*

A Tentative Chronology of the Kingdom of Mittani from its Rise to the Reign of Tušratta

*Stefano de Martino**

Defining the chronology of the kingdom of Mittani in relative and absolute terms is particularly problematic; in fact, not only are references to astronomical details lacking in Hurrian documents – unlike in Mesopotamian, Hittite and Egyptian texts – that could supply us with some objective information, but the sources on the kingdom of Mittani are scant, often indirect and limited to certain periods of the history of this country.

The synchronisms that are seen between the kings of Mittani, and the Hittite, Babylonian and Egyptian kings are useful in placing the history of Mittani into the chronological grid of the ancient Near East; however, problems that inevitably arise in the chronological reconstruction of all these areas – Egyptian, Hittite and Mesopotamian – again fall under the Mittanian chronology.

As we know, the first attestation of the toponym Mittani comes from an Egyptian source. It is the fragmentary inscription on the tomb of an Egyptian official called Amenemhet,[1] who served under three Pharaohs, Ahmose I, Amenophis I and Tuthmosis I; he recalls having participated in a military expedition on Syrian territory and in this context the country of *Mtn* is mentioned, i.e. Mittani.[2] It is thought that this expedition possibly coincides with the one led by Tuthmosis I[3] in Syria; this is the first synchronism that connects the history of Mittani to the history of Egypt, and in this case to the reign of Tuthmosis I, whose ascent to the throne is dated, according to different chronologies, to the end of the 16th or beginning of the 15th century B.C.[4]

Unfortunately, we have no Mittanian sources related to this period that may give us further information on the subject; for this reason, the times and ways in which the kingdom of Mittani was formed are not known.

Nevertheless, some clues on the subject may be gathered from the Hittite sources of the Old Kingdom and, in particular, from the historiographic narrations of the Hittite kings Ḫattušili I and Muršili I. It must be said that the toponym Mittani has never been found in the Hittite texts of the Old Kingdom; the mention of Ḫanigalbat in the Akkadian version of the "Annals" of Ḫattušili I (KBo X 1 Ro 11) might be an interpolation of a subsequent age in this manuscript, since the compilation of it dates to the Imperial Age and, moreover, the textual tradition of this annalistic document is very complex.[5] In all the texts at the time of Ḫattušili I and Muršili I, and also in those of their successors, reference is made to the Hurrian political entities in the Syrian area against whom the Hittites fight only via the ethno-linguistic expression *Ḫurla-*/*Ḫurri* "Hurrian".

As M. Salvini pointed out, Mittani is not even mentioned in the texts of the archive of Tuniptešup, the Hurrian king of the country of Tikunani, which was situated east of the Euphrates;[6] to him Ḫattušili I of Ḫatti sent a letter related to the expedition that both were about to go on against the town of Ḫaḫḫum.[7]

In the military campaigns of Ḫattušili I and Muršili I against Alalaḫ, Aleppo, Uršum, Ḫaššum, Ḫaḫḫum, the Hurrians intervene militarily against Ḫatti, to try and check the Hittite advance, and via operations of military aggression inside the kingdom of Ḫatti.[8] The geographical area in which the presence of the Hurrians is placed, according to the Hittite sources of the Old Kingdom, corresponds more or less to what we know about the kingdom of Mittani then, i.e. south-eastern Anatolia and northern Syria.

* University of Trieste

1 See Porter and Moss 1994, 457.

2 See, recently, Wilhelm 1994, 287; Kühne 1999, 213; De Martino 2000, 68, all with previous bibliography.

3 See Redford 1993, 154 n. 117 with previous bibliography; Wilhelm 1994, 287.

4 See Von Beckerath 1994, 124.

5 See Melchert 1978, 1–22.

6 See Miller 2001, 410–429 with previous literature.

7 See Salvini 1994, 61–68; Salvini 1996, 108–114.

8 See De Martino 1991, 71–84; De Martino 1992, 19–37.

For this area, Hittite documents testify to a political situation that is fragmented; in the text KBo III 60,[9] more Hurrian kings are mentioned to whom the title "Kings of the Hurrian people (ÉRIN)"[10] is given; it is significant that this title, i.e. "King of the Hurrian people" – also documented in another Hittite text of the Old Kingdom, KBo III 46 + II 54, – is borne by the kings of Mittani[11] in a subsequent age. This shows a certain continuity between some Hurrian potentates of this period and the subsequent kingdom of Mittani.

Again from Hittite documentation at the time of Ḫattušili I and Muršili I, a situation of conflict between these potentates can be inferred. In a recent article I put forward the hypothesis that Ḫattušili I exploited and instigated conflicts among some of these potentates of the region in order to overcome the towns in western Syria, supported by Aleppo, which the Hittite king was unable to defeat; in fact, the letter to Tunip-tešup of Tikunani shows that the Hittite king sided with this small eastern Hurrian kingdom, fighting against Ḫaḫḫum. Furthermore, the text KBo I 11,[12] yet again from the time of Ḫattušili I, also makes reference to a dynastic struggle in the royal house of one of the Hurrian principalities in western Syria, enemies of the Hittites.[13]

Therefore, the hypothesis can be made for the formation of the kingdom of Mittani to be placed in this situation of ferment, conflict, and political change in which the Hurrian potentates of Syria found themselves; the fall of the kingdom of Yamḫad and the taking of Aleppo by Muršili I, the destruction of Ebla, the annihilation of towns like Uršum, Ḫaḫḫum and Ḫaššum by Ḫattušili I and Muršili I created a void, which the eastern Hurrian principality of Mittani may have taken advantage of; while the political and military weakness of the Hittite sovereigns, subsequent to Muršili I, may have facilitated its very rapid expansion.[14]

If we accept such a historical scenario about the formation of Mittani, we must conjecture that this kingdom came into existence in the age immediately following that of the Hittite king Muršili I. Now, this sovereign's campaign against Babylon and the end of the first Babylonian dynasty consequent to such expedition are dated depending on the chronologies to 1595 (middle chronology) 1531 (low chronology), or 1499 (according to the chronology suggested by H. Gasche[15]). In the former case, the interval lasting almost a century – between the supposed formation of Mittani and the first attestation of the toponym Mittani to the time of Tuthmosis I – seems to be too long; from this standpoint, as G. Wilhelm already pointed out, it is better to work with the low chronology,[16] or a lower middle chronology, according to what was recently suggested by C. Michel and P. Rocher.[17] According to Gasche's "ultra-low chronology", Mittani, instead, should already exist at the time of Muršili I.

Mittani's first attested king is Parattarna I.[18] Before him, we have to perhaps place the kingdom of Šuttarna, the sovereign documented by the impression of his seal, used in a more recent age by Sauštatar.[19]

As the inscription of Idrimi of Alalaḫ testifies, Parattarna and Idrimi were contemporaries; but not only: the treaty (AlT 3) drawn up between Idrimi and Pilliya,[20] king of Kizzuwatna, also tells us that the latter was a contemporary of Šuttarna. Moreover, the texts of Terqa show that Parattarna was also a contemporary of Qiš-Addu, the king of this country.[21]

Pilliya of Kizzuwatna had also sealed a treaty with the Hittite king, Zidanza (KUB XXXVI 108), and therefore a synchronism can be established between Ḫatti and Mittani.[22] Identifying

---

[9] See, recently, De Martino 2002, 77–85, with previous bibliography.

[10] See Wilhelm 1994, 292; Kühne 1999, 208.

[11] See Wilhelm 1994, 292.

[12] See Beckman 1995, 23–34.

[13] Vo 7: "The sons of the 'Son of the Storm-god' are fighting one another over kingship".

[14] See Klengel 1992, 86.

[15] Gasche, Armstrong, Cole and Gurzadyan 1998.

[16] See Wilhelm 1989, 20.

[17] Michel and Rocher 1997–2000, 111–126; see also, Veenhof 2000, 147–149.

[18] See, recently, Wilhelm 1994, 293 with previous bibliography.

[19] See, recently, De Martino 2000, 76 and no. 41.

[20] On the problem, if there were two sovereigns of Kizzuwatna with this name, see Beal 428–431, who shows convincingly that there was only one king Pilliya.

[21] See Rouault 1992, 254; Rouault 1988, 313.

[22] The excludes the hypothesis put forward by Van Soldt 2000, 111, according to whom Idrimi would be the contemporary of Muršili I.

the Hittite sovereign with whom Pilliya made the treaty – that is, whether it involves Zidanza I or Zidanza II – has been a subject of discussion among scholars.[23] Resolute, however, is the declaration that Kizzuwatna is still under Hittite control during the time of king Ammuna, successor of Zidanza I, as seen in the Edict of the Hittite king Telipinu;[24] therefore, the treaty with Pilliya may be attributed to Zidanza II. In spite of this, the recent hypothesis that the Hittite partner of this treaty may be Zidanza I was reaffirmed by C. Kühne.[25] Such conjecture, however, can no longer be sustained if we also consider how many generations elapse, in the various countries linked by synchronisms, over the same time period, i.e. the one that separates Parattarna, in Mittani, from his successor Sauštatar. As we will note later, between these two Mittanian kings there seems to have been the reign of one or two other sovereigns; in Alalaḫ we find that after Idrimi, there is Adad/Tešup-nirari and then Niqmepa;[26] in Kizzuwatna the sovereigns Pilliya, Talzu and Šunaššura succeded one another.[27] In light of this, it does not seem plausible to retain that in Mittani, Alalaḫ and Kizzuwatna there are three or four sovereigns, whereas over the same time period, in Ḫatti, there are a good twelve of them – as the Hittite kings from Zidanza I to Tutḫaliya I/II were many.

If, therefore, we accept the synchronism between Parattarna of Mittani and Zidanza II of Ḫatti, we also get an idea of how much time elapsed between the rise of Mittani and the reign of Parattarna. Indeed, if we put the first event immediately after the reign of the Hittite sovereign Muršili I, it shows that between Muršili I and Zidanza II seven sovereigns are documented who, according to G. Beckman's study,[28] correspond to five generations, because Ḫuzziya I and Telipinu belong to the same generation, as do perhaps even Taḫurwaili and Aluwamna. Hence, a time lapse equal to about five generations seems to separate Parattarna from the rise of the kingdom of Mittani.[29]

After Parattarna, the king of Mittani of whom we have documents, comes Sauštatar, as previously mentioned. The impressions of this sovereign's royal seal, preserved on a letter from Nuzi and in another letter from Tell Brak,[30] also show the name of Sauštatar's father, Parsatatar. The texts of Terqa, still at the time of the king Qiš-Addu cited above, who was a contemporary of Parattarna, also report a Mittanian king named Sausadat. Sausadat might have been an immediate successor of Parattarna,[31] or, more probably, as O. Rouault[32] has pointed out, this name might be understood as a different writing of the name Sauštatar. Now O. Rouault informs us that in the texts of the king Qiš-Addu also the Mittanian king Šuttarna might be quoted.

Sauštatar is seen in two documents of Alalaḫ. The text AlT 13 preserves a judicial litigation brought by a certain Irib-ḫazi against Niqmepa, king of Alalaḫ and resolved before the king of Mittani. Instead, tablet AlT 14 relates one that is contested between Niqmepa of Alalaḫ and Šunaššura, king of Kizzuwatna due to a border problem between the two countries. This litigation is placed under the judgement of Sauštatar. Šunaššura of Kizzuwatna also draws up an international treaty (KBo I 5) with the Hittite king, Tutḫaliya I/II.[33]

Hence the outcome is that Sauštatar is a contemporary of Niqmepa of Alalaḫ, Šunaššura of Kizzuwatna and Tutḫaliya I/II of Ḫatti; the latter synchronism is also confirmed by the annalistic Hittite text KUB XXIII 14, which describes the military undertakings led by Tutḫaliya I/II and his co-regent Arnuwanda I. On line 14, in a fragmentary passage, where events of the time of Tutḫaliya I/II are narrated, there is also mention of the Hurrians and the person's name Sau[štatar] is partially preserved.

---

[23] See the bibliography cited by Beal 1986, 428 n. 24.

[24] On all this see Beal 1986, 428–430, with previous bibliography.

[25] Kühne 2000, 214 and no. 67.

[26] See Klengel 1992, 243.

[27] See Beal 1986, 443.

[28] Beckman 2000, 24–26.

[29] We cannot take Alalaḫ into consideration, with the aim of defining this time period, because the phase preceding Idrimi still remains obscure; on Alalaḫ in the period before Idrimi see Marquez Rowe 1997, 181–183; on the chronology of Alalaḫ from the archaeological point of view see Gates 1981, 11–49.

[30] Both these letters are subsequent to Sauštatar. For these two documents see, respectively, Stein 1989, 36–60; Illingworth 1988, 99–105.

[31] See also Wilhelm 1994, 293.

[32] Rouault 1992, 254.

[33] See Beal 1986, 442; Wilhelm 1988, 362–370. Different, see Houwink Ten Cate 1998b, 53.

The treaty drawn up by Šunaššura with Ḫatti sanctions the entry of this country into the Hittite sphere of influence and is placed well in the time of the Hittite military expansion, also led into Syria by the king Tutḫaliya I/II and concluded with the conquest of Aleppo. If, therefore, the reign of Sauštatar of Mittani can be placed with a certain precision into the political and chronological context of the Syro-Anatolian area, the comparison becomes more problematic with Egyptian documentation; in fact some scholars think that Sauštatar is a contemporary of Tuthmosis III, and others a contemporary of Amenophis II.[34]

As we know, Tuthmosis III led a series of military campaigns in Syria and fought many times with the Hurrians.[35] In the 22nd/23rd year of his reign, Tuthmosis faced a coalition of Syrian princes in Megiddo, who were commanded by the king of Qadeš and were, presumably, supported by Mittani. The Pharaoh went back to Syria to fight in his 29th, 30th and 31st year; in his 33rd year Tuthmosis fought against a Mittanian army not far from Aleppo, and Egyptian sources hand down to us that Mittani suffered a severe defeat, while the Pharaoh plundered the area along the Euphrates from Karkemiš to Emar. Egyptian documents, however, do not mention the name of the Mittanian king, an adversary of Tuthmosis III.

In trying to contextualize the above-mentioned events in the political situation of the Syro-Anatolian area, it must be pointed out that the expansionistic policies in Syria of the Hittite king Tutḫaliya I/II, i.e. the conquest of Aleppo, and the drawing up of a treaty with Tunip,[36] and yet another with Aštata,[37] might be connected to the weakness of Mittani's authority in these regions, pursuant to the military campaigns of Tuthmosis III. In this political scenario, perhaps the so-called "treaty of Kuruštama"[38] might have been sealed between the Hittites and the Egyptians. This treaty served to tie these two countries, which tried to expand their area of dominion in Syria to the detriment of Mittani and hence had a common interest.

J. Klinger[39] has already pointed out that the period of Hittite political influence in Syria might be placed chronologically between the 32nd and 44th year of the reign of Tuthmosis III, i.e. after the eighth Syrian campaign, the one that broke the Mittanian front, but before the seventeenth expedition of the Pharaoh in Syria when he fought Tunip; in fact, the Egyptian attack on this town might lead us to believe that Tunip had again gone over to the side of Mittani.[40]

As J. Klinger[41] observes, however, the hypothesis of seeing Sauštatar as a contemporary not only of Tuthmosis III, but also of Tutḫaliya I/II of Ḫatti, might appear problematic in the context of the chronological reconstruction of the Hittite kingdom. Indeed, pursuant to a very accurate and critical study on the chronology of the Hittite king Šuppiluliuma I, carried out by G. Wilhelm and J. Boese,[42] most Hittitologists have accepted 1343 as the date when this sovereign's reign begins, thus favoring the low chronology.[43]

It must be pointed out, on this subject, that the reconstruction of the history of the Hittite Middle Kingdom, a subject of discussion among scholars for a long time, now appears clearer; in fact, before Šuppiluliuma, the sovereigns Tutḫaliya I/II, Arnuwanda I and Tutḫaliya III[44] are placed in direct succession, which brings about the elimination of the king Ḫattušili II,

[34] For the first hypothesis see, lastly, Klinger 1995, 234–247; for the second hypothesis see, for example, Kühne 1973, 20 no. 85; Kühne 1982, 222–224. Redford 1992, 161–164 and, in particular, nos. 156 and 171, puts forward the hypothesis that Sauštatar may be a contemporary of Tuthmosis III, but even for the first part of the reign of Amenophis II; see also Kühne 1999, 217. Moreover, Mayer 1995, 340–341; 2001, 15, thinks that Tutḫaliya I/II is a contemporary of Hatshepsut.

[35] See Klengel 1992, 91–95; Redford 1993,160–166 with previous bibliography.

[36] KBo XIX 59 +, See Klinger 1995, 238–241; as this scholar points out, p. 214, the treaty mentions Ilimilimma of Alalaḫ; this means that it was drawn up when Niqmepa was no longer on the throne.

[37] KUB LVII 18, see Klinger 1995, 245.

[38] KUB XL 8, see Klengel 1999, 106, 110 with previous bibliography.

[39] Art. cit. 246.

[40] See De Martino 2000, 84–85.

[41] Klinger 1995, 246–247.

[42] Wilhelm and Boese 1987, 74–117.

[43] For the end of the reign of Šuppiluliuma I and consequently of the ascent of Muršili II to the throne, see now Huber 2001, 640–644.

[44] So this also excludes Ḫantili II.

whose existence was hypothesized by O. Carruba.[45] Furthermore, the proposal[46] to distinguish between one king, Tutḫaliya I, conqueror of Aleppo, and another king, Tutḫaliya II, who led a series of military campaigns in Anatolia described in his "Annals", has by now been abandoned by the majority of scholars.[47]

Therefore, if Tutḫaliya I/II is placed like Sauštatar of Mittani around the middle of the 15th century, based on the synchronism with the 33rd–42nd years of Tuthmosis III,[48] the period, comprising the reign of Tutḫaliya I/II and the ascent to the throne of Suppilulima I, if this is placed in 1344/43, would be about a century. But one century seems too long a period for the reign of only three Hittite sovereigns. From this standpoint, it might appear opportune to raise by about fifteen/twenty years the date of ascent to the throne of Šuppiluliuma I, as recently suggested by some scholars.[49] Consequently, a reign lasting longer than twenty years might be assigned to Šuppiluliuma I; it is true that the Hittite text KUB XIX 9 attributes to him twenty years of reign, but it may be supposed that here only an indicative figure is given, perhaps to signify a long period.[50]

On the other side, the chronological reconstruction proposed by G. Wilhelm and J. Boese is very convincing and we cannot exclude that Tutḫaliya I/II, Arnuwanda I and Tutḫaliya III have ruled for a long time, about 30 years each one.

Otherwise, a lowering of about 20 years for the dates of the reign of Sauštatar of Mittani and of Tutḫaliya I/II might be conjectured if both were supposedly contemporaries of Amenophis II; it is true that this sovereign also carried out an expedition in Syria, however the crisis of Mittani's dominion in western Syria and the Hittite conquest of Aleppo are better placed in the context of the wars in Asia by Tuthmosis III, which took place over a fairly long period of time, rather than in the quick campaign in the 7th year of the reign of Amenophis II.

After Sauštatar, it is not known if Artatama I[51] ascended the throne, or if, prior to him, Parattarna II reigned – the sovereign whose existence is inferred by a Nuzi text.[52] With the reign of Artatama I, we have clear chronological references with Egypt, due to three inter-dynastic marriages that tied the royal house of Mittani to that of the Pharaoh at the time of the sovereigns Artatama I and Tuthmosis IV, Šuttarna II and Amenophis III, Tušratta and Amenophis IV[53] respectively.

The last king of Mittani – before the Hittite conquest of Mittani by the king Šuppiluliuma I – is Tušratta, to whom we owe the letters preserved in the archive of Tell el-Amarna, sent to Amenophis III and Amenophis IV. These documents confirm a series of synchronisms with all the other countries in the ancient Near East.

With Tušratta and with the end of Mittani as an independent state, this quick survey on Mittanian chronology can be concluded. The death of this king might be hinted at in the letter of Tell el-Amarna no. 43,[54] sent by Šuppiluliuma I of Ḫatti to the Pharaoh. Chronologically this event is connected to the request made by an Egyptian queen who asked Šuppiluliuma for his son in marriage. In fact, such a request reached the Hittite king during the siege of Karkemiš, after which Mittani was overcome by the Hittites. So, even though the death of Tušratta can be easily placed into the frame of events known from some Hittite sources, the exact date of it is somewhat difficult to determine, since the Pharaoh, whose widow wrote to Šuppiluliuma, has been identified by scholars either as Amenophis IV, Semenchkare, or Tutanchamon.[55]

[45] See, recently, Dinçol, Dinçol, Hawkins and Wilhelm 1993, 99–105.

[46] See Carruba 1971, 75–94.

[47] See, recently, Taracha 1997, 74 n. 1. Differently, see Carruba 1998, 87–108.

[48] See recently Von Beckerath 1994, 124 with previous bibliography.

[49] See, for example, Na'aman 1996, 257; Houwink Ten Cate 1998, 160; see also Parker 2002, 62.

[50] See, recently, Freu 2002, 88.

[51] See Wilhelm 1989, 28.

[52] HSS XIII 165; See, recently, Stein 1989, 36–60; Wilhelm 1994, 293.

[53] See Wilhelm 1989, 30–32

[54] Na'aman 1995, 116–118; diversely, see Artzi 1993, 7–8 no. 2; Houwink Ten Cate 1998, 160.

[55] See, recently, Wilhlelm and Boese 1987, 74–114; Bryce 1989) 22, 29–30; Von Beckerath 1994, 100; Helck 1994, 15–22; Van Den Hout 1994, 60–88; Hornung 1998, 103; Liverani 1999, 409; Freu 2002, 102–104; Parker 2002, 47–52.

Mittani	Egypt	Ḫatti	Alalaḫ	Kizzuwatna	Terqa
Principate of Mittani Rise of the kingdom of Mittani		Ḫattušili I Muršili I			
First attestation of Mittani	Tuthmosis I				
Kirta (?) Šuttarna I (?)					? Qiš-Addu
Parattarna I	? Tuthmosis III ?	Zidanza II	Idrimi	Pilliya	Qiš-Addu
Sausadat (??)					
Parsatatar					
Sauštatar	? Tuthmosis III ?	Tutḫaliya I/II	Niqmepa	Šunaššura	? Qiš-Addu
ParattarnaII (??)					
Artatama I	Tuthmosis IV				
Šuttarna II	Amenophis III				
Artašumara (Utḫi)					
Tušratta	Amenophis IV	Šuppiluliuma I			

Table 1

Bibliography

ALP, S. and SÜEL, A. (eds.)

1998 *Acts of the IIIrd International Congress of Hittitology*, Ankara.

ARTZI, P.

1993 An (Almost) Forgotten Amarna Letter, in: A.F. RAINEY (ed.) 1993, 7–10.

ÅSTRÖM, P.

1987 *High, Middle or Low?* Gothenburg.

BEAL, R.

1986 The History of Kizzuwatna and the Date of the Šunaššura Treaty, *Or* 55, 424–445.

VON BECKERATH, J.

1994 *Chronologie des ägyptischen Neuen Reiches*, Hildesheim.

BECKMAN, G.

1995 The Siege of Uršu Text (CTH 7) and Old Hittite Historiography, *JCS* 47, 23–34.

2000 Hittite Chronology, *Akkadica* 119–120, 19–32.

BRYCE, T.

1989 Some Observations on the Chronology of Šuppiluliuma's Reign, *AnSt* 39, 19–30.

CARRUBA, O.

1971 Hattusili II, *SMEA* 14, 75–94.

1998 Hethitische Dynasten zwischen altem und neuem Reich, in: S. ALP and A. SÜEL (eds.) 1998, 87–108.

CARRUBA, O., GIORGIERI, M. and MORA C. (eds.)

1995 *Atti del II Congresso internazionale di Hittitologia*, Pavia.

DIETRICH, M. and LORETZ, O. (eds.)

1998 *dubsar anta-men, Festschrift für W.H.Ph. Römer*, Münster.

DINÇOL, A., DINÇOL, B., HAWKINS, D. and WILHLEM, G.

1993 The 'Cruciform Seal' from Boğazköy-Ḫattuša, *IM* 43, 87–106.

FREU, J.

2002 La chronologie du règne de Suppiluliume: essai de mise au point, in: P. TARACHA (ed.) 2002, 87–108.

GASCHE, H., ARMSTRONG, J.A., COLE, S.W. and GURZADYAN, V.G.

1998 *Dating the Fall of Babylon. A Reappraisal of Second-Millennium Chronology*, Ghent.

GATES, M.H.

1981 *Alalakh Levels VI and V: A Chronological Reassessment, Syro-Mesopotamian Studies* 4/2, Malibu.

HELCK, W.

1994 Ägyptologische Bemerkungen zu den Artikel von J. Freu in 'Hethitica XI 39', *Hethitica* 12, 15–22.

VAN DEN HOUT, TH.

1994 Der Falke und das Kücken: der neue Pharao und der hethitische Prinz?, *ZA* 84, 60–88.

HORNUNG, E.

1998 *Akhenaten. La religione della luce nell'Alto Egitto*, Roma.

HOUWINK TEN CATE, PH.

1998 The Scribes of the Maşat Letters and the GAL DUB.SAR(.MEŠ) of the Hittite Capital during the Final Phase of the Early Empire Period, in: M. DIETRICH and O. LORETZ (eds.) 1998, 157–178.

1998b An Alternative Date for the Sunassuras Treaty (KBo 1.5), *AoF* 25, 34–53.

HUBER, P.J.

2001 The Solar Omen of Muršili II, *JAOS* 121, 640–644.

ILLINGWORTH, N.J.J.

1988 Inscriptions from Tell Brak, *Iraq* 50, 87–108.

KLENGEL, H.

1992 *Syria 3000 to 300 B.C.*, Berlin.

1999 *Geschichte des hethitischen Reiches*, Leiden.

KLINGER, J.

1995 Synchronismen in der Epoche vor Šuppiluliuma I. – einige Anmerkungen zur Chronologie der mittelhethitischen Geschichte, 235–248, in: O. CARRUBA, M. GIORGIERI and C. MORA (eds.) 1995.

KÜHNE, C.

1973 *Die Chronologie der internationalen Korrespondenz von El-Amarna*, Neukirchen-Vluyn.

1982 Politische Szenerie und Internationale Beziehungen Vorderasiens um die Mitte des 2. Jahrtausends vor Chr. (zugleich ein Konzept der Kurzchronologie) mit einer Zeittafel, 203–264, in: H.J. NISSEN and J. RENGER (eds.) 1982.

1999 Imperial Mittani: An Attempt at Historical Reconstruction, *SCCNH* 10, 203–221.

LIVERANI, M.

1999 *Le lettere di el-Amarna, vol. 2, Le lettere dei "Grandi Re"*, Brescia.

MARQUEZ ROWE, I.

1997 Ḫalab in the XVIth and XVth Centuries B.C. A New Look at the Alalaḫ Material, *WZKM* 87, 177–205.

DE MARTINO, S.

1991 I Hurriti nei testi ittiti dell'antico regno, *Seminari dell'Istituto per gli studi Micenei ed Egeo-Anatolici (anno 1990)*, Roma, 71–84.

1992 I rapporti tra Ittiti e Hurriti durante il regno di Muršili I, *Hethitica* 11, 19–37.

2000 Il regno hurrita di Mittani: profilo storico politico, *PdP* 55, 68–102.

2002 The Military Exploits of the Hittite King Ḫattušili I in Lands Situated between the Upper Euphrates and the Upper Tigris, 77–86, in: P. TARACHA (ed.) 2002.

MAYER, W.

1995 Die historische Einordnung der 'Autobiographie' des Idrimi von Alalaḫ, *UF* 27, 333–350.

2001 *Tall Munbâqa-Ekalte II*, Saarbrücken, 15.

MELCHERT, H.C.

1978 The Acts of Hattušili I, *JNES* 37, 1–22.

MICHEL, C. and ROCHER, P.

1997–2000 La chronologie di IIe millénaire revue à l'ombre d'une éclipse de soleil, *JEOL* 35–36,111–126.

MILLER, J.L.

2001 Ḫattušili I's Expansion into Northern Syria in Light of the Tikunani Letter, 410–429, in: G. WILHELM (ed.) 2001.

NA'AMAN, N.

1995 Tushratta's Murder in Shuppiluliuma's Letter to Akhenaten (EA 43), *Abr Nahrain* 33, 116–118.

1996 Ammishtamru's Letter to Akhenaten (EA 45) and Hittite Chronology, *AuOr* 14, 251–257.

NEU, E. and RÜSTER, CHR. (eds.)

1988 *Documentum Asiae Minoris Antiquae, Festschrift für H. Otten zum 75. Geburtstag*, Wiesbaden.

NISSEN H.J. and RENGER, J, (eds.)

1982 *Mesopotamien und seine Nachbarn, Berliner Beiträge zum Vorderen Orient* 1, Berlin.

PARKER, V.

2002 Zur Chronologie des Šuppiluliumas I, *AoF* 29, 31–62.

PORTER, S.B. and MOSS R.L.B.

1994 *The Theban Necropolis*, Oxford.

RAINEY, A.F. (ed.)

1993 *kinattūtu ša dārâti, Raphael Kutscher Memorial Volume*, Tel Aviv.

REDFORD, D.B.

1993 *Egypt, Canaan and Israel in Ancient Times*, Princeton.

ROUAULT, O.

1992 Cultures locales et influences extérieurs: le cas de Terqa, *SMEA* 30, 247–256.

1998 Recherches récentes à Tell Ashara-Terqa (1991–1995), *Subartu* 4, 313–323.

SALVINI, M.

1994 Una lettera di Ḫattušili I relativa alla spedizione contro Ḫaḫḫum, *SMEA* 34, 61–80.

1996 *The Ḫabiru Prism of King Tunip-Teššup of Tikunani*, Roma.

VAN SOLDT, W.

2000 Syrian Chronology in the Old and Early Middle Babylonian Periods, *Akkadica* 119–120, 103–116.

STEIN, D.

1989 A Reappraisal of the "Sauštatar Letter" from Nuzi, *ZA* 79, 36–60.

TARACHA, P.

1997 Zu den Tutḫaliya-Annalen (CTH 142), *WO* 28, 74–84.

TARACHA, P. (ed.)

2002 *Silva Anatolica. Anatolian Studies Presented to Maciej Popko on the Occasion of His 65th Birthday*, Warsaw.

VEENHOF, K.R.

2000 Old Assyrian Chronology, *Akkadica* 119–120, 137–151.

WILHELM, G. and BOESE, J.

1987 Absolute Chronologie und die hethitische Geschichte des 15. und 14. Jahrhunderts v. Chr., 74–117, in: P. ÅSTRÖM (ed.) 1987.

WILHELM, G.

1988 Zur ersten Zeile des Šunaššura-Vertrages, 359–370, in: NEU, E. and RÜSTER, CHR. (eds.) 1988.

1989 *The Hurrians*, Warminster.

1994 Mittan(n)i, *Reallexikon der Assyriologie und Vorderasiatischen Archäologie* VIII.

WILHELM, G. (ed.)

2001 *Akten des IV. Internationalen Kongresses für Hethitologie* Wiesbaden.

Abbreviations

AnSt *Anatolian Studies*, London.

AoF *Altorientalische Forschungen*, Berlin.

AuOr *Aula Orientalis*, Barcelona.

IM *Istanbuler Mitteilungen*, Istanbul.

JAOS *Journal of the American Oriental Society*, New Haven.

JCS *Journal of Cuneiform Studies*, Baltimore.

JEOL *Jaarbericht van Het Vooraziatisch-Egyptisch Genootschap Ex Orient Lux*, Leiden.

JNES *Journal of Near Eastern Studies*, Chicago.

Or *Orientalia*, Roma.

PdP *La Parola del Passato*, Napoli.

SCCNH *Studies on the Civilization and Culture of Nuzi and the Hurrians*, Bethesda.

SMEA *Studi Micenei ed Egeo-Anatolici*, Roma.

UF *Ugarit-Forschungen*, Neukirchen-Vluyn.

WO *Die Welt des Orients*, Göttingen.

WZKM *Wiener Zeitschrift für die Kunde des Morgenlandes*, Wien.

ZA *Zeitschrift für Assyriologie und Vorderasiatische Archäologie*, Berlin-New York.

Evidence for the Short Chronology in Mesopotamia?

The chronological relationship between the texts from Emar and Ekalte[1]

*Regine Pruzsinszky**

In the course of the Al-Assad barrage-project in Syria several rescue-excavations took place in the Middle Euphrates region within the past 30–35 years (Margueron [ed.] 1980). Tall Munbāqa and Tall Meskene Qadime are among the best known tells, which were excavated within this period and have also yielded rich text material dating to the second half of the 2nd mill. BC.[2] Based on these numerous texts, which include letters, documents, various kinds of lists, literary, religious and canonical texts, Tall Munbāqa was clearly identified with ancient Ekalte[3] and nearby Tall Meskene with Emar.[4]

Preliminary remarks

The commonly accepted view in secondary literature published so far is that the texts from Ekalte date earlier than the archives of Emar. One crucial impulse for this assumption was presumably the edition of the first known tablet from Tall Munbāqa by W. von Soden 1982, who dated it because of its orthography and language to the late Old Babylonian period. On the other hand Margueron, the first excavator of Tall Meskene Qadime, stressed that Emar, which means specifically the part of the tell from where the tablets derive, was a new foundation by the Hittites dating to the 9th year of Muršili II. Emar then was the capital of the kingdom of Aštata (situated on the west bank of the Euphrates), which was under the supremacy of Karkemiš with its sovereign Šaḫurunuwa.[5] According to this premise the texts, which are generally undated, were chronologically placed in the period starting with the new foundation at the end of the 14th cent. BC (ca. 1310 BC) by the excavator as well as the French field-epigraphist Arnaud. The archaeological finds and results of the Late Bronze Age were consequently interpreted as being strongly influenced by the Hittites. Also the chronological study by Adamthwaite 2001, who believes that the texts belong entirely to the thirteenth century B.C., is based primarily on Margueron's results.

However, most recent excavation results by U. Finkbeiner show that Tall Meskene Qadime has a continuous occupation from the Early Bronze Age to the Late Bronze Age.[6] Part of the material culture of Emar can now be increasingly seen in the light of a Syrian tradition.

Due to the resumption of excavations at Emar as well as the publication of approximately 100 texts from Ekalte by Mayer in 2001 the picture of the chronological setting of the Late Bronze Age tablets and their relationship to each other can be challenged anew. Certainly worth mentioning here is the study by Skaist 1998, who separated the so-called Syrian and Syro-Hittite documents from Emar formally *and* chronologically.[7] In this context it should be emphasized that all the texts from Ekalte belong to the Syrian type of tablets. Syrian documents from Emar are characterized by vertical format tablets, which are impressed with cylinder-seals[8] and have a writing tradition which shows strong affinities with the Alalaḫ IV, the Amurru- and Canaanite Amarna letters and with the texts of the Old Hittite period. Documents from Ugarit, where Syrian traditions remained dominant despite the Hittite sovereignty, also have a vertical format and are written across the short dimension (see lately Faist 2002, 131).

[1] Basic information on these two sites can be found in *Reallexikon der Assyriologie und Vorderasiatischen Archäologie* 8, 1993–1997, 83–93 and 417–419.

* University of Vienna

[2] Tall Ḫadīdī (ancient Azû) will not be further considered within this study, due to the fact that its texts have not been published yet.

[3] In preliminary reports Mayer identified Tall Munbāqa with Uri.

[4] In the 3rd and in the beginning of the 2nd mill. BC this city, which due to its geographical setting was an important center of trade, was known as Imar, as the texts from Ebla and Mari report.

[5] Bryce 1999, 201–203, Klengel 1999, 197–199, Klengel 2001, 270–271.

[6] Finkbeiner 2002, 5–6.

[7] For a differentiation see e.g. Faist 2002, 135. For a more detailed discussion note Seminara 1998, 13–16.

[8] Beyer 2001.

The language of the Emar tablets belongs to the so-called "peripheral" Akkadian featuring Middle Babylonian characteristics, which also comprises Westsemitic substrates[9] and few Assyrianisms. Hurrian lexemes are rarely attested.[10] Wilcke 1992 has already mentioned that less Middle Babylonian features can be found in tablets of the Syrian style than in those belonging to the Syro-Hittite one. He as well as Seminara have pointed out several similarities in the writing system, syllabary and language between the Syrian tablets and the texts from Ekalte. The language of Ekalte, which does not fundamentally differ from the language used at Emar, more precisely from the language of the Syrian type of texts, has been summarized by Mayer 2001, 35–38 ("Die Schreiber und ihre Sprache").[11] According to Mayer the language of Ekalte belongs to the late Old Babylonian, which does not show any Middle Babylonian characteristics. The ductus can be placed between those of Alalaḫ VII and Alalaḫ IV. It should be pointed out that Seminara 1998, 19 did not exclude a chronological division of the documents of the Syrian and Syro-Hittite format when compiling the different characteristics of the Emar tablets.

Let us turn now to the known key-data of the Emar and Ekalte texts, which are partly linked to the archaeological remains. As has already been stated, only few tablets are dated (by year-name or eponym-like dating). Therefore we mostly rely on references to (possibly) determined events and on prosopographical observations.

Emar

According to Arnaud the texts from Emar are to be dated to the period between ca. 1310 and 1187 BC. This dating was established by means of specific absolutely dated events. Firstly, E 26 contains a year-name, which mentions the second year of the Kassite king Meli-Šipak, who reigned between 1188 and 1181 according to Brinkman 1976.[12] We further possess a synchronism between the well known priest (LÚ.ḪAL) of Emar Zū-Baᶜla and the king of Karkemiš Šaḫurunuwa (E 201: note the critical comments by Skaist 1998, 47), who was a contemporary of Muršili II. Muršili II is chronologically determined by an astronomical date, a solar eclipse (basically only a solar omen is mentioned in KUB 14, 4, IV 24'f.) in his 10th year, which is generally dated to 1308 BC. In the course of the chronological evaluation a division in time between tablets of the Syrian and those of the Syro-Hittite style was left unconsidered due to the (limits of the) excavation results proposed by Margueron. This task was undertaken by Skaist 1998, who proposed the following duration for two different and subsequent local royal dynasties at Emar:[13] According to him the Syrian documents cover the period between ca. 1400–1220 BC and the Syro-Hittite ones date between 1275–1210 BC. The following local rulers are therefore attested at Emar:

- Irʾib-^{d}IŠKUR
  - Igmil-Dagān
  - Liʾmi-šarra
    - Išbi-Dagān
      - Zū-Baᶜla

as well as the well-known Emar dynasty, which followed the above mentioned "rulers":[14]

- Iaḫṣi-Dagān
  - ^{d}IŠKUR-kabar I
    - Zū-Aštarti
    - Abbānu
    - Pilsu-Dagān
      - Elli
        - ^{d}IŠKUR-kabar II

---

[9] Seminara 1998; especially the personal names of Emar belong to a Westsemitic language.

[10] Pentiuc 2001

[11] It can be observed that Mayer 2001 generally dispenses from pointing out parallels in Emar (exception on p. 37 on the usage of the subjunctive-marker). Further, another feature is mentioned on p. 36: "Generell scheinen die Schreiber aus *Ekalte* mit ihren Kollegen aus *Alalaḫ* und *Ḫalab*/Aleppo – soweit die aus *Ḫalab* stammenden *Māri*-Texte dies erkennen lassen – eine gewisse Geringschätzung des Tafelrandes zu teilen." This can be observed on Emar tablets as well (see the copies by Arnaud 1985 and 1991). Almost no references can be found to the detailed grammar by Seminara 1998, who has differentiated between Syrian and Syro-Hittite tablets.

[12] Compare also the shortened dates for Meli-Šipak (1186–1179 BC) by Boese 1982. For further notes on E 26 and its archaeological context see Skaist 1998, 46.

[13] The local dynasty is subordinated to the kingdom of Karkemiš: see e.g. Klengel 2001, 270.

[14] I entertain some doubt, whether we are dealing with actual "rulers". See below sub "The earlier 'dynasty' of Emar" and *bēlu*.

In view of Skaist 1998, 62, which is based on a difficult passage in GK 6, Liʾmi-šarra was a dependant of a ruler of Mittani (who is designated as LUGAL KUR *ḫur-ri* "Hurrian king"). Since Šuppiluliuma I, who conquered Syria, brought Mittani to an end, the aforementioned king of Mittani must have ruled before ca. 1325 BC in order to have exercised enough power and pressure on the rulers of Emar, as it is mentioned in GK 6.

1325 BC is the point of time when the ruler of the well-known royal family Iaḫṣi-Dagān ascended the throne (p. 64). Skaist counted back four generations containing 18 years each and obtained ca. 1400 BC for the beginning of the reign of Irʾib-ᵈIŠKUR, the first ruler of the newly established dynasty.[15]

Hurrian troops, who threatened and attacked the city of Emar, are mentioned in texts which can be dated to the reign of the local ruler Pilsu-Dagān, who was a contemporary of Tukultī-Ninurta I.[16] The second dynasty of Emar lasted five generations and was placed accordingly between 1325 and 1220+x years (the actual regnal length of ᵈIŠKUR-kabar II like of all the other rulers is unknown).

Crucial here is the earlier dating of part of the tablets (documents of the Syrian style). Unfortunately the pottery sequences and stratigraphical observations of the French excavation at Emar, which could possibly yield some more information on the chronological sequence of archaeological phases, are still unpublished; the glyptic material, which was published by Beyer in 2001, does not seem to rule out an earlier dating.

Disappointingly the prosopographical data do not allow any links between Emar and Ekalte. However, it has to be stressed that the textual material from Ekalte mostly deals with private matters (family archives from private houses versus archives from the administrative building M_1 at Emar), in which actual contacts between both towns with their own administrative centers (compare the local city-gods ᵈNIN.URTA and Baʿlaka) are unlikely to be expected.

Ekalte

In contrast to Emar no local dynasty is known to have ruled at Ekalte. All texts stem from the local Late Bronze Age phase 4, which is separated from phase 3 by a destruction layer.[17] In the texts an average of three to four generations is attested, which also – depending on the estimation of generation-lengths – is used for the calculation of duration of this phase: according to Mayer 2001, 14 phase 4 lasted 60–80 years. These generations are narrowed down by (reconstructed) absolute dates: On the one hand a year-name in text nr. 80 plays a crucial role for Mayer's reconstruction. In line 32 the author reads MU BA.DU ᴵ*Tu*, which he translated "Jahr nachdem *Tu(ḫalija)* gekommen ist". In spite of the fact that in the past this line was corrected with the more likely reading MU *Ma/Ba?-da/du?* 1 KAM.MA,[18] Mayer 2001, 15 connected the abbreviated spelling ᴵ*Tu* with Tutḫalija I, who reigned at the end of the 15th cent. BC and destroyed Ḫalab.[19] But Klinger 1995, 245[31] has already pointed out that this spelling is only attested for Tutḫalija IV. and that the historical link is therefore unlikely. Further, we do not have any evidence as to whether Tutḫalija I ever crossed the Euphrates during his campaigns against Syria.[20] Next Mayer 2001, 18 attempted to reconstruct the time of destruction of Ekalte by scanning the political situation of this period. He concluded that the town must have been destroyed during the well known 8th campaign of Tuthmosis III (1479–1425), which took place in the latter's 33rd regnal year.[21] Consequently Mayer subtracted three to four generations from 1446 BC and set the beginning of phase 4 around 1530 BC. Though the beginning of this phase is not determined by a layer of destruction, the texts imply a pauperiza-

---

15 Practically nothing is known about the local kings and the conditions which led to their succession. Therefore a calculation of approximate generation-lengths is impossible.

16 Skaist 1998, 65–67 linked these attacks to events reported in KBo 1, 14: here, attacks by "men from Turira" on Hittite territories are mentioned, which presumably took place between 1268 and 1265 BC, when Ḫanigalbat was a vassal-state of Assyria and before an end was put to the independent rule of Ḫanigalbat by Šalmaneser I (ca. 1258 BC).

17 Further occupation is attested after the destruction in phase 3 (but no texts derive from this phase).

18 This date formula is characteristic for Syrian-style tablets (see e.g. Klinger 1995, 245[31]). The PN *Bada* is attested in the Emar onomasticon.

19 This event most probably followed the campaign of Tuthmosis III (Klinger 1995, 244).

20 Klengel 1999, 114, Bryce 1999, 151–154.

21 Ekalte is not mentioned on the northeastern wall of the 7th pylon in Karnak, which contains a list of destroyed towns. See Busch 1998, 141–142

tion of the population, which MAYER attributed to the preceding continous bellicose conflicts between the Hittites and Iamḫad in Northern Syria.[22] Again, these are linked to the campaigns against Syria by Muršili I, who had ultimately caused the fall of the Babylon I dynasty during the reign of Samsuditana.[23]

Following the short chronology, which is based on the observed Venus cycles during the reign of Ammiṣaduqa, the fall of Babylon took place in 1531 BC. MAYER 2001, 18 concluded on behalf of his reconstruction: "Drei bis vier Generationen vor 1446 rückt aber das Ende dieser Phase in etwa auf die Zeit von 1530 – dies spräche eindeutig für die 'Kurze Chronologie', auf keinen Fall ließe sich dieser Befund mit der 'Mittleren' oder der 'Langen Chronologie' in Einklang bringen." As KLINGER 1995 observed, difficulties arise also with the attested number of generations of the Hittite royal family within this period, which is the time between Muršili I and Tutḫalija I (see below).

According to Mayer Ekalte lost its importance after 1446 BC, at the latest after Šuppiluliuma I in the 14th cent. BC, in the course of the breakdown of the Mittanian kingdom and the subsequent reorganization of Syria by the Hittites. Other than in Emar no textual evidence is known from the later phase of the Late Bronze Age. The pottery from Ekalte is still being prepared for publication, which maybe will shed further light on the dating of phase 4 to the 15th cent. BC.

As has been mentioned above no prosopographical links can be established between the materials from Emar and Ekalte, which could help to synchronize both text corpora. But, as expected, it can be noted that in the Ekalte material no Anatolian personal names are attested. Next to the majority of Westsemitic and Akkadian-Westsemitic hybrid names a number of Hurrian personal names are documented, which cannot be found in the Emar onomasticon.[24]

THE EARLIER "DYNASTY" OF EMAR

ADAMTHWAITE 2001, who dealt with the chronology of the Emar texts based on MARGUERON's results, argued for an overall dating to the 13th cent. BC: p. 7: "The fact that the excavated area at Tell Meskéné belongs only to the thirteenth century B.C. since no structures earlier than the Late Bronze Age have been found, supports Margueron's conclusion that the Late Bronze Age Emar was a newly built town, only lately relocated from elsewhere." The author briefly referred to SKAIST's study (1998) and concluded on p. 8: "In summary, his line of argumentation lays too much weight on suggestions in the texts and not on the archaeology of the site ...". Hence ADAMTHWAITE calls SKAIST's earlier dynasty "head of the city council of Emar", which includes also the "city elders of Emar" (^{LÚ}*šībūt* ^{URU}Emar) and was contemporary with the well-known royal family of Emar starting with Iaḫṣi-Dagān.[25]

Texts of the "earlier" dynasty (after Skaist), all belonging to the group of Syrian-type tablets, usually feature an eponym dating: "Year 1 (or 2) of PN". This kind of dating, which names persons without further qualification, is not attested on tablets which mention members of the royal family of Iaḫṣi-Dagān.[26] Following YAMADA 1996 the eponym dating reflects the official dating system of the municipal administration of Emar, which is represented by the city-elders. Otherwise, the city mayor (*ḫazannu*[27]) functions as a representative of the public authority. The elders of Emar are already well attested in the texts of Mari and are known to have already played an important role in the administration in the region of the Middle Euphrates in the first half of the 2nd mill. BC.[28] Also the texts of Ekalte state the importance of

[22] This is indicated by many sale documents (MAYER 2002, 14). See also WESTENHOLZ 2000, xv.

[23] BRYCE 1999, 101–105.

[24] In Emar the following names are attested: *A-ki-ia*, *A-ri-im-mé*, *Eḫli-Addu*, *I-ri-ia*, *Ka-tu-we*, *Ku-ut-pa*, *Ku-ut-ra*, *Ku-ut-ti*, *Pu-ra-me* and *Ta-ki-ia*.

[25] For more prosopographical details of this "family" see pp. 18–21.

[26] As FLEMING 2000, 16 pointed out "many Syrian-type documents involve neither these kings of Emar nor their official scribes".

[27] Mayors usually are attested with names of Westsemitic provenance. Local governors (LÚ.UGULA.KALAM.MA) usually bear Anatolian or Hurrian names. S. BECKMAN 1995, 36 and ADAMTHWAITE 2001, 192, who stresses that the latter are Hittite functionaries. On the role of the LÚ.UGULA.KALAM.MA see lately again HELTZER 2001, 219–236.

[28] Note that at Tuttul a coexistence of a *ḫazannum* and of *šībūtu* is attested as well. Compare also the observations by PODANY 2002, 187 ff.

the elders of the city and the mayor in the city council.[29] ADAMTHWAITE 2001, 191 pointed out that these structures of the local municipal administration represented by the instances mentioned above can be traced back to the 3rd mill. BC.

It has been previously stated that "The elders originally enjoyed complete political and economic powers, but this control was slowly eroded over time." (WESTENHOLZ 2000, xv). The rule of kings at Emar only starts with Iaḫṣi-Dagān and is understood to be an innovation within the administrative structure, which was most probably due to the sovereignty of the Hittites. It can therefore be assumed that during the Mittanian period in Syria, and specifically at Emar, older administrative structures with their representatives *ḫazannu* and *šībūtu* (elders) were still in use,[30] as it is reported in the earlier texts from Ebla and Mari.[31] This scenario is taken for granted at Ekalte and Azû, where no royal family was installed and whose textual evidence is traditionally dated before the one of Emar.

The autonomy of the municipal administration represented by the elders and NIN.URTA has been frequently pointed out before. It can be observed that both were massively involved in numerous transactions and dominated the economic affairs of the city, while the royal family of Emar is not mentioned at all.[32] Combining the evidence it may therefore be concluded that the textual evidence from Emar can be divided into an earlier phase before the Hittites and a later phase.[33] In this case Emar might be chronologically closer to Ekalte than has been proposed so far and the archives of both sites might be possibly brought together in the future (note the unfortunate fact of missing prosopographical links). Most important for chronological considerations is that ADAMTHWAITE's premise can now be dismissed since there is now clear evidence for a continuous occupation from the Early Bronze Age to the Late Bronze Age at Tall Meskene Qadime.

Still, I entertain some doubts as to SKAIST's terminology concerning the preceding "dynasty": Despite the fact that SKAIST has published valuable comments on the formulary and its implications on the sociopolitical situation, I would not go as far as reconstructing another local *royal* family at Emar preceding the well-known one starting with Iaḫṣi-Dagān, who is regularly addressed as LUGAL (URU *E-mar*^{KI}).[34] The sovereigns of the Hittites in Karkemiš (Ini-Teššup, Šaḫurunuwa, Šarri-Kuša and Talmi-Teššup) are designated as LUGAL (KUR/URU *Kar-ga-mis*) as well. But this title is missing with the persons who have been included to the earlier "dynasty" by SKAIST. A hint for the indirect designation of Liʾmi-šarra as a king was seen in text GK 6. In this document, which contains many difficult passages (esp. lines 13 and 14 with the terms É.GAL and LUGAL, which can not be clearly attributed to a specific person in this text[35]), the latter may only be associated with the title *bēlu* ("lord"), which is always mentioned together with the city of Emar (URU^{li}-*šu ù be-li-šu*, note instead in line 36 ^{I}*Li*-LUGAL *ù* URU *E-mar* as witnesses[36]),[37] whereas the term LUGAL ("king") is only attested in connection with the Hurrian king (LUGAL KUR *ḫur-ri*; see below). In this text it is stated that Irʾib-^{d}IŠKUR (father of Liʾmi-šarra?: see lines 1 and 6) is designated as SANGA ("*šangû* priest") of the temple of "Nergal of Trade" for settling the burden of the hostages

[29] The documents from Emar, Ekalte as well as from Azû name a group of brothers (LÚ.MEŠ ŠEŠ.MEŠ/*aḫḫē*) with a "head of the brothers" or "eldest of the brothers" (*rāb aḫḫē* or ŠEŠ.GAL ŠEŠ.MEŠ): MAYER in BUSCH (ed.) 1998, 127–128, ADAMTHWAITE 2001, 191, MAYER 2001, 25 and RE 8, 16.

[30] For a LÚ.UGULA.KALAM.MA from Emar see ADAMTWAITE 2001, 192 ("vestige of the earlier Emarite tradition").

[31] KLENGEL 1989, 61–65. On a "more archaic society" at Emar compared to Ugarit see most recently HELTZER 2001, 236.

[32] They are mostly referred to in Syro-Hittite type of texts. For the use of the Dynastic Seal and the so-called NIN.URTA Seal see SKAIST 1998, 63.

[33] See lately D'ALFONSO 2000, 269–295.

[34] Note that we now know of a king named Iaḫṣi-Baʿl, who ruled at Emar.

[35] Maybe one referred to the family of Iaḫṣi-Baʿl attested in Ekalte texts nr. 9 and 70 (see below)?

[36] *Li*-LUGAL= Liʾmi-šarra. In line 42 Abī-Rašap, the *ḫazannu* is mentioned as well. The same *ḫazannu* acts as a witness in AuOrSI 14 and 87 as well as in E 149. SKAIST 1998, 61 compared lines 20 (LUGAL *ù* URU *E-mar*) and 36 (^{I}*Li*-LUGAL *ù* URU *E-mar*) and concluded that *Liʾmi-šarra* was a king of Emar.

[37] In RE 34 a certain Ikūn-Dagān committed an offense against his city (URU^{KI}-*šu*) and his lord (*be-li-šu*), which resulted in confiscation of his property by ^{d}NIN.URTA. On the chronological significance of this text see FLEMING 2000, 23. Document E 1 also reports an offense against the lord.

that was on the city and its *bēlu*. Otherwise, neither Liʾmi-šarra[38] nor Irʾib-^{d}IŠKUR ever bear a title. Studying the role of the city-elders in Ebla and Mari, Klengel 1989, 63[23] mentioned that it is uncertain whether the EN of Ebla, who often is attested together with the city-elders, is to be regarded as the "king" (Archi) or rather as a "chief administrator" (Michalowski).[39] Discussing the evidences Klengel further proposed the translation "Stadtherrscher (ohne monarchische Gewalt)" or "Verwaltungschef", which might be compared with Adamthwaite's "head of the city council" cited above.

The circle of persons around Irʾib-^{d}IŠKUR is mostly mentioned as witnesses at various transactions. It may be concluded that these persons were representatives of the city, comparable with the city-elders who were heavily involved in economic life.[40] It is worth mentioning that in these documents the payment of penalty usually goes to the city, which is represented by the elders of the city and ^{d}NIN.URTA. Just in one case (AuOr SI 14) also the palace receives part of the fine. It remains unclear why – in the case of the palace as the recipient – no member of the royal family is explicitly mentioned, which is why Skaist (1998) 61 then assumed that the mentioned group of persons around Irʾib-^{d}IŠKUR acting as witnesses in this sale document represented members of a *royal* family (dynasty).[41]

Further and even more important, the identification of Irʾib-^{d}IŠKUR (first witness) in AuOrSI 14 (see Skaist 1998, 61) with the one of the earlier "dynasty" is not secured yet and highly problematic. But nevertheless this text can be dated within this period of time, due to the fact that it belongs to the so-called *arana*-documents.[42] Based on GK 6 and the *arana*-documents Skaist 1998 argued for an earlier Hurrian domination (Mittani) over Emar before the Hittite takeover of power in Northern Syria. GK 6 as well as the *arana*-documents report on payments of tribute (Hurrian term *arana*) to a Hurrian king, who was most likely a Mittanian ruler. As a result of these external contacts mentioned in the Emar texts Skaist proposed an earlier dating of the Syrian-style tablets.

Due to the statement in the starting line "in the days of Liʾmi-šarra, son of Irʾib-^{d}IŠKUR" of AuOrSI 87 it becomes evident that Liʾmi-šarra was certainly an important person at Emar (see lately also Fleming 2000, 25). This introduction referring to a certain period is only attested in texts by the hand of the scribe Eḫli-Kuša (also E 149, AuOrSI 18 and GK 6). Interestingly, both texts GK 6 and AuOrSI 87 deal with the appointment of two different SANGA of Nergal-temples (Irʾib-^{d}IŠKUR and Pilsu-Dagān).[43] In both instances the city is involved; only text GK 6 further notes a LUGAL in this respect, who is to be related to the Hurrian king of line 13.

It is not fully proven whether Liʾmi-šarra and his family can be entirely placed chronologically before the reign of Iaḫṣi-Dagān or whether they overlap with the latter's dynasty.

An indication on the concurrence of the texts from Ekalte and Emar may be found in the badly preserved text nr. 1 from Ekalte, which was written on behalf of the city-council (URU.KI GAL.GAL ù TUR.TUR ù LÚ.MEŠ *ab-bu*[44]): here the Ekaltean mayor Muḫra-aḫī and the Emarite king ^{d}IŠKUR-kabar (I ?) are mentioned together. It is reported that copper instead of [...] of the property of Muḫra-aḫī is to be delivered to the king. Both persons are again attested together in the sale-document nr. 24 from Ekalte.

In the case of the king (LUGAL) Iaḫṣi-Baʿl, who is named in the Ekalte texts nr. 9 and nr. 70 but not in the archives of Emar, no further solution can be offered here: As Mayer has already pointed out, Iaḫṣi-Baʿl seems very likely to represent a yet unknown king of Emar,[45] possibly preceding the well-known royal family of Emar.[46]

[38] Seminara 1996, 79–92: on the meanings of LUGAL/ *šarru* ("governor" and "king") in Emar and Ebla.

[39] See lately again Pettinato (1995) 99–104 and Pitard 1997, 399–416.

[40] Referring to the Ebla evidence Klengel 1989, 63 states: "Es ist unklar, ob der EN selbst aus dem Ältestenrat hervorgegangen ist oder sogar von diesem bestimmt wurde."

[41] One would expect that the members of this family were designated as LUGAL regularly.

[42] Skaist 1998a, 169–171.

[43] Fleming 2000 24[33].

[44] See Mayer 2001, 25.

[45] Further evidence must be awaited whether Zū-Baʿla of text nr. 9, line 35 really is to be regarded as the son of the king Iaḫṣi-Baʿl, and therefore as a prince of Emar.

[46] Note that the palace mentioned in GK 6, 13 most probably refers to the palace of Emar. It is not clear whether the LUGAL of line 14 is to be identified with the Mittanian king (see above) or possibly with Iaḫṣi-Baʿl known from the Ekalte texts.

Unfortunately, none of the other persons in the text can be found in the prosopographical data of Emar, which could indicate that the mentioned LUGAL preceded the family of Iaḫṣi-Dagān and somehow links to the family of Irʾib-^{d}IŠKUR. Yet, we do have to await further evidence to fit in this king chronologically; but he can be taken as a proof that in texts nr. 9 and 70 one referred to Emar's role of the late 15th or 14th cent. BC.

The "missing link" between Egyptian and Mesopotamian chronology?

Despite the fact that Mayer has repeatedly published his line of argumentation stressing Ekalte's importance for Mesopotamian chronology, we are still confronted with a number of difficulties arising around the Dark Age of Mesopotamia. The link between Ekalte and the campaign of Tuthmosis III is by no means proven and relies solely on doubtful as well as indirect connections (note the date-formula with ^{I}*Tu*). In view of the references to Hittite rulers and their campaigns against Syria one has to consider the long and assured line of Hittite kings within the mentioned period. No matter how long each of the generations actually lasted, this succession of kings does not allow to fit the evidence of Ekalte – as understood by Mayer – within the framework of a short chronology for Mesopotamia.[47] Phase 4 of Ekalte cannot be correlated with known historical events for the time being; especially the beginning of this layer, which according to Mayer does not show any destruction or any other significant characteristics, can hardly be linked with the campaign of Muršili I against Babylon, despite the attempt of the re-calculation of generations starting with Tutḫalija I. Regardless of the question of generation-lengths and the dating of Ekalte, one should perhaps consider a chronology for Mesopotamia which is *not* based on the observations of Venus cycles. The evaluation of astronomical data has repeatedly shown that no satisfying results can be achieved, which implies that alternative approaches should be considered in the future.

Much as we would like to find a solution for absolute chronology in Mesopotamia, one cannot do so by neglecting important sources of the Ancient Near East which cover the Dark Age.

Bibliography

Adamthwaite, M.R.

2001 *Late Hittite Emar, The Chronology, Synchronisms, and Socio-Political Aspects of a Late Bronze Age Fortress Town*, Ancient Near Eastern Studies Supplement 8, Leuven.

Beckman, G.

1995 Hittite Provincial Administration in Anatolia and Syria, in: O. Carruba *et al.* (eds.), *Atti del II. Congresso Internazionale di Hittitologia*, Studia Mediterranea 9, Pavia, 19–37.

Beyer, D.

2001 *Emar VI - Les sceaux, Mission archeologique de Meskéné-Emar, Recherches au pays d'Aštata*, Orbis Biblicus et Orientalis Series Archaeologica 20, University Press Fribourg.

Boese, J.

1982 Burnaburiaš II, Melišipak und die mittelbabylonische Chronologie, *Ugarit-Forschungen* 14, 15–26.

Brinkman, J.A.

1976 *Materials and Studies for Kassite History, vol. 1, A Catalogue of Cuneiform Sources Pertaining to Specific Monarchs of the Kassite Dynasty*, The Oriental Institute, Chicago.

Bryce, T.

1999 *The Kingdom of the Hittites*, Oxford University Press.

Busch, R.

1998 Der achte Feldzug des Tutmosis III. in seinem 33. Regierungsjahr, in: R. Busch (ed.), *Tall Munbāqa – Bronzezeit in Syrien*, Wachtholz Verlag: Neumünster, 139–144.

d'Alfonso, L.

2000 Syro-Hittite Administration at Emar: New Considerations on the Basis of a Prosopographic Study, *Altorientalische Forschungen* 27, 269–295.

[47] Klinger 1995, 245.

Faist, B.

2002 Die Rechtsordnung in Syrien nach der hethitischen Eroberung: Wandel und Kontinuität, in: H. Blum *et al.* (eds.), *Brückenland Anatolien? Ursachen, Extensität und Modi des Kulturaustausches zwischen Anatolien und seinen Nachbarn*, Attempto Verlag: Tübingen, 129–146.

Finkbeiner, U.

2002 Neue Ausgrabungen in Emar, *Alter Orient* 3, 4–6.

Fleming, D.E

2000 *Time at Emar, The Cultic Calendar and the Rituals from the Diviner's Archive*, Mesopotamian Civilizations 11, Eisenbrauns: Winona Lake, IN.

Heltzer, M.

2001 The Political Institutions of Ancient Emar as Compared with Contemporary Ugarit (13. - Beginning of the 12. Century B.C.E.), *Ugarit-Forschungen* 33, 219–236.

Klengel, H.

1989 „Älteste" aus Ebla und Mari, in: M. Lebeau and Ph. Talon (eds.), *Reflets des deux fleuves, Volume de Mélanges offerts à André Finet*, Akkadica Supplementum VI, Peeters: Leuven, 61–65.

1999 *Geschichte des Hethitischen Reiches*, Handbuch der Orientalistik I/34, Brill: Leiden-Boston-Köln.

2001 Einige Bemerkungen zur hethitischen Herrschaftsordnung in Syrien, in: G. Wilhelm (ed.), *Akten des IV. Internationalen Kongresses für Hethitologie Würzburg, 4.–8. Oktober 1999*, Studien zu den Boğazköy-Texten 45, Harrassowitz Verlag: Wiesbaden, 255–271.

Klinger, J.

1995 Synchronismen in der Epoche vor Šuppiluliuma I. – einige Anmerkungen zur Chronologie der mittelhethitischen Geschichte, in: O. Carruba *et al.* (eds.), *Atti del II. Congresso Internazionale di Hittitologia*, Studia Mediterranea 9, Pavia, 235–248.

Margueron, J.-Cl. (ed.)

1980 *Le moyen Euphrate, Zone de contacts et d'echanges, Actes du Colloque de Strasbourg 10–12 mars*, Strasbourg 1977.

Mayer, W.

2001 *Tall Munbāqa – Ekalte II, Die Texte*, in: D. Machule (ed.), Ausgrabungen in Tall Munbāqa - Ekalte, Wissenschaftliche Veröffentlichungen der Deutschen Orient-Gesellschaft 102, SDV: Saarbrücken.

Pentiuc, E.J.

2001 *West Semitic Vocabulary in the Akkadian Texts from Emar*, Harvard Semitic Studies 49, Eisenbrauns: Winona Lake, IN.

Pettinato, G.

1995 "Napoleone" ad Ebla: un generale o un verbo, *Aula Orientalis* 13, Editorial Ausa: Sabadell (Barcelona), 75–106.

Pitard, W.T.

1997 The Meaning of EN at Ebla, in: G.D. Young *et al.* (eds.), *Crossing Boundaries and Linking Horizons, Studies in Honor of Michael C. Astour*, CDL Press: Bethesda, MD, 399–416.

Podany, A.H.

2002 *The Land of Hana, Kings, Chronology and Scribal Tradition*, CDL Press: Bethesda, MD.

Seminara, St.

1996 Il "lugalato" da Ebla a Emar, Sopravivenze emarite della terminologia e della prassi eblaite della gestione del potere, *Aula Orientalis* 14, Editorial Ausa: Sabadell (Barcelona), 79–92.

1998 *L'accadico di Emar*, Materiali per il Vocabulario Sumerico 6, Rom.

Skaist, A.

1998 The Chronology of the Legal Texts from Emar, *Zeitschrift für Assyriologie und Vorderasiatische Archäologie* 88, 45–71.

1998a A Hurrian Term at Emar, *Studies on the Civilization and Culture of Nuzi and the Hurrians* 9, CDL Press: Bethesda, MD, 169–171.

Soden, W. von

1982 Eine altbabylonische Urkunde (79 MBQ 15) aus Tall Munbāqa, *Mitteilungen der Deutschen Orient-Gesellschaft* 114, 71–77.

Westenholz, J.G.

2000 *Cuneiform Inscriptions in the Collection of the Bible Lands Museum, The Emar Tablets*, Cuneiform Monographs 13, Styx Publications: Groningen.

Wilcke, C.

1992 AḪ, die „Brüder" von Emar, Untersuchungen zur Schreibertradition am Euphratknie, *Aula Orientalis* 10, Editorial Ausa: Sabadell (Barcelona), 115–150.

Yamada, M.

1996 The Eponymous Years and Ninurta's Seal, Thoughts about the Urban Authority of Emar, in: Prince T. Mikasa (ed.), *Essays on Ancient Anatolia and Syria in the Second and Third Millennium B.C.*, Bulletin of the Middle Eastern Center in Japan 9, Harrassowitz: Wiesbaden, 297–308.

Abbreviations

AuOrSI Arnaud, D., 1991, *Textes syriens de l'âge du bronze récent*, Aula Orientalis Suppl. 1, Sabadell: Barcelona.

E Arnaud, D., 1985, *Recherches au pays d'Aštata, Emar VI, Textes sumériens et accadiens 3*, ÉRC: Paris.

GK Sigrist, M. 1993, Seven Emar Tablets, in: A.F. Rainey (ed.), *kinattūtu ša dārâti*, Raphael Kutscher Memorial Volume, Tel Aviv, 165–184.

RE Beckman, G., 1996, *Texts from the Vicinity of Emar in the Collection of Jonathan Rosen*, History in the Ancient Near East/ Monographs II, Sargon srl: Padova.

Chronological Problems Concerning the Middle Euphrates during the Bronze Age

Olivier Rouault[*]

1. Introduction

Terqa – modern Ashara – and two other nearby sites have furnished a lot of information about the history and chronology of the Middle Euphrates area after the fall of Mari. Indeed, this region is a good observation point for what was happening in Mesopotamia in that period. Observing the location of the Middle Euphrates, we can immediately see that the region is situated on one of the most important highways linking southern and central Mesopotamia to its northern areas and to the Syro-Palestinian countries. Despite the other route following the Tigris river, the Euphrates remains the most important route easily linking the south to the prosperous valleys of the Habur and the Balih, or to the Mediterranean coast following the fringe of the plain. Moreover, by taking this route, it is exactly in the Middle Euphrates region where one can turn westwards to the Mediterranean coast, or continue north towards the Habur and Balih valleys. Alternatively one can turn north-east and reach the Tigris and the Assyrian regions through the wadi Ajij.

All these roads run mainly through subdesertic and inhospitable areas, which at the time were rather dangerous because of the frequent presence of plunderers, especially when the local kingdoms were weak. Hence, the rulers of the northern or southern countries, when necessary, sought to take over and maintain control of these important crossroads. Nevertheless, for long periods, the local powers in the Middle Euphrates – also shielded by the long distances typical of this region – were usually strong enough to preserve their autonomy and could control the region to their own advantage. We must also note that there are some mountains or "djebels" in this area: in the north, the Djebel Abd-el-Aziz (900 m) and the Djebel Sindjar (1400 m), to the west the Djebel Bishri (850 m). Since prehistoric times these mountains served as a refuge for semi-nomadic populations, allowing them a safe haven from dangers.

This geopolitical situation explains some of the economic and cultural characteristics of this region: in certain periods it became an important crossroad, where trade afforded local kingdoms the opportunity to become wealthy and powerful. In other more turbulent times, when commerce halted, the area reverted back to its autonomous and autarchic origins – but without severing all ties to neighbouring countries. This oscillation can explain the coexistence of very strong clearly external influences from a variety of outside countries together with enduring local characteristics, which have remained unchanged for centuries, in the regional culture of the Middle Euphrates.

2. History of research

The main goal of the research program of our team was to study, from proto-historic times (6000 BC) down to the end of the classical period, the social, economic and cultural history of the Terqa-Ashara area, exploring both the Terqa site as well as others in the same territory. Terqa has been considered an important site for research on Mesopotamian history since the end of the nineteenth century. It was the area in the deep north of the Euphrates valley where the first cuneiform tablets were found, often in unofficial or illegal diggings, and brought to Europe by dealers. F. Thureau-Dangin, amongst others, published some of these texts, and it became apparent right from the beginning that Terqa, at least at a certain stage of its history, had been the capital city of a kingdom, Hana.[1] The localization of these findings at Ashara seemed reliable, because it was a rather important Tell, beneath a modern village. Hence, it was quite likely that this kind of discovery should have been made by villagers digging in their courtyards, or digging foundations

* University of Lyon

[1] Thureau-Dangin 1897, 1908 et 1909.

for new houses. Further, the village of Ashara has been identified with ancient Terqa since 1908. A tablet coming indisputably from this site, commemorated the construction of a temple in Terqa dedicated to the god Dagan by the king Šamši-Adad, known to have ruled Assur.[2] Further confirmation came in 1910, when E. HERZFELD, who travelled through the region, passed through Ashara and bought several tablets and fragments. Among these, one, coming from a foundation deposit with an inscription of Zimri-Lim, king of Mari, commemorated the building of an ice house.[3] During the same period, A. MUSIL travelled throughout this area and wrote a very important book providing information which is still useful today.[4]

For all these reasons Terqa appeared to be the most suitable place to start a program of excavation aimed at enhancing our understanding of the history of the Middle Euphrates and the relationship between southern and northern Mesopotamia. It was in this spirit that in 1923 F. THUREAU-DANGIN and E. DHORME, during a trip to Syria, decided to spend five days in Ashara. They made a deep sounding there, clearly hoping to find more tablets, this time in their true archaeological context. With the help of French *légionnaire* soldiers, they dug an 18 metre pit, but with meagre results. Nevertheless, they could identify some ceramics and proposed a stratigraphic sequence for the occupation of Terqa from the beginning of the Early Bronze to around the end of the Middle Bronze Ages. They immediately published their results,[5] also editing some new tablets found by the villagers. However, they omitted to mark the exact position of their sounding on the surface of the Tell. THUREAU-DANGIN and DHORME were confident of the importance of the site and planned to continue excavations on a regular basis. But a few years later, the discovery of a statue on the site of Tell Hariri changed the archaeologists' priorities. This was because one of the proposed identifications of Hariri was Mari, certainly a more important city than Terqa. Moreover, Tell Hariri was free of modern houses, while Terqa was covered by a village, making archaeological work difficult. Although the early confirmation of the identification of Hariri with Mari, already during the first season by A. PARROT, pushed Ashara-Terqa back into the shadows, the Middle Euphrates area nevertheless emerged into the full light of historical importance.

Later exploitation of the Mari archives provided a lot of information mainly about the period of the Amorite kingdoms, not to mention the reign of Hammurapi of Babylon. However, it also became clear that after its fall the city of Mari was never rebuilt again and that Terqa then became the new political centre of the region. Therefore, documents from Terqa could shed light on the periods not attested in nor covered by the Mari archives. In addition, by chance, the distribution of the Terqa epigraphic documents appears to be largely complementary with the materials from Mari. We have few tablets dating from the time of Šamši-Adad and Zimri-Lim, while the most important part of the corpus belongs to later epochs, mainly the Hana period. A good summary of the knowledge available at the time can be found in the article by F. THUREAU-DANGIN and E. DHORME published after their expedition in the region. The chronological problems were first reviewed by A. GOETZE.[6] The most important issue regarding the chronology of Terqa at the time was the placing of king Kaštiliašu. Was he only a local king or one of the first of the Kassite dynasty? Could then the presence of a Kassite king in the Middle Euphrates be connected with the raid of Muršili I. on Babylon, and the subsequent foundation of a Kassite dynasty in Babylon? Many different hypotheses have been put forward, but the solution is still not forthcoming even if our texts do provide some new information. Moreover, another king attracted the attention of scholars: Hammurapi of Terqa, whose name has a widely varying spelling. On the basis of some characteristics of the texts, at the beginning of our research on the period, it was thought that he was a king from a late period.

3. Recent Research

I must also mention that in 1948 a basalt stela representing a god killing a snake[7] was found by

[2] EBELING *et alii* 1926, 27
[3] HERZFELD 1914, 131 ss.
[4] MUSIL 1927.
[5] THUREAU-DANGIN and DHORME 1924.
[6] GOETZE 1957, 63 ss.
[7] TOURNAY and SAOUAF 1952, TOURNAY 1995.

a peasant in the Terqa area. It was immediately considered an Assyrian provincial work, because the cuneiform inscription contained the name of the Neo-Assyrian king Tukulti-Ninurta II. However, this subject lies outside of our topic today. Terqa only seriously re-emerged in research during the seventies, when regular digging began on the site under a joint mission led by the University of California in Los Angeles. The expedition was directed by GIORGIO and MARILYN BUCCELLATI, and I participated as epigrapher and archaeologist. Most of the first texts found in regular excavations in Ashara-Terqa were retrieved from the house of Puzurum, in area C, in front of the Ninkarrak temple, during the third and fourth seasons in 1977 and 1978.[8] Their publication substantially increased our knowledge of the kings ruling in Terqa during the Hana period, allowing us to add the name of several new kings to the previous list. One of the most important pieces of new information in those texts was the discovery of the name of the king Yadih-Abu, because he was probably the same as Yadih-Abu defeated by Samsuiluna of Babylon. According to the twenty-eighth regnal year name of this king, Samsuiluna defeated Yadih-Abu at about the same time as Muti-Huršana, another king. This event was so important that it was used to name three successive years. The king of Babylon probably maintained control over the region at least for a number of years, given that his twenty-third year name mentions some construction activities in Saggaratum, a place which was then part of the Hana region. This synchronism provided a good basis for the reconstruction of the Hana dynasty.

Other texts were found from the fifth to the ninth season (TQ5 = 1979, TQ6 = 1981, TQ7 = 1982, TQ8 = 1983 and TQ9 = 1985) under American guidance. I have already published an initial report on their content,[9] but I have still to complete their publication which is scheduled for the end of 2004. This group of tablets does not provide any important new information about the chronology of the Hana period; most of them seem more relevant to the Old Babylonian and the so-called "Šakkanakku period". For the period we are now dealing with, I can say that we have three new year names for Kaštiliašu. One mentions public works in the Lower Habur, "the year when Kaštiliašu changed (unakkiru) the course of the Habur", perhaps an allusion to the restoration of the great canal of the west bank called today Nahr Dawrin. Another year name commemorates the crushing of the Sutean population by this king, while the third commemorates the construction of some object or a building. This last tablet is not a contract, but a list of personal names, worshippers or servants of the goddess Ninkarrak, found in a temple and confirming the identification of this building within area C. We have also a new year name for Šunuhru-Ammu, recording the rebuilding of a town gate in Saggaratum, and a letter sent to Isih-Dagan, known as a king of Hana, probably by another king. The message deals with problems of grain and crop supplies. The finding of this document in Terqa is significant: we know another year name of a king called Isih-Dagan, which I think may be the same man as Yassi-Dagan. This year name commemorates the construction of a new palace in a place called Biddah. Some colleagues have proposed the hypothesis that at that time, Terqa was no longer the capital city of the Hana kingdom, as it had been replaced by Biddah. But the discovery of this letter in Terqa, probably sent by a foreign king, leads me to think that Terqa was still the capital city.

4. A NEW LIST OF KINGS

A very important discovery occurred during the twelfth season. That year, after I became director of the mission, we decided to begin a large excavation on the highest point of the Tell, in front of the ancient mosque, on the edge of an eighteen metre cliff cut by erosion due to the Euphrates. G. BUCCELLATI had already done some soundings in this area,[10] but he did not excavate much deeper than the two metres of Islamic deposits. He exposed the top of some walls he attributed to a large old Babylonian monument: high walls were still visible from the bank of the Euphrates in the natural cut along the cliff. Just at the beginning of our operations, while cleaning the top of the

[8] ROUAULT 1984.

[9] ROUAULT 1992.

[10] BUCCELLATI 1979, 41 and fig. 4 (SG 40). ROUAULT *et al.* 1997, 99 ss.

cliff, we discovered two jars, one almost complete and one broken, which were full of very badly preserved tablets because for years they had been filled with all the garbage and waste water from the neighbouring modern houses. Nevertheless, we could save around twenty-five documents, mainly contracts, with significant new information regarding the dynasty of Hana.[11] Then by excavating from the top of the cliff, we exposed the archaeological context of this epigraphic discovery along a rather narrow strip, between the edge of the cliff and the modern buildings. We found a succession of small rooms separated by larger spaces, probably courtyards without a roof. In these larger rooms there were small platforms built with baked bricks, often with traces of fire to one side. These platforms had been rebuilt several times roughly in the same place, and were used for crafts. All around there were remains of crucibles or melting pots made of a very rough clay, with drops of bronze in them. In neighbouring rooms we found coloured pigments in small bowls, and an ingot of glass with some fragments of figurines made from the same glass as the ingot. The jars of tablets were located in the same context in a small room. We believe that these rooms did not belong to private houses, but were rather the adjuncts of an official building, in an area devoted to small and luxury industries and crafts, and to storage.[12]

Thanks to these new documents, we discovered the name of several kings of Hana, substantially modifying our list. The list of names I propose here is in a tentative chronological order and we will see that some further changes can be proposed: Yapah-Sumu-[Abu], Iṣi-Sumu-Abu, Yadih-Abu (synchronism with Samsuiluna of Babylon), Zimri-Lim (son of Yadih-Abu/ Idi-Abu), Kasapan, Kuwari, Hanaya (under control of Ya'usa), Kaštiliašu, Šunuhru-Ammu, Ammi-madar (son of Šunuhru-Ammu,) Ammiṣaduqa of Babylon, Samsuditana of Babylon, Idin-Kakka, Išar-Lim (son of Idin-Kakka), Igid-Lim, Isih-Dagan/ Yassi-Dagan son of Igid-Lim, Ahuni,[13] Hammurapi (son of Ahuni), Qiš-Addu (under the control of the Mittani kings), Pagiru, Tukulti-Ninurta I./ Šalmaneser I. of Assyria (*līmu* of Libur-zanin-Aššur), Ilu-iqiša and Tukulti-Mer (king of Hana, son of Ilu-iqiša).

From this new list it emerges that the Babylonian presence was still strong during the reign of the first kings of Hana. Yapah-Sumu, a name which in its complete form may have been Yapah-Sumu-Abu, could have been the first king in the region after the fall of Mari. At this juncture we must point out that this reference to the first king of the Babylonian Hammurapi-dynasty, Sumu-Abum, would be a remarkable coincidence, because the name of our first king in association with the second, Iṣi-Sumu-Abu, where the "abu" is certain. Both pay special deference to the Babylonian dynasty whose latest representative had just destroyed the neighbouring Mari. We can safely suppose that these kings were, at that time, still under the close control of Babylon, and probably of Hammurapi's successor, the king Samsuiluna.

The following king of Terqa was probably Yadih-Abu, already known from the Puzurum archive. We have already mentioned how Samsuiluna tried, at the time, to maintain control of the northern regions of the Euphrates and Habur valleys. We know that in his twenty-third year he invaded the region of Apum and defeated Yakun-Ašar, the king of the capital city, Šehna/ Šubat-Enlil, the ancient names of the Tell Leilan site. Later, following the same path as Šamši-Adad, he attacked the Middle Euphrates and the kingdom of Hana, and, in his twenty-eighth year defeated Yadih-Abu. It appears then that after the first two kings of Hana, who were vassals of Babylon, the third, Yadih-Abu, embarked on a more independent policy and was punished as a result.

Among the new tablets, two contracts were dated by year names referring to a king called Zimri-Lim, son of Idi-Abu. Another later text again mentions a Zimri-Lim, son of Yadi-Abu, but not Yadih-Abu. As it is not rare for the spelling of names to shift from Amorite to Akkadian, as for Yassi-Dagan/ Isih-Dagan and others,

[11] Rouault 1992.

[12] Rouault 1998b, 320.

[13] Ahuni, father of Hammurapi of Hana, and also a king himself, appears in unpublished texts found during the twelfth season of excavations in Terqa. The ancient reading *Azilia(?)* (Podany 2002, 240 and Rouault 2001, 16) should be abandoned.

I think it is possible to identify Idi-Abu and Yadi-Abu with Yadih-Abu.

If this hypothesis is correct, Zimri-Lim should be the son of Yadih-Abu, who rebelled against Babylon, and who reigned between Yadih-Abu and Kaštiliašu. After his father's defeat by the Babylonian king, the very choice of this king's name, which is a reference to the last king of Mari, perhaps signalled new aspirations to political independence by Terqa. However, it should be noted that during the reign of Zimri-Lim, there was a clear change in the legal formulae, with the emergence of typical Babylonian forms. It surely was an important change at that time, and again may be direct evidence of Babylonian control over Terqa. This impression is strengthened by another contract, dated from the reign of king Kasapan (*Ka-sa-pa-an*), confirming a royal grant to a certain Sin-imguranni, previously bestowed on him by king Zimri-Lim, son of Yadi-Abu. This confirmation of an ancient donation occurred during the first year of the reign of the new king, "the year when Kasapan sat on the throne of his father", and it was written by the same scribe who had drafted the contract with Babylonian characteristics dating from the time of Zimri-Lim. It is important to remark that this new contract no longer showed Babylonian characteristics, but followed the ancient Hana tradition. Therefore, Kasapan appears not only to have restored the local legal formulae, but also confirmed and gave back royal donations probably annulled during the preceding period, when the kingdom was under direct Babylonian control. That is, between Zimri-Lim and Kasapan, during the reign of Samsuiluna or of Abi-ešuh.

According to the prosopographical data two kings with Hurrian names, Kuwari and Hanaya, must be inserted in our list at this juncture. Kuwari had to confront the soldiers sent by Hattum, written also Hattu and Hatte. This is probably a reference to the country of Hatti[14] and we can consider these year names as one of the earliest citings of conflicts between Syrian or Mesopotamian peoples and the Hittites. According to this chronology, we have reached the beginning of the seventeenth century. One of the sons of Sin-imguranni, who received the grant under Zimri-Lim (which was confirmed by Kasapan), also received a donation from two kings whose names were previously unknown, Ya'usa and Hanaya. These two kings appear to have ruled together: they are both mentioned in the oath formula, but unfortunately the year name is broken. This association of two kings is not rare, and we will witness another example in Terqa later. The name Hanaya has sometimes been ascribed to the Hurrian language. As for Ya'usa, which seems to be an Amorite form, it is difficult to tell: if it really is the name of a foreign king, of whom the local king was a vassal, the spelling could be approximate, and so we must look for different names for comparison. The only possible parallel I have found until now is Ušše, a king of the Kassite dynasty ruling later over Babylon: Ya'usa could be the Amorite interpretation of this name. Ušše would then be the sovereign of Hanaya, the local king. But since this reading of Ušše itself is uncertain, this tantalising interpretation remains a rather feeble one. Nonetheless, the overall hypothesis that Terqa was under the control of a Kassite king before Muršili conquered Babylon, is still in my opinion quite attractive.

If we follow this reconstruction of the list, we must place Kaštiliašu just after or before Ya'usa and Hanaya, around the middle of the sixteenth century. Kaštiliašu is attested in five contracts, some of which are still unpublished, showing that during his reign the local legal style, restored by Kasapan after the Babylonian intrusion, was still in use. Generally speaking, these texts resemble the documents written during Yadih-Abu's period. If Kaštiliašu of Terqa is one of the kings of the Kassite dynasty, he could only be Kaštiliašu II, and according to the middle chronology his reign should be contemporary to that of Ammiṣaduqa of Babylon. Moreover, if we consider Yadih-Abu and Idi-Abu as two different kings,[15] we must now add another king to our list, Idi-Abu, who is not Yadih-Abu, and place him after the trio Kaštiliašu, Šunuhru-Ammu, Ammi-madar. The principal result would be to put Kaštiliašu before the very beginning of the Kassite dynasty of Babylon in

[14] Cf. Nashef 1982, 123.

[15] For this opinion, see Podany 2002, 42.

the chronology, making him contemporary with the end of the reign of Samsuiluna.

When I read the tablets from the jar for the first time, one of the surprises was to find two contracts mentioning Ammiṣaduqa and Samsuditana, the kings of Babylon. The first tablet is characterised by a Babylonian formulary. In contrast, the second from the time of Samsuditana, shows the typical Terqa formulary, with the traditional penalty using asphalt. This return to Terqa of the last kings of Babylon sheds new light on the end of the first dynasty of Babylon. A consensus has existed until now among most historians that after Samsuiluna, the Babylonian kingdom shrank to a relatively limited territory in the south of Mesopotamia.[16] H. GASCHE, after examining all the archaeological data concerning the end of the first dynasty of Babylon, arrived at the similar conclusion that the kingdom had shrunk to a very limited territory surrounding the capital city. The Terqa texts therefore show that not only was Ammiṣaduqa perfectly right to claim control over the Middle Euphrates in the introduction of his edict, but that even his successor, Samsuditana, the last king of the dynasty, hitherto presented as a very weak ruler governing just a small kingdom, in fact maintained control over the same region, probably in order to stop the movement of peoples from the north and east. As a result, the Terqa documents shed new light on events leading to the fall of Babylon.

The possible involvement of the kingdom of Hana in the downfall of the Amorite dynasty of Babylon has been the object of much debate. The presence in Terqa of at least one king carrying a Kassite name, Kaštiliašu, has led some scholars to see in the Terqa kingdom an important step in the Kassite advance towards Babylon. Some authors have even envisaged an objective alliance between Muršili I. and a possible Kassite power entrenched in the Middle Euphrates, the first looking for an alliance against the Hurrians, and the second soliciting help against Babylonian designs over the Middle Euphrates. According to this theory, after the Hittite raid on Babylon the Kassites took advantage of the situation to settle in Babylon themselves.[17] Despite the fact that a Hana king had a Kassite name, we now know that the Babylonians controlled the Middle Euphrates, and it becomes clear that Muršili's real goal was to fight against Babylon and contrast its influence in the Syrian territories along the Euphrates valley. Hence, the continuation of his expedition all the way down to Babylon was in fact a logical move, and it was probably achieved with the help of the populations living in the Middle Euphrates region.

5. THE LIST AFTER THE FALL OF BABYLON

We are unsure whether to place this series of kings, which we shall now discuss, before or after the end of the first Babylonian dynasty. At the present stage of our analysis, the textual elements in favour of one hypothesis or the other do not appear to be absolutely definitive. Nevertheless, in general terms one can argue that the insertion of Idin-Kakka, Išar-Lim, Igid-Lim, Isih-Dagan and Hammurapi before the end of the first dynasty of Babylon would add too many kings in a too short period. Moreover, it would leave open a large gap in attempts to cover the whole period between the end of the first dynasty of Babylon and the Mittanian domination. Finally, the stratigraphy of Area E in Terqa shows us that king Išar-Lim ruled in a later period, just before the Mittanian kings took over control of the region.

For this period, the unpublished Terqa documents allow us to draft a list of part of the dynasty ruling after the fall of Babylon.[18] We now know that Idin-Kakka, father of Išar-Lim, was king himself, and the succession from father to son works out this way: Idin-Kakka, Išar-Lim, Igit-Lim, Isih-Dagan and maybe Hammurapi.[19] It is interesting to note that after the reign of Išar-Lim, the legal formulas in the contracts revert to their ancient form, mentioning in the oath the local gods Šamaš, Dagan and Itur-Mer (cf. GC1-1 and TQ12-3). Later at the time of king Paratarna, Terqa passed under Mittanian control. In the oath formulas, Paratarna is associated with a man named Qiš-Addu, who was probably the local king. The name has several spellings: *Pa-ra-tar-na* (TQ12-10 and 15), *Pa-ri-tar-na* (TQ12-9 and 16). Another name, which we

[16] See for instance GASCHE 1989 and PONS 1996.

[17] For a summary of these positions, see GARELLI 1997, 133, 307 s., et 338.

[18] ROUAULT 1992.

[19] For the hypothesis that there were two different Hammurapi kings at the end of the dynasty of Hana, see PODANY 2002.

first read as *Pa-i-tar-na*,[20] should probably read *Sa-i-tar-na*, and it could be a variant of the spelling of Šuttarna, the Mittanian predecessor to Paratarna.

A third king with the name of Sausadat or better, Sausadatra,[21] appears as a partner of the same Qiš-Addu in other documents. Again, it is probably a local spelling of the name of Saustatar, one of the successors of Paratarna to the throne of Mittani. At this time, oddly, the Babylonian legal formulas reappear in the texts, and it is the southern list of gods that is the most current, with Šamaš, Addu, Marduk, Almuš and Annunitum. But this is not a systematic rule, and we also possess two dated tablets of Paratarna and Qiš-Addu, recording the same transaction, but giving two different lists of gods in the oath formula, one again mentioning Šamaš, Dagan and Itur-Mer!

From an archaeological viewpoint, the history and the development of the cultural, political and economic structures of Hana society are difficult to elicit and to understand. At the present stage of our study, the ceramic production of the Hana period seems to show remarkable unity and a very slow evolution over the whole post-Mari period, always reproducing the same shapes, exhibiting very few outside influences. In contrast, the glyptic documentation is much more varied, and it clearly shows all the foreign influence already suggested by the texts, not only Hurrian, Hittite or Babylonian, but also Western. All these outside contributions were often mixed and later merged to form the distinguishing characteristics of local styles.[22] But as everybody knows, the diachronic evolution of this type of material is very difficult to use as a chronological index.

The archaeological context of the archive recovered during our twelfth season of excavation may even be more recent than the most recent tablets in the collection. Hovever, in a room close to where the jars were found, on a floor apparently corresponding to the same context, we found a letter (TQ13-154), giving us the name of a certain Pagiru, whose name also appears in two contracts of the archive in the jar (TQ12-26 and 29). He is cited at least once as king in the oath formula. This leads us to believe that our archive could date back to the time of this Pagiru, unless two different kings bore the same name. The stratigraphic and archaeological evidence seem to show that the site was abandoned from the second half of the fourteenth century.

6. The end of Hana

Nevertheless, this system of local monarchies could have survived in the Middle Euphrates region until the very end of the Late Bronze Age, because the last known tablet showing the legal tradition of Hana, belongs to the time of Tukulti-Ninurta I. of Assyria. However, this tablet has been found outside of Terqa and it is dated by indication of the *limmu*, following the Assyrian chronology.[23] The city of Terqa itself had probably already lost its central role, possibly during the struggle for control over the Jezirah and northern Mesopotamia between Assyria and the waning Mittani kingdom during the fourteenth century. After the Hana structures, we encountered no later archaeological levels in Terqa. In the thick layer pertaining to the abandonment period covering the remains of the last Hana constructions, we found mainly Islamic graves or pits. But in area E, we also found a pit and a tomb surely older than the Islamic levels, associated with some characteristic "late Kassite" goblets.[24] It was mainly in order to understand this "dark" period, the "late Kassite" Iron Age, so badly documented in Terqa, that we undertook a survey in the surrounding areas. The site of Tell Mashtale, about five kilometres south of Terqa, but on the opposite bank, provided interesting information about the relations between the Middle Euphrates and Babylonia during that period. Relatively large – close to nine hectares – but rather shallow – about five meters above the level of the plain, Tell Mashtale is cut by a wadi or an ancient channel. It is partly occupied by a cemetery still in use today and by a large school. Its roughly rectangular shape induced several scholars to see in it a sort of a military encampment, possibly Neo-Assyrian. Some late Kassite goblets had already been collected during previous surface surveys, and our sounding confirmed this date for the main occupation. In a small sounding we found hundreds of goblets, jars and other ceramic forms characteristic of the southern Babylonian/ Kassite assem-

---

20 Rouault 1992, 254.

21 I thank D. Charpin for this correction of my first lecture.

22 Gualandi 1997 and 1998.

23 Kümmel 1989.

24 Rouault 1998.

blage. The tall bottles had the characteristic filled annular base, often reinforced by the addition of clay to the centre. The ceramic production of Mashtale corresponds precisely enough to the craft traditions typical of the end of the Kassite dynasty in Babylon, or belonging to the Isin II dynasty, at the end of the twelfth century.

One may wonder whether this "late Kassite" southern influence, also attested in Mari, constitutes the sign of an important and unexpected cultural phenomenon. We could perhaps link this surprising Babylonian presence in the Middle Euphrates to the reign of Nebuchadnezzar I (1124–1103), who drove the Elamites out of Babylon through alliances he had forged in the valley of the Middle Tigris, ultimately not too distant from the Hana region, during a period when Assyria, under the rule of Assur-reša-iši I., was relatively weak. This situation should probably also be connected with a particular event of the reign of Tukulti-Mer, king of Hana, son of Iluiqiša, who was also king of Hana,[25] showing that the region was then strongly oriented towards the south: a votive object,[26] bearing an inscription, and dedicated by this king to the god Šamaš has been recovered in Sippar, and it is probably this same king – called "king of Mari" in the Assyrian royal inscriptions – who was defeated by the Assyrian king Aššur-bel-kala, at the beginning of the eleventh century.

The information provided by the archaeological and historical research conducted in Terqa itself and in the surrounding region[27] offers fresh insight into relations between the Middle Euphrates and southern Mesopotamia, especially at the end of the Old Babylonian period, after Hammurapi of Babylon. The control of the Middle Euphrates area probably continued to be an extremely important objective for the dominant states, and despite the emergence of new powers, first Mittanian then Assyrian, Babylonia always managed to project its presence over the region, at least in the form of a certain cultural influence. The Middle Euphrates valley and the Hana country represented a sort of fluctuating border, a contact zone, between all the empires of the Ancient Near East before the time of the Neo-Assyrian hegemony, which conquered and destroyed the local cultures forever.

The Terqa documentation clearly shows how this process was a continuous one, lasting over most of the period. However, we are still left with a gap and very obscure interlude corresponding roughly to the thirteenth century, between the documentation coming first from Terqa and then Mashtale. It is clear that Terqa ceased to be the centre of the kingdom of Hana at the beginning of this "dark" period. However, if we must look for an alternative centre, Mashtale – which shows only a brief period of human occupation – is certainly not the best candidate. We believe Tell Hariri would be a possible candidate, because of the permanence of the title of king of Mari,[28] even if the more recent Bronze Age levels in this site are very rare and eroded, and mainly documented by graves.

---

[25] Perhaps the same as the "king of the land of Mari": Grayson 1991, 89 and 111.

[26] Thureau-Dangin and Dhorme 1924, 279

[27] The last reports have been published in Rouault *et al.* 2001 and Rouault and Mora 2002.

[28] Masetti-Rouault forthcoming.

Bibliography

BUCCELLATI G.

1979 *The Fourth Season: Introduction and the Stratigraphic Record*, Bibliotheca Mesopotamica 10, Terqa Preliminary Reports 10, Malibu.

EBELING E., MEISSNER B. and WEIDNER E.

1926 *Die Inschriften der altassyrischen Könige, Altorientalische Bibliothek*, Erster Band, Leipzig, 1926.

GARELLI P.

1997 *Le Proche-Orient asiatique, Tome 1, Des origines aux invasions des peuples de la mer*, Nouvelle Clio, édition refondue, Paris.

GASCHE H.

1989 *La Babylonie au 17ème siècle avant notre ère: approche archéologique, problèmes et perspectives*, Mesopotamian History and Environment, Series II, Memoirs I, University of Ghent, Ghent.

PONS N. and GASCHE H.

1996 Du Cassite à Mari, in : *Collectanea Orientalia. Histoire, arts de l'espace et industrie de la terre. Etudes offertes en hommage à Agnès Spycket* (CPOA 3), Neuchâtel et Paris, 287–298.

GRAYSON A.K.

1991 *Assyrian Rulers of the Early First Millennium BC, 1 (1114–859 BC)*, University of Toronto Press, Toronto.

GUALANDI G.

1997 Terqa. Rapport préliminaire (1987–1989). Les sceaux-cylindres, étude préliminaire, *Mari Annales de Recherches Interdisciplinaires*, 8, ADPF, Paris, 149–157.

1998 *Les styles de Terqa. Glyptique et Histoire du Moyen-Euphrate au IIème millénaire av. J.-C.*, Thèse de l'Ecole des Hautes Etudes en Sciences Sociales, Paris.

HERZFELD E.

1914 Hana et Mari, *Revue d'Assyriologie* 11, 131–139.

KÜMMEL H.M.

1989 Ein Kaufvertrag aus Hana mit mittelassyrischer limu-Datierung, *Zeitschrift für Assyriologie* 79, 191–200.

MASETTI-ROUAULT M.G.

forthc. Mari et le Moyen-Euphrate au Bronze Récent et à l'âge du Fer: problèmes historiques. *Actes de la table ronde "Travaux récents sur et autour de Mari"*, Strasbourg, 20–21 Juin 1997.

MUSIL, A.

1927 *The Middle Euphrates. A Topographical Itinerary*, American Geographical Society, Oriental Explorations and Studies N° 3, New York.

NASHEF K.

1982 *Die Orts- und Gewässernamen der mittelbabylonischen und mittelassyrischen Zeit*, Répertoire géographique des Textes Cunéiformes, Band 5, Wiesbaden 1982.

PODANY A.

2002 *The Land of Hana. Kings, Chronology, and Scribal Tradition*, CDL Press, Bethesda.

ROUAULT O.

1984 *L'Archive de Puzurum*, Bibliotheca Mesopotamica 16, Terqa Final Reports 1, Undena, Malibu.

1992 Cultures locales et influences extérieures: le cas de Terqa, *Studi Micenei ed Egeo-Anatolici* 30, 247–256.

1998 Villes, villages, campagnes et steppe dans la région de Terqa: données nouvelles, Canadian Society for Mesopotamian Studies, Bulletin 33 = TMO 28, Québec, M. FORTIN (éd.), *Actes du colloque «Espace naturel, espace habité en Syrie du Nord (10e–2e millénaires av. J.-C.)»*, 191–198.

1998b Recherches récentes à Tell Ashara-Terqa (1991–1995), *Subartu* IV/1, Brepols, Turnhout, 1998, 313–330.

ROUAULT O. *et al.*

1997 Terqa. Rapport préliminaire (1987–1989), *Mari. Annales de Recherches Interdisciplinaires* 8, 73–178.

2001 Missione archeologica di Terqa-Ashara: Rapporto preliminare 2000, *Athenaeum - Studi di Letterature e Storia dell'Antichità, Università di Pavia*, vol. 89, 621–644.

ROUAULT O. and MORA C. (eds.)

2002 Dossier "Progetto «Terqa e la sua regione»: rapporto preliminare 2001", *Athenaeum - Studi di Letterature e Storia dell'Antichità, Università di Pavia*, vol. 90, 564–565.

THUREAU-DANGIN F.

1897 Tablettes chaldéennes inédites, *Revue d'Assyriologie* 4, 69–78 et pl.32.

1908 Un nouveau roi de Hana, *Orientalistische Literaturzeitung* 11, 93.

1909 Un contrat de Hana, *Journal Asiatique* 1909/II, 149–155.

THUREAU-DANGIN F. and DHORME E.

1924 Cinq jours de fouille à Asharah, *Syria*, 5, 265–293.

TOURNAY R.J.

1998 La stèle du roi Tukulti-Ninurta II. Nouvelle interprétation, *Subartu* IV/1, Brepols, Turnhout, 273–278.

TOURNAY R.J. and SAOUAF S.

1952 Stèle de Tukulti-Ninurta II, *Annales Archéologiques Arabes Syriennes* 2, 169–190, pl. 1–3.

Babylonian Chronology of the 2nd Half of the 2nd Millennium B.C.

*Leonhard Sassmannshausen**

Connecting Kassite chronology with the 1st millennium

The most important source for the chronology of the Kassite and Post-Kassite periods is Babylonian King List A[1] which gives the lengths of the reigns of all kings of Babylon from the first dynasty of Babylon to the Neo-Assyrian period. Unfortunately we know so far only one copy of this text which has three gaps and lacks the beginning and the end. Because of the gaps there is no direct connection from the 2nd millennium rulers to the 1st millennium. However, the gap can be bridged, because there are 14 synchronisms of Assyrian rulers with Kassite rulers which allow to parallel the Babylonian King List with the Assyrian King List,[2] and since we have for Assyria the uninterrupted sequence of regnal dates we can thereby connect Kassite chronology with 1st millennium chronology (Table 1).

A possibility to check the accuracy of Babylonian King List A is provided by the administrative archives found at Nippur, from the time of Burna-Buriyāš II to Kadašman-Ḫarbe III (usually called K.-Ḫ. II[3]), 1359 to 1223, according to Brinkman's chronology.[4] Much less dense is the documentation for the last 67 years of the late Kassite period, from which we have dates in texts found in Ur, Dūr-Kurigalzu, Tell Zubeidī and in the unpublished documents found in Babylon.

The late and middle Kassite period

Babylonian King List A provides dates for the reigns back to the time of ***Kurigalzu II.*** The administrative texts give a minimum of 27 years for his predecessor ***Burna-Buriyāš II*** and at least 15 years for ***Kadašman-Enlil I.*** Thus the accession of Kadašman-Enlil I has to be dated at 1374 B. C. at the latest.

For the middle Kassite period we have a good sample of dated documents from Nippur for the 125 years from the first year of Burna-Buriyāš II to Kaštiliyāš IV. These dates confirm the general reliability of the Babylonian King List A at least for the middle Kassite period. We only have minor problems, the most serious of which is the 25th year of king Nazi-Maruttaš. King List A gives 26 years for this king. We have documents from his 24th year and the year of his death (MU.ÚS.SA) which should be the 26th year, if the king list is correct, but texts from the 25th year are still wanting. Another problem is posed by a tablet in which a king with the name of Kadašman-Enlil is placed before Kadašman-Turgu.[5] Kadašman-Turgu is known to have been the predecessor of Kadašman-Enlil II., his predecessor was Nazi-Maruttaš.

A particular problem are the years following the deposition of Kaštiliyāš, especially the statement of Chronicle P that Tukultī-Ninurta I of Assyria administered Babylonia for seven years. King List A does not mention this administration and gives one and a half year for Enlil-nādin-šumi, the same duration for Kadašman-Ḫarbe III,[6] and six years for Adad-šuma-iddina. From documents we have the accession year of Tukultī-Ninurta as king of Babylonia, the first year of Enlil-nādin-šumi, the accession year and the first year of Kadašman-Ḫarbe III and the accession year of Adad-šuma-iddina. Since we know that Adad-šuma-uṣur came to the throne through a revolt of the Babylonian magnates, that he was said to have been a member of the old Kassite royal family,

* Albstadt, Germany

[1] Most recent edition by Grayson 1980–1983, 90–96.

[2] Edited by Grayson 1980–1983, 101–115.

[3] Karaḫardaš of the Synchronistic History is apparently a garbled form of Kadašman-Ḫarbe; the latter form is given for the predecessor of Kurigalzu II in Chronicle P. I do not think, as does Brinkman 1976, 146, that the chronicle "mistakenly inserts the name of Kadašman-Ḫarbe as a predecessor of the later Kurigalzu", but rather that we should refer to the predecessor of Kurigalzu II as Kadašman-Ḫarbe II.

[4] Brinkman 1976, 31.

[5] Donbaz 1982, 207–212, cf. Brinkman 1983, 67–74.

[6] In his chronological scheme Brinkman assigned only one year to Enlil-nādin-šumi and Kadašman-Ḫarbe each. Cf. Brinkman 1976, 26f. footnote 76.

and attacked Assyria, in all likelihood his three predecessors were more or less Assyrian puppets. So their three reigns combined, nine years according to the king list, come close to the seven years of Chronicle P for Tukultī-Ninurta's administration of Assyria.

In the late Kassite period we have the problem of double datings for the kings Adad-šuma-uṣur, Mele-Šīḫu, and Marduk-apla-iddina.[7] For whatever reasons, these three kings seem to have had a second and partly third accession after which a new numbering of years began.[8] For Mele-Šīḫu we have his 12th year in an unpublished text from Babylon and his second 4th year in a text from Ur. Therefore there seem to have been at least 16 years of this king while the king list attributes 15 years to him.

Vexing as these problems are, they are only minor and just show us that King List A, while generally reliable for the middle and late Kassite period, may need some adjustment.

The early Kassite period

The direct predecessor of Kadašman-Enlil I was ***Kurigalzu I.*** He was one of the most active builders among the Ancient Near Eastern kings. He had not only built the residential city Dūr-Kurigalzu, which must have been still one of the important centers of Babylonia during the 2nd quarter of the 12th century, although no traces of construction activity of any of the successors of Kurigalzu I have been found in Dūr-Kurigalzu. He initiated an ambitious program aiming at the renovation of the main temples of the important Babylonian cities (Table 2). He is known to have cultivated the relations with Egypt[9] and married a sister of his to the Elamite king Paḫir-iššan, and a daughter to the next Elamite king, Ḫumban-numena.[10]

We have no concrete dates for his reign, but since Kurigalzu I was one of the most important Kassite rulers, even one of the most significant kings in the entire history of Mesopotamia, and since Kassite rulers with much less profile such as Nazi-Maruttaš and Kadašman-Turgu had reigns of 26 and 18 years, it is realistic to reckon for Kurigalzu I with a reign of at least three decades. Thus we reach the last decades of the 15th century (Table 3).

The predecessor of Kurigalzu I was ***Kadašman-Ḫarbe I.*** On a tablet which was found at Nippur a date "year in which king Kadašman-Ḫarbe dug the canal of Diniktum" is attested. Chronicle P[11] ascribes to him a campaign against the Suteans. These pieces of information show that he was a king who, unlike several other Kassite rulers, left some historical traces. Although the few data do not allow us to assess the length of his reign, he – in all likelihood – ruled at least a few years. Thus the end of his predecessor ***Karaindaš*** may have been around the last but one or last but two decade of the 15th century.

Karaindaš did not only rebuild a part of the Eanna in Uruk. He also took up relations with Egypt[12] and concluded a border treaty with Aššur-bēl-nišēšu, a ruler of Assur.[13] Thus he was one of the more prominent rulers of the Kassite dynasty. Most probably his reign was not short. For a ruler, who undertook such significant activities in the early Kassite period, I would assume that he reigned for more than a decade, possibly much more, and that his reign therefore started somewhere in the second third of the 15th century. It is very likely that Karaindaš was the Babylonian king who sent precious gifts, particularly lapis-lazuli, to pharao Thutmosis III during the 8th campaign of this pharao, according to the annals of Thutmosis III. If Karaindaš is not the king in question, it must be one of his rather obscure predecessors, which does not seem very likely. According to the Egyptian chronology of von Beckerath[14] which is not the only possible one,[15] the

[7] Brinkman 1976, 410.
[8] The 2nd and 3rd accession years of Marduk-apla-iddina are attested in unpublished documents from Babylon. I owe the correct interpretation of these dates to O. Pedersén.
[9] Amarna letter EA 11, 47'f.
[10] van Dijk 1986, 163.
[11] Grayson 1975, Chronicle 21.
[12] EA 10, 8–10.
[13] Synchronistic History, Grayson 1975, Chronicle 22.
[14] Beckerath 1997, 108–111 and 189.
[15] One of the greatest problems is the controversy concerning the several co-regencies that have been assumed by some scholars. Because of the problems of Egyptian chronology of the New Kingdom the attempt of Boese 1982, 15–26 to arrive at a more precise Middle Babylonian chronology through links with Egypt is based on conditions which are not given. This is also the case for Boese's linking of the supposedly simultaneous destruction of Emar, Ugarit and Ḫattuša. For Ḫattuša see now Seeher 2001, 623–634. For Emar the excavator U. Finkbeiner informs me that there is no evidence for a large destruction layer that seals the Late Bronze Age remains.

8th campaign of Thutmosis III took place in 1447. This date fits well with my assumption on the probable beginning of the reign of Karaindaš. Unfortunately, both Babylonian King List A and the Synchronistic King List[16] have gaps where the reign of Karaindaš should be listed. The only clues for the chronological placement of Karaindaš can be found in the Synchronistic History and Chronicle P. Thus we do not know who was the immediate predecessor of Karaindaš. The reign of king Aššur-bēl-nišēšu of Assur, with whom Karaindaš concluded a treaty, has to be dated according to BRINKMAN's chronology to the years 1417–1409. Presumably the reign of Karaindaš ended in the first years of Aššur-bēl-nišēšu. As a rough estimate for the reign of Karaindaš I suggest 1450–1415, on the basis of the data mentioned above.

One of the predecessors of Karaindaš was one ***Burna-Buriyāš*** who concluded a treaty with Puzur-Aššur III of Assur, according to the Synchronistic History. Puzur-Aššur III must have ruled around the first quarter of the 15th century. Unfortunately the reigns of the two predecessors of the Assyrian ruler Enlil-nāṣir II, Aššur-rabi I and Aššur-nādin-aḫḫē I, are lost in the Assyrian King List. The reign of the quite obscure Aššur-nādin-aḫḫē I was probably short. Not too short was the reign of Aššur-rabi I, since four generations later this king was still included in the royal genealogy[17] and an inscribed clay nail documents his construction activity[18]. So two decades for both rulers combined seems a good guess. This Burna-Buriyāš of the Synchronistic History was perhaps (but not necessarily) the same person as Burna-Buriyāš, the father of Ulam-Buriyāš. The Synchronistic King List names one Burna-Buriyāš as tenth Kassite ruler who was contemporary of Išme-Dagan II, who is separated from Puzur-Aššur III by 42 regnal years. This looks as if there were at least two early Burna-Buriyāš, one contemporary with Puzur-Aššur III and one roughly contemporary with Išme-Dagan II. It has to be stressed, however, that the Synchronistic King List is very far from being a chronologically precise source and can be shown to be inexact at several places. Unfortunately our sources for this stretch of history are too few and too fragmentary. So far there is no contemporary material to confirm or disprove the chronological sources for most of the early Kassite period. But since Išme-Dagan II lived around 1557–1542, and since the discussion below will show that this was during the final years of Samsu-Ditāna, the first Burna-Buriyāš should have lived after Išme-Dagan II of Assyria.

A successor of Burna-Buriyāš I seems to have been ***Agum***, son of Kaštiliyāš (usually called Agum III), because Agum is mentioned in the Chronicle of Early Kings[19] after Ulam-Buriyāš, who was a son of a Burna-Buriyāš.[20] This Agum led a campaign into the Sealand, according to the Chronicle of Early Kings. He conquered the city Dūr-Enlil which is otherwise unknown and destroyed its temple Egalga'uruna. Annoyingly the text ends right here. Whether this king[21] Agum is the same person as the king Agum whose 4th year and perhaps also his 3rd year are attested in the dates of texts found in the area of the Qalʿat al-Baḥrain,[22] is not yet clear. If yes, then Agum conquered the Sealand in his first year, crossed over to Baḥrain, had a new palace built, set up a functioning administration there in his second year, so that already in his third and fourth year administrative documents could be dated after his reign. Not impossible, but not too likely. I would prefer to see these two kings named Agum as two different persons.

Several ***earlier Kassite kings*** are mentioned both in the Babylonian King List A[23] and in the Synchronistic King List,[24] partly not in the same sequence. The Synchronistic King List states that eight of these Kassite rulers were contemporary with Šamšī-Adad II who died 58 years before Puzur-Aššur III, thus around the middle

[16] GRAYSON 1980–1983, 116–121.

[17] Cf. ALBRIGHT 1942, 30. Not only his grandson Aššur-rîm-nišēšu (RIMA I A.0.70) and the son of his great-grandson, Aššur-uballiṭ (A.0.73.1-3), but also Erība-Adad I. mention Aššur-rabi I.

[18] RIMA I A.0.65.

[19] GRAYSON 1975, Chronicle 20.

[20] Note, however, that while the inscriptions of Ulam-Buriyāš state that his father was king, they do not specifically call him king of Babylon.

[21] He is not explicitly called a king, but the text is one that deals with the exploits of kings.

[22] ANDRÉ-SALVINI - LOMBARD 1997, 165–170.

[23] I 16–22.

[24] I 18–20.

of the 16th century, and ruled for eight years. Whether this is really true is doubtful. If yes, it would mean that these early Kassite rulers either had short reigns or/and were partly contemporary rivals for power. The chronological data given by the Assyrian King List (see below) also do not necessitate too long reigns for the early Kassite rulers.

A crucial question is, how the dates on the ***texts from Tell Muḫammad*** can be fitted into our chronological mosaic.[25] A number of these texts bear dates of the type MU.x.KAM.MA *ša* KÁ.DINGIR.RA[ki] *uš-bu*, with the "x" standing for numbers between 36 and 41. S. COLE translated this phrase as "year x that Babylon was resettled", a translation that seems reasonable.[26]

It seems not very likely to me that Babylon, at least nominally the capital of the country, was resettled only in the final phase of the consolidation of Babylonia, after a treaty with Assyria was concluded and texts were dated after Kassite kings all the way down to Baḫrain. It is more likely that Babylon was rebuilt provisionally soon after the Hittite sack. Also the war events, which are mentioned in several year names on Tell Muḫammad texts, indicate a somewhat chaotic time of transition. The Old Babylonian kingdom consisted in its final years only of the city of Babylon and its close surrounding. It seems reasonable to assume that the reestablishment of the Babylonian Kingdom required some time. Therefore Cole's chronological placement of the Tell Muḫammad texts after Agum seems forced. But in view of the paltry data for the 15th century it is not yet possible to disprove COLE's arrangement[27] definitively.

Since the somewhat chaotic era of the Tell Muḫammad texts has to be placed in all likelihood at the beginning of the Kassite period, the titles of Gandaš and Agumkakrime "king of the four world quarters" and "king who causes the four world quarters to exist permanently" in their inscriptions of disputed authenticity[28] do not fit into the early Kassite period and this speaks against the authenticity of these inscriptions.

THE END OF THE FIRST DYNASTY OF BABYLON

The lengths of the reigns given in the Assyrian King List permit to compute approximately the end of the first dynasty of Babylon, despite some dispute over some of the lengths of reigns and and the fact, that there are attested rulers who do not appear in the King List. If we depart from the reign of Enlil-nāṣir II and follow BRINKMAN in dating it to 1430–1425 and assume as a very rough estimate for the reigns of Aššur-rabi I and Aššur-nādin-aḫḫē I, which are not preserved in the Assyrian King List, roughly 20 years, as I suggested above, we arrive at a date around 1725 or 1715 for the final year of Šamšī-Adad I.[29] If we follow CHARPIN and DURAND who assumed the death of Šamšī-Adad I in the 17th year of Ḫammurapi,[30] we arrive at an estimated date around 1544 or 1534 for the end of Samsu-Ditāna.

An old question that is at the heart of the Assyriological chronology debate is the fact that the Assyrian King List cannot be reconciled with the Babylonian King List A, which gives a length of 576 years and 9 months for the entire Kassite period – this would bring us to the year 1733 for the beginning of the Kassite period, which is totally impossible, because this date is early in the reign of Ḫammurapi or even before the accession of Ḫammurapi and therefore half a century before the first safe references for Kassites.

The Old Assyrian eponym lists indicate, as far as they are published, that the length of the reigns of the Old Assyrian rulers in the Assyrian King List are generally correct. The "new" Kültepe eponym list[31] gives exactly the forty years for Irīšum I that we find in the king list, as well. Furthermore there are headings in the Kültepe eponym list at the beginning of each reign. This

[25] For these year names see my paper "Kassite Nomads: Fact or Fiction?", Amurru 3, Paris, in press.

[26] In 1999, 414 and in my book of 2001, 456 I suggested to translate the phrase "38th year, after x sat down in Babylon". Now, while elliptic versions of Old Babylonian year names are common, it is never the subject that is omitted in such phrases. Therefore Cole's solution is definitely preferable.

[27] In: J. A. ARMSTRONG, S. W. COLE, H. GASCHE, V. G. GURZADYAN 1998, 66.

[28] STEIN 2000, 149–165.

[29] Puzur-Aššur III ruled for 14 or 24 years, depending on which copy of the Assyrian King List one follows.

[30] CHARPIN - DURAND 1985, 306.

[31] VEENHOF 2003.

makes it likely that the figures given in the Assyrian king list are based on eponym lists from which the length of reigns could be most easily taken. It is also interesting to see that the eponym list begins with Irīšum I who is also the first Assyrian ruler who is listed with the length of his reign in the Assyrian King List – certainly not a coincidence. Therefore the Assyrian King List should be seen as generally reliable, and the figure of 576 years and 9 months of the Babylonian King List A, of which we do not yet know how it came about, should not be seen as something that would render the figures of the Assyrian King List questionable.

Thus the written documents which are available at present speak in favour of an end of the first dynasty of Babylon shortly after the middle of the 16th century.

The "Venus tablet of Ammiṣaduqa"

It is not possible to discuss the chronology of Mesopotamia in the 2nd millennium without considering the so-called "Venus tablet of Ammiṣaduqa" which is a traditional designation for the 63rd tablet of the astrological omen series Enūma Anu Enlil,[32] a composition of the first millennium without 2nd millennium forerunners in which king Ammi-ṣaduqa is not mentioned at all. The tenth omen on this tablet reads: "If Venus sets in the east on the 25th of Addaru, it is the year of the golden throne". The apodosis of that omen was seen since more than 90 years[33] as referring to the date formula for the 8th year of Ammi-ṣaduqa which reads in its complete form: "Year in which king Ammi-ṣaduqa brought a throne of red gold which is fit for the distant place, and his forward rushing(?) statue into the Enamtil". One could, however, as well see the apodosis as referring to the 21st year of Samsu-Ditāna which reads: "year in which king Samsu-Ditāna brought his princely statue and a throne of red gold for the distant place into the Enamtil."[34]

A golden throne is also mentioned in several other Old Babylonian date formulas. There it is however not called dúr-gar, but gišgu-za, mostly in connection with bára "temple".[35]

Since the tradition of the days on this tablet is notoriously bad and this specific omen is preserved only on two of the five known copies of this tablet, this text can at the most function as a possible additional confirmation for a chronology which has to rely on other sources. Therefore the question of "high, middle or low chronology" should not be asked any more, at least not in the way it has been done since the early 1940's, when these chronologies were first established.

Prospects for Mesopotamian chronology

The open chronological questions can only be clarified through new text finds. This requires new excavations. Excavations in the cultural sphere of Assyria like the ones at Assur seem particularly promising, because this is where the most important chronological sources like the Assyrian King List and the Synchronistic King List come from. A complete edition of the Assyrian King List would bridge the chronological gap in the 15th and 16th centuries. Finds of additional copies of Assyrian eponym lists of the 2nd millennium have been made and more can be expected, which is important as possible confirmation of the King List. Dated documents from Babylonia are still wanting for large parts of the 2nd millennium, like the years of stability under Karaindaš and Kurigalzu I. In recent years sources appeared for periods where they were previously lacking, as was the case with the Tell Muḫammad texts and the new finds from Baḫrain. This shows that it is realistic to reckon with the possibility that in the future dark decades may become illuminated by new finds of texts, if the sites are not destroyed.

Also material for dendrochronology would be very important, especially for the sites in Babylonia and Assyria where dendrochronological evidence might be correlated with building inscriptions.

The continued edition of the tens of thou-

[32] Reiner 1975

[33] Kugler 1912

[34] Pientka 1998, 141. The end of the year name reads according to my collation of VS 22, 45: É-nam-ti-la-šè in-ni-en-ku$_4$-ra.

[35] Sumu-la-el years 22, 23, Apil-Sîn 3, 9, 10, 15, 17, 18, Sîn-muballiṭ 16, Ḫammu-rapi' 3, 12, 14, 16, 18, 20, Samsu-iluna 5, 19, 21, Ammi-Ditāna 6, 19, 31.

sands of unpublished legal and administrative texts in the museums and the collation of the published material is also important since these texts allow sometimes to check the accuracy of the King Lists.

Thirty years ago John Brinkman expressed this wish: "In conclusion, if one may look forward to the future, it would be a great service to students of Mesopotamian history if all the various Assyrian and Babylonian kinglists were available in more accessible and reliable form. It is essential that these documents be carefully re-edited from the original tablets, since some of the present disagreements concern even the basic reading of the text. ... At this stage in the history of the discipline, we would all derive much more benefit from an adequate and reliable text edition than from further elaborate theorizing on an unevenly edited jumble."[36]

Brinkman's wish was so far only partly fulfilled through the article "Königslisten und Chroniken" in the Reallexikon der Assyriologie. That article gives the desired overview, but does not make up for an edition that shows how the tablets look precisely and what is exactly on the tablets. Since all historical chronologies for the entire Near East in the 2nd and 3rd millennia B. C. are entirely or to a larger or smaller degree dependent on the Assyrian King List, this new edition is most urgently needed.

[36] Brinkman 1973, 316f.

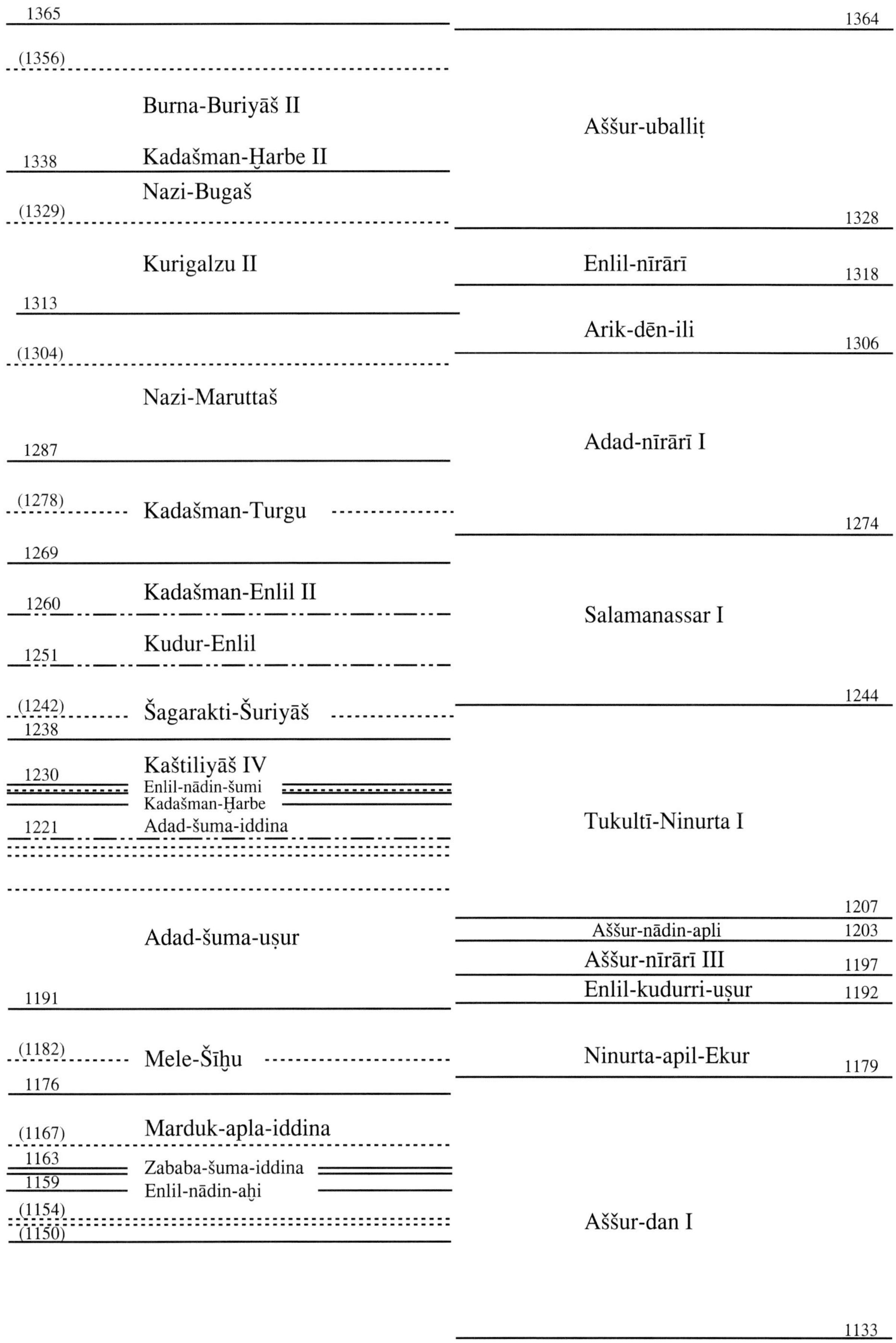

Table 1 Kassite - Middle Assyrian synchronisms (Brinkman 1976, 30)
The highest possibility for the reigns of the Kassite rulers is represented by the unbroken lines on the left side, the lowest possibility (9 years lower) by the dotted lines. 1 year ≅ 1 mm.

King	City	Temple
Karaindaš		
	Uruk	Eanna of Inanna
Kurigalzu		
	Adab	Emaḫ of Ninḫursag
	Akkade	Emegalam of Ištar of Akkade for the *akītu*-festival (Neo-Bab. copy)
		Attempted rebuilding of the Eulmaš
	Borsippa?	... of Enlil (inscription said to come from Borsippa)
	Dēr	Edimgalkalama of Ištarān
	Dūr-Kurigalzu	E'ugal of Enlil
		Egašanantagal of Ninlil
		Esagdingirene of Ninurta
		Šarrat-Nippur
	Isin	Egalmaḫ of Gula
		Cella of Ninurta in the Egalmaḫ
	Kiš	Zababa
	Nippur	Ekurigibara of Enlil
	Sippar	Ebabbar of Šamaš
	Ur	Ekišnugal of Sîn
		Edublalmaḫ of Sîn
		Eganunmaḫ of Sîn
		Ningal
		Egabur of Ningublaga
	Uruk	Eanna of Inanna
Kadašman-Enlil		
	Isin	Egalmaḫ of Gula
	Larsa	Ebabbar of Šamaš
	Nippur	Ekur
Burna-Buriyāš		
	Larsa	Ebabbar of Šamaš
	Nippur	Ekiur of Ninlil
Nazi-Maruttaš		
	Uruk	*Eḫiliana of Nanâ*
Kadašman-Turgu		
	Marad	E'igikalama of Lugalmarada
Kudur-Enlil		
	Nippur	Enlil
Šagarakti-Šuriyāš		
	Sippar-Annunītu	*Eulmaš of Ištar-Annunītu*
Adad-šuma-uṣur		
	Nippur	Ekur of Enlil
Mele-Šīḫu		
	Isin	Egalmaḫ of Gula
	Nippur	unpublished inscriptions from the Ekur area
Marduk-apla-iddina		
	Borsippa	Ezida of Marduk

Table 2 Known temple constructions of Kassite Babylonian Kings in chronological order[37]
(Data taken from inscriptions of Esarhaddon and Nabonidus are given in *italics*)

[37] Cf. SASSMANNSHAUSEN 2001, 157f. It is unclear whether the inscriptions of Kadašman-Enlil were commissioned by the first or the second king of that name. I consider it likely that they have to be attributed to Kadašman-Enlil I who may have tried to bring the ambitious program of his predecessor to an end, and not to Kadašman-Enlil II who ruled only for nine years at a time that is characterised by little construction activity still visible.

Kadašman-Enlil I	1374 (+x)–1360
Kurigalzu I	ca. 1410–1380
Kadašman-Ḫarbe I	ca. 1415–1410
Karaindaš	ca. 1450–1415
Predecessor of Karaindaš	?
Agum "III" son of Kaštiliyāš = (?) Agum of Baḫrain-texts	
Burna-Buriyāš, contemporary with Puzur-Aššur	ca. 1480
Burna-Buriyāš father of Ulam-Buriyāš and Burna-Buriyāš I of the Synchronistic King List the same person?	
Tell Muḫammad texts	ca. 1540–1490

Table 3 Suggested chronology for Kassite Babylonia in the 15th–16th centuries

Bibliography

ALBRIGHT, W.F.

1942 A Third Revision of the Early Chronology of Western Asia, *Bulletin of the American Schools of Oriental Research* 88, 28–36

ANDRE-SALVINI, B. - LOMBARD, P.

1997 La découverte épigraphique de 1995 à Qal'at al-Bahrein, *Proceedings of the Seminar of Arabian Studies* 27, 165–170

ARMSTRONG, J.A., COLE, S.W., GASCHE, H., GURZADYAN, V.G.

1998 *Dating the Fall of Babylon*, Mesopotamian History and Environment Memoirs 4, Gent

VON BECKERATH, J.

1997 *Chronologie des pharaonischen Ägypten*, Münchner Ägyptologische Studien 46, Mainz

BOESE, J.

1982 Burnaburiaš II., Melišipak und die mittelbabylonische Chronologie, *Ugarit-Forschungen* 14, 15–26

BRINKMAN, J.A.

1973 Comments on the Nassouhi Kinglist and the Assyrian Kinglist Tradition, *Orientalia N.S.* 42, 306–319

1976 *A Catalogue of Cuneiform Sources Pertaining to Specific Monarchs of the Kassite Dynasty*, Chicago

1983 Istanbul A. 1998, Middle Babylonian Chronology, and the Statistics of the Nippur Archives, *Zeitschrift für Assyriologie und Vorderasiatische Archäologie* 73, 67–74

CHARPIN, D. - DURAND, J.-M.

1985 La prise du pouvoir par Zimri-Lim, *Mari. Annales de Recherches Interdisciplinaires* 4, 293–342

VAN DIJK, J.

1986 Die dynastischen Heiraten zwischen Kassiten und Elamern: eine verhängnisvolle Politik, *Orientalia N.S.* 55, 159–170

DONBAZ, V.

1982 A Middle Babylonian Legal Document Raising Problems in Kassite Chronology, *Journal of Near Eastern Studies* 41, 207–212

GRAYSON, A. K.

1975 *Assyrian and Babylonian Chronicles*, Texts from Cuneiform Sources 5, Locust Valley NY

1980–1983 Königslisten und Chroniken, B. Akkadisch, in: *Reallexikon der Assyriologie* 6, Berlin - New York, 86–135

1987 *Assyrian Rulers of the Third and Second Millennia BC*, The Royal Inscriptions of Mesopotamia, Assyrian Periods 1, Toronto

KLENGEL, H.

1983 *Altbabylonische Texte aus Babylon*, Vorderasiatische Schriftdenkmäler 22, Berlin

KUGLER, F.X.

1912 *Sternkunde und Sterndienst in Babel*, 2. Buch, Teil 2, Heft 1, Münster

PIENTKA, R.

1998 *Die spätaltbabylonische Zeit*, Teil 1, Münster

REINER, E.

1975 *The Venus Tablet of Ammiṣaduqa*, Bibliotheca Mesopotamica 2/1, Malibu

SASSMANNSHAUSEN, L.

1999 The Adaptation of the Kassites to the Babylonian Civilization, in: K. Van LERBERGHE - G. VOET (eds.), *Languages and Cultures in Contact*, OLA 96, Leuven, 409–424

2001 Beiträge zur Verwaltung und Gesellschaft Babyloniens in der Kassitenzeit, *Baghdader Forschungen* 21, Mainz

in press Kassite Nomads: Fact or Fiction?, *Amurru* 3, Paris

SEEHER, J.

2001 Die Zerstörung der Stadt Ḫattuša, in: G. WILHELM (ed.), *Akten des IV. internationalen Kongresses für Hethitologie, Studien zu den Boğazköy-Texten* 45, Wiesbaden, 623–634

STEIN, P.

2000 *Die mittel- und neubabylonischen Königsinschriften bis zum Ende der Assyrerherrschaft,* Wiesbaden

VEENHOF, K.R.

2003 *The Old Assyrian List of Year Eponyms from Karum Kanish and its Chronological Implications,* Publications of the Turkish Historical Society, Serial VI No. 64, Ankara

Generation Count in Hittite Chronology

Gernot Wilhelm[*]

In studies on Ancient Near Eastern chronology Hittite history has often been considered a cornerstone of a long chronology. In his grandiose but – as we now see – futile attempt to denounce the Assyrian Kinglist as a historically unreliable source for the Assyrian history of the first half of the 2nd millennium B.C., LANDSBERGER 1954: 50 only briefly commented on Hittite history.[1] A. Goetze, however, who at that time had already repeatedly defended a long chronology against the claims of the followers of the short chronology (GOETZE 1951, 1952), filled the gap and supported Landsberger's plea for a long chronology, though not as excessively long as Landsberger considered to be likely.[2] Thirty years later, when in a strongly low-chronology-minded atmosphere at the "High, Middle or Low?" meeting at Gothenburg the audience was invited to take a vote, Oliver Gurney was one of three participants who voted for the high chronology without hesitation (ÅSTRÖM 1989: 76). At a colloquium organized by advocates of an ultra-low chronology at Ghent, another hittitologist, BECKMAN 2000: 25, deviated from the mainstream by declaring that from his viewpoint, "the Middle Chronology best fits the evidence, although the High Chronology would also be possible".

Those hittitologists who adhered to the low chronology (which means, sack of Babylon by Mursili I: 1531) had to solve the problem of squeezing all the kings attested between Mursili I and Suppiluliuma I into appr. 150 years, provided that there was agreement on Suppiluliuma's accession to the throne around 1380 B.C. None of the solutions proposed have stood the test of time.[3] The scholars who suggested the (moderate) ultra-short chronology (which means, sack of

* University of Würzburg

[1] No longer valid is Landsberger's argument that the "author" of the Puzur-Sîn inscription is omitted by the king-list (see READE 2001). The correctness of the tradition on the Old Assyrian dynasty is proven by the Kültepe eponym list published by VEENHOF 2003 (for a preliminary overview cf. already VEENHOF 2000). The figures given there for the reigns from Irīšum I to Šamšī-Adad I match well the *Distanzangaben* of Shalmaneser I's and Esarhaddon's inscriptions. The *Distanzangabe* was certainly computed by using the king-list or an eponym list of the Kültepe type with summary figures of reigns. Down to the Middle and Neo-Assyrian period the Assyrian archival data were evidently not altered because of ideological purposes. In their tradition they were, however, at times subject to mistakes. The early portion of the list had been compiled by using Assyrian archival data supplemented by Amorite tribal traditions (ancestors list) and *Urzeit* constructions (kings in tents), as has been shown convincingly by LANDSBERGER 1954, KRAUS 1965 and YAMADA 1994, but, as is clear now, even for the old Assyrian history prior to Šamšī-Adad, the available sources were carefully reproduced: The division line between Ilušūma and his son and successor Irīšum can be explained by the fact that only from Irīšum onwards was information on the length of reigns available, as is now shown by the Kültepe eponym list and the Mari eponym canon.

[2] For a detailed summary and bibliography of the discussion on the Ancient Near Eastern chronology especially during the 40ies and 50ies cf. KAMMENHUBER 1968: 34–40, ZEEB 2001: 75–87. Zeeb pronounces himself in favor of the ultra-short chronology (p. 123), but since he – unfortunately – follows MAYER 1995, 2001:15f., in linking Tudḫaliya I to the "evil" (*mašiktu*) which led to Idrimis flight from Ḫalab (ZEEB 2001: 106f., 112, 122; see, however, WILCKE 1992: 124f.), he is forced to concede only 24±5 years for the span of time between Mursili I's sack of Babylon and Tudḫaliya I's conquest of Aleppo, which is impossible. For an excellent résumé of the data and problems with rich literature cf. DE MARTINO 1993.

[3] Before the discovery of middle-Hittite *Landschenkungsurkunden* in the late 80ies and early 90ies which proved beyond doubt that there was a double sequence of Hittite kings with identical names (old Kingdom: Ḫantili I, Zidanta I, Ḫuzziya I; middle Kingdom: Ḫantili II, Zidanta II, Ḫuzziya II), some scholars had suggested that the duplication had to be omitted (LAROCHE 1955: 5, CORNELIUS 1958: 103, VON SCHULER 1965: 16f. with n. 168; for older literature cf. GOETZE 1957b: 54 n. 13). OTTEN 1951: 60, while accepting the middle-Hittite kings, nevertheless remained a supporter of the low chronology by hypothesizing two parallel lines of kings. HELCK 1979: 244, another advocate of the low chronology, suggested a family tree in which Suppiluliuma I was a grandson of Tudḫaliya I, the conqueror of Aleppo and husband of Nikkalmati, and a cousin of Tudḫaliya "III" (who was Suppiluliuma's father as we know today). ASTOUR 1989 was the last author who tried to reconcile an early date

Babylon by Mursili I: 1499) more or less dismissed Hittite data.[4]

The exact figures for the different Ancient Mesopotamian chronologies from the sack of Babylon onwards still rest on the venus data of *Enuma Anu Enlil* tablet 63, though astronomical criticism has lead to questioning its usefulness. Do the astronomical data belong to a continuous series of observations or is the tablet the result of compilation?[5] It has been argued that only the first 10 omens (recording 5 synodic periods, i.e. one 8-years-cycle) belong to the reign of king Ammiṣaduqa whose 8th year is mentioned in the 10th omen instead of the apodosis.[6] If this is correct, EAE 63 does not provide enough data for identifying a venus period of 64 or 56 years. Some scholars dismiss any chronological value of the venus dates.[7] Two Ur III lunar eclipses mentioned in EAE 20 and 21 have been used in support of the long as well as of the (moderate) ultra-short chronology (GASCHE *et al.* 1998: 74ff.), but they have also been dismissed for chronological purposes by HUNGER 2000. For our discussion of the Hittite chronology of the pre-Amarna period, the exact figures provided by astronomically based chronological systems cannot be proven or challenged in detail. What can be expected is that the Hittite data might exclude one of the extreme positions (high, ultra-low). This is to be examined on the following pages.

In 1987, the present writer in cooperation with J. Boese submitted a reassessment of the chronology of Suppiluliuma's reign (WILHELM and BOESE 1987). They questioned the traditional view[8] – best expressed and reasoned by KITCHEN 1962 – that Suppiluliuma I ruled for approximately 40 years after ascending the throne between 1386 and 1372 (KITCHEN 1962: 39).

Lowering the chronology of the Hittite Empire period had become urgent after most Egyptologists agreed upon a low chronology for the Egyptian New Kingdom with the key-date 1279 for Ramses II's accession to the throne,[9] while older calculations depended on higher accession dates (1304, 1290, with wide-spread preference for the last date). Lowering Ramses II's accession date from 1290 to 1279 would have "automatically" lowered Suppiluliuma's accession from 1372 to 1361, still maintaining a 40 years reign.[10]

for Suppiluliuma's accession (1386) with the low chronology, by eliminating Ḫantili II, Zidanta II and Ḫuzziya II as kings of Ḫatti and making them local kings or princes (p. 34–37; for a critique cf. WILHELM 1991: 471).

4 GASCHE *et al.* 1998: 6f. seem to imply that the Telipinu edict – "perhaps as much as a century after the event" – is not sufficient evidence of Mursili's sack of Babylon. They duly quote, however, HOFFNER 1975, who edited and discussed the fragment KBo 3.45, in which a contemporary critic of Mursili's sack of Babylon decrees the *damnatio memoriae* of this king. The combined evidence of the Hittite and Babylonian sources – which are independent of each other – leaves no doubt that the duration of Hittite history between the two synchronisms produced by Mursili's sack of Babylon (by plausibility including the end of Samsuditana's reign) and Suppiluliuma's appearance on the Syrian theatre has to be compatible with the dates provided by any chronology of the mid-second millennium B.C.

5 REINER and PINGREE 1975: 21ff.; HUBER 1982: 19; KUDLEK 1985: 114f.

6 GASCHE *et al.* 1998: 72.

7 KÜHNE 1999: 203 n. 1; MICHEL 1997–2000.

8 Cf., e.g., GOETZE 1933: 79 ("etwa 1395–55").

9 For recent overviews cf. VON BECKERATH 1997 and KITCHEN 2000; Kitchen, however, does not take into account that the Middle Babylonian chronology depends on the Middle Assyrian one and that there is wide agreement now that the latter one has to be reduced; thus the reign of the Babylonian king Burnaburiaš is not an argument for 1334 as a *terminus ante quem* for Amenophis IV's death, nor is 1332 a *terminus ante quem* for Tutanḫamun's accession; cf. BOESE 1982 for the Middle Babylonian chronology (Burnaburiaš 1354–1328[+2/–3]) and BOESE and WILHELM 1979, FREYDANK 1991 for the Middle Assyrian chronology. GASCHE *et al.* 1998: 66 follow Boese (without quoting him) for the Middle Babylonian chronology. They do not, however, follow BOESE and WILHELM 1979 in reducing the Middle Assyrian dates prior to 1169 by 10 years (p. 51); for the 14th century they nevertheless reach figures that come close to the reduced Middle Assyrian chronology, because they calculate shorter year lengths prior to Tiglathpileser (that is prior to the adoption of the Babylonian solar calendar in Assyria) based on a lunar calendar without intercalation. WILHELM 1994: 551 had already tested this theory, but left the question open. VEENHOF 2000: 141f., quoting KOCH 1989, argues in favor of a special kind of intercalation: According to this hypothesis a month was added after the last month of the year and given the same name as the previous one, but was counted as the first month of the new year. This would speak against the assumption that Assyrian regnal years followed the lunar year of 354 days instead of the solar year.

10 WENTE and VAN SICLEN III 1976: 250 had already (implicitly) noticed this consequence (cf. also BOESE and WILHELM 1979: 37 n. 67). However, it has not always been observed since, especially not in general books on Ancient Near Eastern history. NISSEN 1998: 246f. follows the Egyptian low chronology (Ramses' accession year 1279), while giving 1375 as Suppiluliuma's accession year, a date that is not only based on a reign of 40 years, but also on a higher Egyptian chronology (Ramses' accession year 1290).

What established the assumption of a 40-year-reign is a late source from the time of Ḫattusili III saying that Suppiluliuma campaigned for 20 years in Anatolia, and that he needed 6 years to subdue the Hurri lands. Conventionally, Suppiluliuma's conquest of Syria and the struggle with Egypt had been estimated to have lasted from 12 to 14 years. This span of time had been combined in one way or the other with the 20 years of Anatolian fightings and the 6 years of the Hurrian war, thus adding up to 40 years for the whole of Suppiluliuma's reign.

Our analysis of the very fragmentary text of the "Deeds of Suppiluliuma, as told by his Son Mursili II" leads us to the conclusion that it is virtually impossible that Suppiluliuma campaigned for 20 years before entering Syria. The details of our analysis cannot be repeated here, but since the results saw highly controversial judgements,[11] the basic lines[12] of the argument are summarized here.

The Deeds of Suppiluliuma are preserved in several copies which differ in the length of columns (caused by differences in the size of the handwriting and/or the tablet). One copy (e.g. KBo 14.3) with very small handwriting is numbered "tablet 2" within the series of 7 to 12 tablets which contained the whole *res gestae* of Suppiluliuma. Another copy (KUB 19.18) is labeled "tablet 3", but its first column corresponds to the last column of "tablet 2" due to its larger script. Still another tablet is numbered "tablet 7". Its handwriting is "extremely large". The columns of this tablet amount to only 62 lines, whereas the "tablet 2" has 78 lines per column. The content of this "tablet 7" must have been recorded at the end of tablet 5 and the beginning of tablet 6 of the version with the small handwriting.

In the copy of the version with small script, the tablets no. 1 and no. 2 (until col. iii inclusively) record events which took place while Suppiluliuma was still serving as a general during his father's reign. The death of Suppiluliuma's father and the events leading to Suppiluliuma's accession to the throne may have been told at the beginning of tablet 2 col. iv (which is not preserved) or even later. "Tablet 7" of a series with "short columns" reports the so-called *daḫamunzu* episode, the story of an Egyptian queen who after the death of her husband Nipḫururiya asked for a son of Suppiluliuma's to become her husband and king of Egypt.

The beginning of this report in column iii of "tablet 7" (tablet with "short columns", large handwriting) would correspond to the first column of tablet 6 (tablet with "long columns", small script). Our calculation proved that the space between the (lost) report on Suppiluliuma's seizure of the throne and the *daḫamunzu* episode is not larger than three tablets of the largest size. To judge from the preserved parts of the "Deeds of Suppiluliuma" we calculated appr. 10 years.[13]

It is evident that the *daḫamunzu* affair provides

---

[11] Kitchen 1989: 157 („W. & B. indulge in very speculative reconstructions of broken Hittite tablets"; in his further critical remarks the author is mistaken in keeping up his former argument [Kitchen 1962: 1f., especially p. 2 n. 2] that all of Suppiluliuma's "three queens" [p. 156] were his successive wives, though today there is no doubt that Taduḫepa is the [second?] wife of Suppiluliuma's father Tudḫaliya II. [cf. Kammenhuber 1976: 166–171, 176, corrected by Gurney 1979; cf. also Bryce 1989: 26]. Kitchen also misses the point when reproaching us to "rely in highly uncritical fashion upon the *diktat* of Krauss and Fecht" [p. 156] – actually we had quoted their theory in indirect speech [German *Konjunktiv*] and tried to put forward a counter-argument against the linguistic identification of *Nipḫururiya* with *Nfr-ḫpr.w-rʿ*, cf. Wilhelm and Boese 1987: 100f.). Freu 1992: 87–90 (critical review, accepting a moderate reduction of Suppiluliuma's reign to 31 years; Freu bases his reconstruction of events on a co-regency of Amenophis III and Echnaton of appr. 11 years and dates Suppiluliuma's accession to the throne to 1353; cf., however, von Beckerath 1997: 110, who states that the question can be regarded as being solved; a long co-regency can be excluded, a short one of one or two years is possible, but cannot be proven and is chronologically irrelevant). - Bryce 1989 accepts the method of textual analysis employed by us, suggesting some changes in the course of events and gives 1344–1322 as the dates of Suppiluliuma's reign, i.e. 22 years. O.R. Gurney (who, according to an oral communication Gothenburg 1987, had carefully cross-checked our analysis of the Deeds of Suppiluliuma), follows Bryce in his 4th edition of his standard work on the Hittites and attributed the same dates – 1344–1322 – to Suppiluliuma's reign (Gurney 1990: 22, 181); in the latest general histories of the Hittites, Bryce 1998 repeats his views of 1989, whereas Klengel 1999 refers to the length of Suppiluliuma's reign only vaguely and avoids giving absolute dates.

[12] A more extensive English summary was provided by Bryce 1989: 21.

[13] Bryce 1989 basically follows these calculations, though he is forced to extend the span of time to 17 years, because he – as most scholars – dates the *daḫamunzu* episode to the time following Tutanḫamun's death. According to his reconstruction of the sequence of

an important synchronism between Hittite and Egyptian history. If it were possible to fix this event exactly within the Egyptian history of the late 18th dynasty and within Suppiluliuma's career and subsequently calculate the time between this date and Mursili's sack of Babylon, the central riddle of the Ancient Near Eastern chronology would be solved, and the "floating block" of ca. 700 years of Late Early Bronze and Middle Bronze Age Mesopotamian history would be tightly knotted to the chronologically well-established younger history of the Ancient Near East.

In the context of this colloquium it is not necessary to discuss the many details which are still more or less controversial. For our purposes it suffices to state that Suppiluliuma I ascended the throne in the 40ies of the 14th century.

The difficulties of Hittite chronology are obvious: There are no year-names, no eponyms, no counting of regnal years, no era, no kinglist. There is, however, institutional continuity, despite the many political disruptions apparent in regicides, dethronements and usurpations, and this continuity is embodied in the royal clan that seems to have ruled the country from the earliest old Hittite period to the end of the empire period (and in some regions beyond). Thus generation count is the best Hittitology can offer to help solve the problems of Ancient Near Eastern chronology. In addition to this, there is a much-debated solar omen that took place in Mursili II's 10th regnal year on a campaign to the land of Azzi in northeast Anatolia. It is likely to be an eclipse, but the possibility of a different phenomenon cannot be excluded. If indeed it is an eclipse, two dates can be calculated that belong to the period defined by synchronisms with Egyptian history: June 24, 1312[14] or April 13, 1308.[15]

The generation count is necessarily rather inaccurate and only applicable for long periods in which irregularly long or short generation intervals are evened out.[16] How is a generation interval defined? The most regular result would be a count based on regular natural[17] conditions: The distance between the birth of a man's eldest surviving son and the birth of this son's eldest surviving son. But even here culture mixes with biology: It makes a big difference whether any son, regardless of what rank within the harem his mother enjoys, is eligible for office (as the princes in the Ottoman house) or whether the role the mother plays is mirrored in the rank of the king's sons (as in Hatti). Even more so, if the eldest son is not automatically heir apparent (also, as in Hatti), then in the case of the death of or divorce from the first queen, the second queen will be likely to scheme against the king's elder sons in favor of one of her own sons. Apart from that, the culturally defined marriage age of the crown prince is unknown.

Various calculations of the lengths of generation intervals have led to very different results. This is not astonishing because the variables mentioned above are mostly unknown or differ from one another. Rowton 1958: 100–102 checked various Ancient Near Eastern dynasties for a seven years' generation sequence and calculated a generation interval between 21.1 and 31.7 years. Comparing the British royal family, Gurney 1974: 108f. established a generation interval of 29/30 years. Wilhelm 1990: 523 n. 97 used the Ottoman dynasty for the same purpose and calculated 21.5 years. More extreme positions have

events, the „one year's war" ("First Syrian war") took place four years before Aḫenaten's death. This, however, seems to be excluded by EA 75, which clearly refers to the "one year's war" ("May the king be informed that the king of Ḫatti has seized all the countries *that were vassals* of the king of Mitta<ni>." Moran 1992: 145), a passage which belongs to the older group of vassal letters still mentioning Abdi-Aširta of Amurru as an active opponent. EA 75 cannot be dated that late; Boese and Wilhelm 1987: 88 calculated what they considered as the lowest possible date, namely seven years before Amenophis IV's death and opted for a slightly higher age. Freu 1992: 53 even thinks the addressee is Amenophis III, but at a time when Amenophis IV was already in his seventh year as coregent (p. 94). Also Moran 1992: XXXV f. n.127 puts forward an argument in favor of Amenophis III as addressee.
Considering the many difficulties of an identification of the Nipḫururiya of the "Deeds" with Tutanḫamun (Krauss 1978 passim, Murnane ^{2}1990: 131–136) it seems still to be a preferable option to think of Smenḫkare-Anḫḫeperure, survived by his powerful wife Meritaten, who made herself reigning queen under the feminine form of her deceased husband's name, Anḫetḫeperure, buried her husband's mummy in due time, tried to solve two problems at the same time – the Hittite military threat and her domestically difficult situation –, and when failed, was killed to be replaced by the boyish husband of her younger sister (cf. also Krauss 1994: 76).

[14] Wente and Van Siclen III 1976: 250.

[15] Wilhelm and Boese 1987: 107 (as a possible alternative to the earlier date).

[16] Rowton 1958: 101.

[17] Goetze 1952: 72 n. 32 quoted by Gurney 1974: 108: "after all there is a biological factor involved".

been expressed by STEINER 1989, who suggested a generation interval of 40 years, and HAGENBUCHNER 1992: 116, who quotes the middle-Assyrian laws for a marriageable age minimum of 10 years. In the case of the Hittite royal house, there are so many open questions and irregularities that the lack of agreement among scholars is not astonishing. Nevertheless, the available data have to be examined again by using the method of defining maxima and minima of possible dates as far as possible. In a generation count this has to be done on two levels: the number of generations and the average lengths of generation intervals.

In the line of Hittite kings between Mursili I[18] and Suppiluliuma I there are several kings who are (a) the sons of their respective predecessors, several others who are (b) sons-in-law or (c) brothers-in-law of their predecessors. The relation of some kings (usually called (d) "usurpers" by modern hittitologists) with the royal clan is unknown. At least in one case it is likely that a king is an (e) adopted son.

A minimal count would only ascribe the full length of a generation interval to case (a). Taking into consideration the relationship between Tušratta and his "son-in-law", the much older Amenophis III, one could even speculate about a "negative generation interval". One should not argue that this is typical of political marriages, and that it does not apply to marriages of all members of the royal clan; within a political elite every marriage is likely to be "political". The same, of course, is even more true of brothers-in-law. Here a "negative generation interval" is even more probable. On the other hand, it can reasonably be excluded that an adopted son is older than his adoptive father. Fig. 1 lists all the attested Hittite great kings together with the available information on their family relationship.

(a) sons of their predecessors: (8) Ammuna, (13) Ḫantili II, (18) Tudḫaliya I,[19] (20)Tudḫaliya II, (21–22)(Tudḫaliya III[20])/Suppiluliuma.
(b) sons-in-law: (7) Zidanta I, (12) Alluwamna, (19) Arnuwanda I.
(c) brothers-in-law: (6) Ḫantili I, (10) Telipinu
(d) "usurpers": (9) Ḫuzziya I, (11) Taḫurwaili, (16) Muwattalli I
(e) adopted sons: (19) Arnuwanda I (?)
(f) unclear: (14) Zidanta II, (15) Ḫuzziya II, (17) Kantuzzili

In a radical minimal calculation of attested generation intervals we get the following sequence: Mursili I – Ammuna – Telipinu (?) – Ḫantili II – Tudḫaliya I – Tudḫaliya II – Suppiluliuma I.

In an equally radical maximal calculation we attribute half a generation interval (symbol: **-½-**) to every son-in-law and a full generation interval (symbol: **–1–**) to adopted sons and to the kings (14) and (15). Though the family relationship of kings (14) and (15) is unclear, they seem to have had a legitimate claim to the throne (at least this is suggested by the offering-lists). Only brothers-in-law and the "usurpers" are not counted: Mursili I **–½–** Zidanta I **–1–** Ammuna **–1–** Telipinu **–½–** Alluwamna **–1–** Ḫantili I **–1–** Zidanta II **–1–** Ḫuzziya II **–1–** Kantuzzili **–1–** Tudḫaliya I **–1–** Arnuwanda I **–1–** Tudḫaliya II **–1–** Suppiluliuma. In the first count the addition results in 6, in the second case in 11 generation intervals.

In the following diagram we combine these figures with the lengths of generation intervals according to the aforementioned suggestions (leaving aside the two most radical and less than likely ones, 10 and 40) and in a parallel column we add them to Suppiluliuma's rounded accession year 1350:

Author	generation interval	Maximum (11)		Minimum (6)	
ROWTON (low)	21.1	232.1	1582	126.6	1477
ROWTON (high)	31.7	348.7	1699	190.2	1540
British Royal Family (GURNEY)	29/30	319–330	1669–1680	174–180	1524–1530
Ottoman Imperial Family (WILHELM)	21.5	236.5	1587	129	1479

[18] It is not known whether Mursili was murdered upon his return from his Babylonian campaign or whether he had a couple of years to enjoy his unheard-of achievement. The question is irrelevant for the following count of generations.

[19] Tudḫaliya I is a son of Kantuzzili (OTTEN 1987, 2000), who is not attested independently as a king, but who took part in killing (16) Muwattalli I. Since Tudḫaliya's annals (CARRUBA 1977; DEL MONTE 1993: 143ff.; for the Middle Hittite origin of the annals cf. NEU 1986) refer to his father's death ("father" restored), Kantuzzili should be included in the king-list.

[20] Tudḫaliya was killed to be succeeded by his (half)brother Suppiluliuma I. It is unknown whether Tudḫaliya had already been formally established as a king, though this is likely. In a generation count he is negligible.

	Hittite Kings	Family Relationship	Dates
1	Ḫuzzia[1]		
2	Papaḫdilmaḫ		
3	Labarna		
4	Ḫattusili I	nephew of (3) (?)	
5	Mursili I†	grandson[2] (?) of (4)	
	sack of Babylon		high: 1659 middle: 1595 low: 1531 ultra-low (a):[3] 1499 ultra-low (b):[4] 1467
6	Ḫantili I	brother-in-law of (5)	
7	Zidanta I†	son-in-law of (6)	
8	Ammuna	son of (7)	
9	Ḫuzziya I#		
10	Telipinu	son of (8) (?) brother-in-law of (9)	
11	Taḫurwaili ¶		
12	Alluwamna	son-in-law of (10)	
13	Ḫantili II	son of (12)	
14	Zidanta II		
15	Ḫuzziya II†[5]		
16	Muwattalli I†[5]		
17	Kantuzzili (?)*[6]		
18	Tudḫaliya I (= "II")	son of (17)	
19	Arnuwanda I	(adopted) son, son-in-law of (18)	
20	Tudḫaliya II (= "III")	son of (19)	
21	Tudḫaliya III (?)*†	son of (20)	
22	Suppiluliuma I	son of (20)	
	daḫamunzu episode		after death of Amenophis IV:[7] 1341/1333 after death of Smenḫkare:[7] 1340/1332 after death of Tutanḫamun:[7] 1330/1322
23	Arnuwanda II	son of (22)	
24	Mursili II	son of (22)	
	omen of the sun in Mursili's 10th year (if eclipse)		June 24, 1312 or April 13, 1308
25	Muwattalli II	son of (24)	
	Battle of Qadeš		1274[8]
26	Mursili III (Urḫi-teššub)#	son of (25)	
27	Ḫattusili "III"	son of (24)	1265±2 – 1236±2[9]
	Treaty with Egypt		1259[9]
28	Tudḫaliya IV	son of (27)	
29	Arnuwanda III	son of (28)	
30	Suppiluliuma II	son of (28)	

* no proof for kingship; † assassinated; # deposed; ¶ position not clear

Fig. 1

1) According to Dinçol *et al.* 1992. 2) According to the Aleppo treaty; Steiner 1996: son. 3) Gasche *et al.* 1998. 4) Åström, 1992. 5) Otten 1987. 6) Otten 2000. 7) Dates according to von Beckerath 1997: 119 (the low versus high dates are based on 11/15 regnal years for Sethos I, 26/31 regnal years for Haremhab and 3/4 regnal years for Aya. 8) In Ramses II's 5th regnal year (1275/74); Ramses ascended the throne "ab 31. Mai 1279" (von Beckerath 1997: 118), Ramses left his residence for the campaign on day 9 of 2nd *šmw*, i.e. in the middle of April 1274. (According to von Beckerath 1997: 10, during the New Kingdom the regnal year was counted from the day of the accession to the throne until the same date in the following calendrical year.) 9) Boese and Wilhelm 1979: 36 n. 65. In the chronological system suggested by Gasche *et al.* 1998 Ḫattusili's last year would be 1243.

The extreme dates, 1477 and 1699, are certainly highly unlikely. In theory one could narrow the probability by mathematical procedures, but this would leave aside the different aspects of each individual case, which are subject to ongoing philological and historical debates. The only chronology which can be confidently excluded is the variant of the ultra-low chronology which dates the sack of Babylon to 1467.

Though the present writer himself used lengths of generation intervals in the past when arguing about Hittite history,[21] he would like to suggest that one should rather neglect the Hittite data in the discussion of Ancient Near Eastern chronology, as long as we do not have more information.

Bibliography

ASTOUR, M.C.

1989 *Hittite History and Absolute Chronology of the Bronze Age* (Studies in Mediterranean Archaeology and Literature, Pocket-book 73), Partille.

ÅSTRÖM, P.

1987a, 1987b, 1989 *High, Middle or Low? Acts of an International Colloquium on Absolute Chronology held at the University of Gothenburg 20th–22nd August 1987, Part 1–3* (Studies in Mediterranean Archaeology and Literature, Pocket-book 56, 57, 80), Gothenburg.

1992 Implications of an Ultra Low Chronology, *Ägypten und Levante* 3, 19–21.

VON BECKERATH, J.

1997 *Chronologie des pharaonischen Ägypten* (Münchner Ägyptologische Studien 46), Mainz.

BECKMAN, G.

2000 Hittite Chronology, *Akkadica* 119–120, 19–32.

BIETAK, M. (ed.)

2000 *The Synchronisation of Civilisations in the Eastern Mediterranean in the Second Millennium B.C., Proceedings of an International Symposium at Schloß Haindorf, 15th–17th of November 1996 and at the Austrian Academy, Vienna, 11th–12th of May 1998*, Wien.

BOESE, J.

1982 Burnaburiaš II., Melišipak und die mittelbabylonische Chronologie, *UF* 14, 15–26.

BOESE, J. and WILHELM, G.

1979 Aššur-dān I., Ninurta-apil-Ekur und die mittelassyrische Chronologie, *WZKM* 71, 19–38.

BRYCE, T.R.

1989 Some Observations on the Chronology of Šuppiluliuma's Reign, *AnSt* 39, 19–30.

1990 The Death of Niphururiya and its Aftermath, *JEA* 76, 97–105.

CARRUBA, O.

1977 Beiträge zur mittelhethitischen Geschichte I, *SMEA* 18, 137–174.

CORNELIUS, F.

1958 Chronology. Eine Erwiderung, *JCS* 12, 101–104.

DEL MONTE, G.F.

1993 *L'annalistica ittita* (TVOA 4/2), Brescia.

FREU, J.

1992 Les guerres syriennes de Suppiluliuma et le fin de l'ère amarnienne, *Hethitica* 11, 39–101.

FREYDANK, H.

1991 *Beiträge zur mittelassyrischen Chronologie und Geschichte* (SGKAO 21), Berlin.

GASCHE, H., ARMSTRONG, J.A., COLE, S.W. and GURZADYAN, V.G.

1998 *Dating the Fall of Babylon. A Reappraisal of Second-Millennium Chronology* (MHE 2, Memoirs 4), Ghent - Chicago.

GOETZE, A.

1933 Kleinasien, in: *Kulturgeschichte des alten Orients* (Handbuch der Altertumswissenschaft), München.

1951 The Problem of Chronology and Early Hittite History, *BASOR* 122, 18–25.

1952 The Date of the Hittite Raid on Babylon, *BASOR* 127, 21–26.

1957a Alalaḫ and Hittite Chronology, *BASOR* 146, 20–26.

1957b On the Chronology of the Second Millennium B.C., *JCS* 11, 53–61, 63–73.

GURNEY, O.R.

1974 The Hittite Line of Kings and Chronology, in: *Anatolian Studies Presented to Hans Gustav Güterbock on the Occasion of his 65th Birthday* (PIHANS 35), Istanbul, 105–111.

[21] WILHELM and BOESE 1987: 109, WILHELM 1989: 65f.

1979 The Anointing of Tudhaliya, in: O. Carruba (ed.), *Studia Mediterranea Piero Meriggi dicata I*, Pavia, 213–223.

HAGENBUCHNER, A.

1992 War der ^{LÚ}*tuḫkanti* Neriqqaili ein Sohn Ḫattušilis III?, *SMEA* 29, 111–126.

HELCK, W.

1979 Die Vorgänger König Šuppiluliumas I., in: *Festschrift Elmar Edel* (Ägypten und Altes Testament 1), Bamberg, 238–246.

HOFFNER, H.A.

1975 Propaganda and Political Justification in Hittite Historiography, in: H. GOEDICKE and J.J.M. ROBERTS, *Unity and Diversity. Essays in the History, Literature, and Religion of the Ancient Near East*, 49–62.

HUBER, P.J.

1982 *Astronomical Dating of Babylon I and Ur III* (OPNE 3, 4), Malibu.

HUNGER, H.

2000 Uses of Enūma Anu Enlil for Chronology, *Akkadica* 119–120, 155–158.

KAMMENHUBER, A.

1968 *Die Arier im Vorderen Orient*, Heidelberg.

1976 *Orakelpraxis, Träume und Vorzeichenschau bei den Hethitern* (Texte der Hethiter 7), Heidelberg.

KITCHEN, K.

1989 Supplementary Notes on "the Basics of Egyptian Chronology", in: ÅSTRÖM 1989, 152–159.

2000 Regnal and Genealogical Data of Ancient Egypt (Absolute Chronology I). The Historical Chronology of Ancient Egypt, A Current Assessment, in: BIETAK 2000, 39–52.

KRAUS, F.R.

1965 *Könige, die in Zelten wohnten. Betrachtungen über den Kern der assyrischen Königsliste* (Mededelingen der Koninklijke Nederlandse Akademie van Wetenschapen, Afd. Letterkunde N.R. 28 no. 2), Amsterdam.

KRAUSS, R.

1994 Nur ein kurioser Irrtum oder ein Beleg für die Jahre 26 und 27 von Haremhab?, *Discussions in Egyptology* 30, 73–85.

KUDLEK, M.

1985 [Review of] HUBER 1982, *AfO* 32, 114–115.

KÜHNE, C.

1999 Imperial Mittani: An Attempt at Historical Reconstruction, *SCCNH* 10, 203–221.

LANDSBERGER, B.

1954 Assyrische Königsliste und "Dunkles Zeitalter", *JCS* 8, 31–73, 106–133.

LAROCHE, E.

1955 Chronologie hittite: état de question, *Anadolu* 2, 1–22.

DE MARTINO, S.

1993 Problemi di cronologia ittita, *PP* 270, 218–240.

MAYER, W.

1995 Die historische Einordnung der "Autobiographie" des Idrimi von Alalah, *UF* 27, 333–350.

2001 *Tall Munbāqa - Ekalte II: Die Texte* (WVDOG 102), Saarbrücken.

MICHEL, C.

1997–2000 La chronologie du IIe millénaire revue à l'ombre d'une éclipse de soleil, *JEOL* 35–36, 111–126.

MURNANE, W.J.

1990 *The Road to Kadesh. A Historical Interpretation of the Battle Reliefs of King Sety I at Karnak, Second Edition Revised* (SAOC 42), Chicago.

NEU, E.

1986 Zum mittelhethitischen Alter der Tutḫalia-Annalen (CTH 142), in: W. MEID / H. TRENKWALDER, *Im Bannkreis des Alten Orients. Studien zur Sprach- und Kulturgeschichte des Alten Orients und seines Ausstrahlungsraumes Karl Oberhuber zum 70. Geburtstag gewidmet* (IBK 24), Innsbruck.

NISSEN, H.J.

1998 [1999] *Geschichte Altvorderasiens* (Oldenbourgs Grundriss der Geschichte 25), München.

OTTEN, H.

1951 Die hethitischen "Königslisten" und die altorientalische Chronologie, *MDOG* 83, 47–71.

1987 Das hethitische Königshaus im 15. Jahrhundert v.Chr., *AOAW* 123, 21–34, Abb. 1–8.

2000 Ein Siegelabdruck Dutḫalijas I.(?), *ArchAnz* 2000, 375–376.

READE, J.

2000 Absolute Dates and Assyrian Calendars, *Akkadica* 119–120, 151–153.

2001 Assyrian King-Lists, the Royal Tombs of Ur, and Indus Origins, *JNES* 60, 1–29.

ROWTON, M.B.

1958 The Date of Hammurabi, *JNES* 17, 97–111.

REINER, E. and PINGREE, D.

1975 *The Venus Tablet of Ammiṣaduqa* (BM 2,1), Malibu.

VON SCHULER, E.

1965 *Die Kaškäer. Ein Beitrag zur Ethnographie des alten Kleinasien* (UAVA 3), Berlin.

STEINER, G.

1989 Die Dauer einer Generation nach den Vorstellungen des Alten Orients, in: ÅSTRÖM 1989, 170–195.

1996 Muršili I: Sohn oder Enkel Labarna-Ḫattušilis I?, *UF* 28, 561–618.

VEENHOF, K.R.

2000 Old Assyrian Chronology, *Akkadica* 119–120, 137–150.

2003 *The Old Assyrian List of Year Eponyms from Karum Kanish and its Chronological Implications* (TTKY VI/64), Ankara.

WENTE, E.F. and VAN SICLEN III, Ch.C.

1977 A Chronology of the New Kingdom, in: *Studies in Honor of George R. Hughes* (SAOC 39), Chicago 1976, 217–261.

WILCKE, C.

1992 AḪ, die "Brüder" von Emar. Untersuchungen zur Schreibtradition am Euphratknie, *AuOr* 10, 115–150.

WILHELM, G.

1990 Marginalien zu Herodot, Klio 199, in: T. ABUSCH, J. HUEHNERGARD and P. STEINKELLER, *Lingering over Words. Studies in Ancient Near Eastern Literature in Honor of William L. Moran* (HSS 37), Atlanta.

1991 Probleme der hethitischen Chronologie, *OLZ* 86, 469–476.

1994 [Review of] H. Freydank, *Beiträge zur mittelassyrischen Chronologie und Geschichte*, *OLZ* 89, 549–552.

WILHELM, G. and BOESE, J.

1987 Absolute Chronologie und die hethitische Geschichte des 15. und 14. Jahrhunderts v.Chr., in: ÅSTRÖM 1987a, 74–117.

YAMADA, SH.

1994 The Editorial History of the Assyrian Kinglist, *ZA* 84, 11–37.

ZEEB, F.

2001 *Die Palastwirtschaft in Altsyrien nach den spätaltbabylonischen Getreidelieferlisten aus Alalaḫ* (Schicht VII) (AOAT 282), Münster.

Abbreviations

AfO *Archiv für Orientforschung*
AnSt *Anatolian Studies*
AOAT Alter Orient und Altes Testament
AOAW Anzeiger der phil-hist. Klasse der Österreichischen Akademie der Wissenschaften
ArchAnz *Archäologischer Anzeiger*
AuOr *Aula Orientalis*
BASOR *Bulletin of the American Schools of Oriental Research*
BBVO Berliner Beiträge zum Vorderen Orient
BM Bibliotheca Mesopotamica
HSS Harvard Semitic Studies
IBK Innsbrucker Beiträge zur Kulturwissenschaft
JCS *Journal of Cuneiform Studies*
JEA *Journal of Egyptian Archaeology*
JEOL *Jaarbericht "Ex oriente lux"*
JNES *Journal of Near Eastern Studies*
MDOG *Mitteilungen der Deutschen Orient-Gesellschaft*
MHE Mesopotamian History and Environment
OLZ *Orientalistische Literaturzeitung*
OPNE Occasional Papers on the Near East
PIHANS Publications de l'Institut historique et archéologique néerlandais de Stamboul
PP *La Parola del Passato*
SAOC Studies in Ancient Oriental Civilizations
SCCNH *Studies on the Civilization and Culture of Nuzi and the Hurrians*
SGKAO Schriften zur Geschichte und Kultur des Alten Orients
TTKY Türk Tarih Kurumu Yayınları
TVAO Testi del Vicino Oriente antico
UAVA Untersuchungen zur Assyriologie und Vorderasiatischen Archäologie
UF *Ugarit-Forschungen*
WVDOG Wissenschaftliche Veröffentlichungen der Deutschen Orient-Gesellschaft
WZKM *Wiener Zeitschrift für die Kunde des Morgenlandes*
ZA *Zeitschrift für Assyriologie*

The History of Alalaḫ as a Testcase for an Ultrashort Chronology of the Mid-2nd Millennium B.C.E.

*Frank Zeeb**

Preliminary remarks

The following paper[1] examines the Alalaḫ texts as to their relevance and possible conclusions for the chronological problems in the mid-second millennium B.C.E. It is structured in six main sections with three digressions. After a brief introduction I present some methodological remarks concerning the Alalaḫ material and the data as found in Alalaḫ.[2] The third section highlights the history of research, inasmuch as data from Alalaḫ have been discussed to determine an absolute chronology of the time in question. In the next step we will have to evaluate the material itself and in the next to last section I will try to embed Alalaḫ in the framework of international history. The final conclusion appears to favour an absolute chronology which is even shorter than the so-called "Short Chronology".[3] However, the approach does not answer all the questions and remains open to discussion. The aim of the present paper consists therefore rather in presenting the material and the questions and presuppositions that lead to the given proposal than in attempting a definite solution. It goes without saying that different answers and decisions must lead to other conclusions. For the time being it would be unwise to head towards a generally accepted consensus on chronology.

1. Introduction

It must be borne in mind that the trivial distinction between absolute and relative chronology is always to be observed. Both frameworks have their own right and their respective consequences. The general public is normally more interested in absolute chronology while the historian may be content with a relative chronology that enables him to connect historical events and their mutual impacts on each other.[4]

However, much work and an immense amount of scholarly sharp-wit has been spent to build up a network of absolute dates. In fact, it would not be too hard a task to show that harsh arguing is often not very far when it comes to establish an absolute chronology, especially when the data is as ambiguous and scarce as in the case of the mid-second millennium B.C.E.

I presume that human consciousness is in some way dependent on organised structuring of data in order to be able to include new or unknown facts into a secure framework. The most secure principle of structuring things appears to be pure mathematics, and therefore, the sometimes vivid struggle for absolute data that one can learn by heart may be the (unconscious) expression of a desire to perceive a secure structure in an unorganised collection of different facts and bits of information so that the human brain can handle them in a more convenient way. If this is true, our scholarly attention must be drawn to this our very own – perhaps unconscious – presupposition: We would like to establish an absolute chronology as precise as possible, but perhaps we must realize that the desired precision is not always achievable. In sum, both relative and absolute chronology can enhance our knowledge considerably.

---

* Nellmersbach, Germany

[1] Paper as read at the workshop on Nov 08, 2002. The oral form has been widely preserved.

[2] For a more detailed discussion see Zeeb 2001, 67–124. The most recent discussions on the chronological issues of the Alalaḫ material are those by van Soldt 2000 and Oliva 1999/2000, see below.

[3] For convenience we will use the following terms for the respective chronological systems; the supposed date for the fall of Babylon is given in brackets: Ultra-Short (1499, cf. Gasche *et al.* 1998a); Short (1531, cf. Albright 1957), Middle (1595, cf. Smith 1940), Long (1651, cf. Huber 2000), Ultra-Long (~1700; cf. Landsberger 1954).

[4] Schoolbooks even for advanced pupils generally rely on absolute dates. The pupil may perfectly acquire them by heart and still miss a historical understanding. E.g. the battle of Tours and Poitiers (732 C.E.) should not only be treated as an isolated event, but ought to be seen in the context of the geo-political situation of the then not yet consolidated Frankish kingdom – the historical impact will then be more than mere year dates.

2. A Few Words on Methodology

2.1. The value of the Alalaḫ material for the question

If we take these introductory remarks seriously, then a few words on methodology are in order.[5] It goes without saying that textual sources and archaeological data need to complement each other.[6] Both sets of data cannot be seen on their own, but must interpret each other mutually, and any results are void if texts and archaeology contradict each other. Furthermore, it must not be forgotten that our sources of insight are as limited as our positive knowledge of events. At best, we can aim to connect as much data as possible with known events in history but it must be clear from the very beginning that we are simply not aware of all events. It remains possible that a given date seems to fit a certain event but in reality is to be connected to something different that we do not know about.

In any case the material from Alalaḫ is not really unambiguous in this respect. We must take into account that archaeological remains[7] in most cases allow more than one interpretation, and the best we can make of them is normally an evaluation of time periods rather than exact dates. On the other hand, the same is true for written sources. The bulk of material cannot be dated exactly without further suppositions and needs careful interpretation, which means that we must be aware that any absolute chronology based on the Alalaḫ material is open to question. The best we can achieve is to present our own interpretations and show their respective impact on absolute chronology as it can be proposed with the present state of knowledge.

Even with this *caveat* in mind, Alalaḫ is a good starting-point for discussing the matter of absolute chronology for various reasons. The North Syrian area is a melting-pot of cultures and influences from different parts of the world then known.[8]

- For the Hittites Alalaḫ and its surroundings were always a kind of entrance gate to the areas lying beyond the Mukiš plain.[9]
- Contacts between the Alalaḫ region and the Mesopotamian kingdoms are attested as being highly regular, even if it were only the connection between Aleppo and Mari in the Old Babylonian time.[10]
- The relationship between Alalaḫ and far away Egypt will form a corner-stone of the discussion later[11] and it is evident that Egyptian art influenced at least the seal-cutting of Northern Syria.[12] Of course in the Late Bronze Age the political impacts of Egypt on Syria are even more important than they were in the Middle Bronze Age.[13]
- Even the Aegean cultures left material remains in Alalaḫ itself.[14]

A last remark that is crucial for the importance of the Alalaḫ material: Alalaḫ has been settled over the complete time period of the so-called Dark Ages and may therefore serve as a bridge between the chronologically well documented second half of the 15th century and the Old Babylonian time as the textual sources[15] either coming from Alalaḫ itself or stemming from other find-spots but connected with Alalaḫ are divided into two time periods: For the Later Old Babylonian period, the text finds from Alalaḫ VII are interwoven with the Mari texts, a coincidence that allows a fairly certain location within the OB time and for the later level IV we can connect the evidence with

5 Cf. Zeeb 2001, 67–73; 87–89.

6 So far no data from Alalaḫ have been brought forth that might be treated with modern methods like thermoluminiscence, ^{14}C dating, dendrochronology or the like. Therefore, we need not discuss the relevance of these methods in this context.

7 As for Alalaḫ see the excavation report by Woolley 1955, for the seals Collon 1982, for seal impressions Collon 1975. A stratigraphically-based analysis of the ceramics found at Tell Açana by Gates 1982 (cf. Gates 1987) has provided important insights.

8 The following remarks will only mention a few points without attempting to cover all aspects. Therefore only a couple of references will be given that highlight some central features.

9 Cf. any history of the Hittites, e.g. Klengel 1998 or Miller 2001.

10 Cf. Villard 1986.

11 Cf. Mayer 1995.

12 Cf. Eder 1995 and Otto 2000.

13 Cf. Kühne 1982 or Klengel 1992, 84–180 and most recently Warburton 2001, 39–98.

14 Cf. Niemeier 1991.

15 Mainly published for the first time by Wiseman 1953, cf. for more recent reassessments of Old Babylonian tablets the references given in Zeeb 2001, 31–66 (with new numbering according to literary genres), for the Middle Babylonian corpus still Hess 1988 (new numbering by Niedorf 1998).

Egyptian and Mittani history. It is fortunate that the archaeological remains from Alalaḫ are described and interpreted in a very convenient way as well, so that the tell of Alalaḫ provides enough material to become a chronologically interesting, if not deciding place.

2.2. The line of the present argument

The evidence of all these cultures and regions makes Alalaḫ a valuable testcase. In fact, it is methodologically a minimal condition that an absolute chronology must be compatible with known events in other areas of the world. Therefore, our methodological task consists obviously first in establishing a close network of relative data that can be taken from Alalaḫ and then see how this sample can fit chronologically into the broader frame of international history.

In a second step we will have to examine whether there are absolute data that may be connectable to the above-mentioned framework of relative data in order to get a workable absolute chronology. For obvious reasons, we must refrain from taking the ANE chronology as a starting point, as this framework is just being the question rather than an answer. More valuable are any chronological coincidences with Egypt as they make us stand on firmer grounds. Both archaeological and textual sources from Alalaḫ give no direct hints on astronomical data[16], so that we need not go deeper into this field, while of course the chronology of Egypt – as is well known – needs an astronomically based assessment of the absolute data, which in our case concerns the accession year of Thutmosis III.[17] As this date forms the cornerstone of any absolute chronology in the mid-second millennium B.C.E., it must be mentioned explicitly that the present paper accepts 1479 B.C.E. as beginning of Thutmosis' reign, which implies a date of 1457 for the siege of Megiddo in his 23rd year.[18]

To sum up, our own methodological procedure is an attempt to connect both the textual sources of level VII and IV to their respective international counterparts and fill up the time between, i.e. level V and VI with their mostly archaeological remains by questioning them if and how they possibly fit in the political history of the time in order to make this collection of data a reliable basis for an absolute chronology.

2.3. The analysis of political situations

I will introduce the analysis and evaluation of political situations in the discussion about relative chronology as I consider this an essential tool for the transition from relative chronology to absolute data. Where exact data are missing and we need to deal with more or less indefinable periods of time, the analysis of political backgrounds of a given situation may be a useful means.[19] The crossover from relative to absolute chronology must be tested against the political situation of both sets of data. We have to show that the political ambience of the period in question can be explained by the known facts from the chronology of the culture with which we want to connect our relative chronology in order to get absolute data. It is especially necessary to explain the actions of the persons and powers in the plot by their personal and political interests. Should this not be possible or only on the basis of further and less probable assumptions, then the hypothesis loses probability and the proposed chronology may need to be rejected. For the question dealt with in this paper, the appropriate testcase is of course the political situation in Syria influenced by local powers as well as by the external powers of Egypt, Mittani and the Hittites respectively in the time period between Aḫmose and Thutmosis III.

2.4. The length of generations

Another set of data is sometimes overestimated. The average length of generations[20] is only help-

[16] With the only possible exception that our reconstruction of the Alalaḫ calendar and its method of intercalation (Zeeb 2001, 164.173f) suggests – if correct – that in the next to last year of the Alalaḫ VII archive a new lunar month began at a solar date of about October 21st. Of course, this evidence is too scanty to be really relevant to the chronological discussion, the more so, as this correspondence occurs about every five years.

[17] Kitchen 1987, cf. for astronomical backgrounds Casperson 1986 and for Egyptian chronology in general von Beckerath 1997.

[18] This seems to be broad consensus among Egyptologists and need not be discussed at length here as I laid my understanding of the topic open in Zeeb 2001, 117–122.

[19] This is generally agreed upon and most historical analyses use this tool as a matter of course. However, it is only rarely that one finds a methodologically considered assessment of the method.

[20] Cf. Steiner 1989.

ful if we consider a time period that is sufficiently long to rule out statistical mischiefs, in other terms, it doesn't really make sense to calculate time differences by multiplying a given number of generations by an average number of years, as often has been done, if there are less than, say, five generations involved – just because fortunate or unfortunate statistics may invalidate our calculation.[21] Another point that is sometimes overlooked is the fact that two lines of generations or dynasties in different places seldom run exactly parallel, i.e. it may occur that one line appears to be one generation longer, just because the first representative of line A is ten years older than his counterpart of line B. However, it is sensible to use such data as check cases if possible.[22] Especially helpful are cases in which two given events are connected to one single person. Then the conclusion is sound that the time difference between the two events must not exceed 90 years as a reasonable lifespan of a human being.

3. History of Research

It may suffice here to recall the various positions only insofar as the Alalaḫ material played a major role in the discussion. I follow the now traditional division of long, middle and short chronology.

• The ***long chronology*** has recently been favoured in an article by Wolfram Nagel and Christian Eder.[23] The two authors aim to parallel the Mari letters with the 12th dynasty of Egypt (e.g. p. 5.46.66), but their reconstruction is in my opinion not very convincing.[24] The crucial point is the number of kings that reigned during the time of the Alalaḫ VII archive.[25] The argument that Aleppo was ruled in the time under discussion by about four generations of kings must be dismissed on the very fact that Abban of the first generation of Aleppo was obviously a couple of years older than his brother Jarimlim who was given the city of Alalaḫ as his residence. The same holds true for the last king of Aleppo during the archive of level VII, Jarimlim III, who was the younger brother of Irkabtum. If we further take into account that Ammitaqum, the last ruler of Alalaḫ VII, reigned for quite a long time, it is not very hard to see that Ḫammurapi, his heir, was not too young at the time when Alalaḫ perished. He might have well represented a third ruling generation if his father had died earlier. Therefore there is no need to multiply the kings in Alalaḫ, as Nagel and Eder suggest, just to parallel their order to a generation-sequence in Ḫalab.[26] The textual evidence from Alalaḫ also does not support their view. Easier solutions to all the problems that the two scholars discuss can be provided, if the argument is based on a sequence of only two rulers at Alalaḫ, of which especially the second, Ammitaqum, lived very long. To sum up, the attempt to make the evidence from Alalaḫ fit into the scheme of a long chronology must be rejected as it is based on suppositions that are obviously not very well-founded.

• The ***middle chronology*** that used to be very much en vogue and is still widely used in both scholarly and popular literature[27] was developed by Sidney Smith[28] mainly on the basis of the Alalaḫ material. He recognised that the wares of Alalaḫ are not in favour of too long a time-span between the Old

---

[21] E.g. statistics of the last rulers of the Habsburg dynasty between the French Revolution and the end of the monarchy are biased by the extremely long reigns of Franz I (43 years) and Franz Joseph (68 years): three generations for 124 years from 1792–1916 makes an average of about 42 years. If the last emperor, Karl, is accounted for, then the respective figures are four generations in 126 years, average 31.5 years. The average generation length of the Dukes (later kings) of Württemberg (1450–1918, 14 generations) is 33.4 years.

[22] Generation lengths should not be estimated too long in the Ancient Near East. The 1st dynasty of Babylon has an average of 30 years per generation, the kings of Juda (excluding David and Salomon with their idealized rules of 40 years each) of about 28 years (depending on whether the final figure is the fall of Jerusalem or the death of Jojakin), so that 28–30 years should be appropriate.

[23] Nagel and Eder 1992.

[24] Cf. for a more detailed discussion of their arguments Zeeb 2001, 95–100.

[25] This is a very much debated question. Cf. Landsberger 1953, 51f; Albright 1957, 27; Collon 1975, 145–152; Na'aman 1979; Oliva 1999/2000. The discussion is summed up in Zeeb 2001, 89–95.

[26] The same is of course true for similar proposals as given by Na'aman 1979, Gaál 1982 and most recently Oliva 1999/2000 that base their respective reconstructions on a number of more than two kings during the time of level VII.

[27] Recent reference works that use the middle chronology are e.g. CivANE (1995) and OxfEncANE (1997).

[28] Smith 1940.

Babylonian period and the 15th century. The archaeological data allow the connection of Muršili's campaign with the end of level VI rather than the end of level VII. The end of level V may be ascribed to the time of Thutmosis III.[29] However SMITH was still clinging to the Venus data of Ammiṣaduqa, which he had newly calculated to find a new basis for a shortened chronology and could therefore propose the still widely accepted figure of 1595 for the fall of Babylon and Aleppo.

- The so-called ***short chronology*** was – as is well-known – proposed mainly by WILLIAM FOXWELL ALBRIGHT,[30] and once more, Alalaḫ was one of the most important arguments in the discussion. Within a framework of synchronisms in Syria and taking the textual evidence from Alalaḫ VII as well as the archaeological remains into account, ALBRIGHT reached the conclusion that the fall of Babylon has to be dated in 1531 B.C.E. As the Mari texts never mention the 12th dynasty of Egypt, it is reasonable enough to conclude that the prime of Mari must be dated after the fall of this dynasty. The same is then, of course, true for Ḫammurapi of Babylon and the Alalaḫ VII archive.
- I do not need to refer to the ***ultra-short chronology*** by GASCHE and his co-authors[31] here, as they don't mention Alalaḫ, but will rather turn now to the Alalaḫ material itself.

4. THE ALALAḪ MATERIAL AND ITS HISTORICAL IMPACT

The archive of Alalaḫ VII consists of about 300 tablets, of which about two thirds are published. The bulk of the tablets are economic records that have little, if any, historical relevance. One main insight in this kind of texts is the provenance of the latter part of the archive, due to the fact that such texts are kept only as long as they are of practical use and juridical relevance.[32] However, there is a couple of texts that record events from law-courts and even some historical texts have survived.[33] The facts that are reported or can at least be concluded from these tablets permit a relatively certain reconstruction of the events.[34] At the present state of the argument, we must of course refrain from making any direct chronological connections with Mesopotamia.

In the Old Babylonian time Alalaḫ was a kind of "secundogenitur" for the royal family of Ḫalab/Aleppo. Jarimlim, the younger brother of Abban, king of Ḫalab, was at first ruler of Irride.[35] After a revolt he had to give up Irride and was given Alalaḫ as his city by his older brother and overlord.[36] From the time of king Jarimlim only a few tablets have been discovered as those tablets were not preserved any more once they lost their practical value (e.g. as proof documents for economic transactions). Still we can see that Jarimlim survived his brother and even his brother's son, king Jarimlim II of Ḫalab. In the time of the latter's son, king Niqmepuḫ of Ḫalab, Jarimlim of Alalaḫ died and left the kingdom to his son, king Ammitaqum. As mentioned above, I don't see any reason to consider that there was more than one Ammitaqum or one Jarimlim. It seems reasonable that Ammitaqum was born more or less at the time of the foundation of Alalaḫ VII, and that he was not too young when he ascended the throne of Alalaḫ. With this in mind, we can conclude that level VII – which came to an end late in the reign of Ammitaqum – covered a time-span of about 80, but not more than 90 years. Ammitaqum survived his distant relative and even the next generation. He bequeathed his rulership and his possessions to his heir, a certain Ḫammurapi.[37] Ḫammurapi didn't come to rule during level VII, but there is one tablet on his behalf that probably belongs to level VI, in other terms, the local family survived the fall of the

[29] Note that Smith could not yet be aware of the fact that Ḫattušili claimed to have destroyed the city of Alalaḫ as this text was only published in 1958.

[30] Cf ALBRIGHT 1942 and1957 (still without the Annals of Ḫattušili).

[31] GASCHE *et al.*1998a and 1998b, cf. WARBURTON 2001.

[32] Cf. ZEEB 2001, 167–169. The so-called "ration lists" or "grain delivery lists" (our category 41, 94 texts) derive from the last three years of the palace.

[33] Our categories 10 (3 historical texts); 20–24 (53 juridical texts) and 30–32 (42 texts dealing with debts).

[34] The arguments are more precisely presented in ZEEB 2001, 89–101. Cf. VAN SOLDT 2000, esp. 104–108.

[35] Cf. ZEEB 1998, 834.

[36] Texts 10.01 and 10.02, cf. ZEEB 1991 with the correction by VAN SOLDT 2000, 104 n. 16.

[37] Text 21.01, cf. ZEEB 2001, 37f.; VAN SOLDT 2000, 105f. The same Ḫammurapi is probably mentioned in KUB XXXI 5.

city and Ḫammurapi could continue the dynasty.[38] The greater part of the economic texts belongs to the last years of Ammitaqum's reign and the grain delivery lists indicate that the last months of the archive were already under a military threat.[39] We know from the annals of the Hittite king Ḫattušili that he destroyed Alalaḫ during his second campaign, which means probably rather early in his reign.[40] With this campaign, level VII and its archive came to an end. Level VI and level V didn't produce much written material, but the textual documentation continued with the archive from level IV.

5. Embedding in the historical contexts

5.1. General remarks

Our next task is obviously to see how the texts from level VII can be embedded in the international history of the Old Babylonian period. As there are no direct connections and references in the Alalaḫ VII texts, our duty is twofold:

- To start with, we have to place the end of level VII in the framework of relative chronology,
- then we have to look for connections between Aleppo and the Mesopotamian world that allow us to embed the facts from Alalaḫ within this general framework.

I would like to call attention to the point that we are still dealing with relative chronology rather than absolute dates. Accordingly we take the accession year of king Ḫammurapi of Babylon as a reference point without using any absolute date.

It goes without saying that we got already one criterion to falsify our results: If the alleged time-span for the duration of level VII is longer than one person – Ammitaqum – can reasonably live, then our argument has proven wrong.

5.2. Alalaḫ VII: Its foundation, its destruction and the time-length in between

Let us begin with the end of level VII. I can see no reason to doubt that Ḫattušili was in fact responsible for the destruction of Alalaḫ as he claims in his annals.[41] There have been various attempts to attribute the destruction to Muršili,[42] but they appear to have been motivated mainly by the interest or supposition that the events ought to fit into a Middle Chronology. The simple question is in this regard: Why attribute a military success to a king who doesn't even claim it, instead to attribute it to the king who mentions it – as long as there is no reason to doubt the veracity of the text in question.[43]

I cannot deal here with the relationship between Muršili and Ḫattušili and their degree of kinship[44] in detail but it should be clear that the destruction of Alalaḫ took place in the beginning of the latter's reign[45] and Muršili's campaign to Babylon and Aleppo a few years after Ḫattušili's death.[46] As we know that the fall of Babylon was 197 years after the accession of Ḫammurapi, it seems reasonable to date the destruction of Alalaḫ VII about 150–160 years after this reference date, allowing for about 30–40 years as reign-length of Ḫattušili.

We now turn to the more difficult part, the foundation of Alalaḫ. Here we are forced to rely on external evidence from other sources, for example a synchronism between Aleppo and Tell Leilan that allows the conclusion that Abban did not come to power before the time of Samsuiluna.[47] On the other hand, there is a letter (AbB VII,7) from Samsuiluna that may be related to

---

38 Text 30.09. The proposal by Na'aman 1976 and 1979 is entirely dependent on the attribution of this text to level VII.

39 Cf. Zeeb 2001, 168; 486–488.

40 First publication by Otten 1958, cf. Klengel 1998, 38–59, esp. 47f.50.53.

41 Texts see CTH 4, the main texts are KBo X 1 l. 6 (Akkadian) and KBo X 2 l. 15 (Hittite); cf. Astour 1997, 19f.

42 E.g. Klengel 1992, 82 who doesn't rule out this possibility.

43 Annals like the *res gestae* are in general relatively trustworthy. The mention of Alalaḫ is not very likely to be introduced for rhetorical purposes or the like. The destruction of Alalaḫ by Ḫattušili may therefore be taken for granted.

44 Cf. Steiner 1996 for a detailed presentation of the question.

45 As the *res gestae* mention a "following year", the destruction of Alalaḫ is generally dated in Ḫattušili's second year. This may indeed be probable even if the text doesn't state this explicitly.

46 The exact difference of time between the two events cannot be determined with desirable accuracy. It should not be neglected that most of the sources are younger than the events (cf. Klengel 1998, 59–64).

47 Cf. Zeeb 1991.

the death of Abban,[48] in which case the foundation of Alalaḫ must be dated within the 38 years of this Babylonian king, i.e. between 42 and 80 years after the accession of Ḫammurapi of Babylon, which in turn would determine the length of level VII between 122 years at the longest and 70 years at the shortest.

If both assumptions are correct then the result may be tested against the given falsification criterion: The time-span for level VII must not exceed the live-span of king Ammitaqum who was born at about the time when Alalaḫ was given to his father Jarimlim by the latter's brother Abban. This is perfectly fitting into the framework if we assume that the contract between Abban and his brother was concluded not too early in Abban's reign.[49] The foundation of Alalaḫ can therefore be reasonably dated in the last third of Samsuilunas reign. This result is confirmed when we consider the references to Aleppo in the Mari texts.[50] Still we are only dealing with relative data and have carefully avoided absolute figures.

5.3. The beginning of level IV

To proceed a step further towards the question of absolute chronology, we must now leave the Old Babylonian time of level VII and take a look at the transition from level V to level IV. Archaeologically level IV begins by definition with the building of this level's palace.[51] I take it for granted[52] that the builder must have been king Idrimi as he claims himself in his statue.[53] If this is correct, then the change from level Vb to level IV is marked by Idrimi's return to Alalaḫ. The statue of this ruler provides further insights into the political and historical situation of the time which is worthy to recall: Aleppo was suffering a *mašiktu* (l. 4), a mischief, which is not specified. We may leave the matter aside for the moment but have to keep in mind, that, once again, the *mašiktu* and the return of Idrimi must fit into one person's lifespan.

5.4. The events according to Idrimi's statue

As a consequence of the *mašiktu* the royal family[54] to which Idrimi belonged had to seek refuge at Emar (l. 5–12). After a certain time, he took his fate into his own hands and joined the Ḫapiru in Canaan for seven years (l. 17–28). Whether we take this number literally or not, it is easily understandable that Barattarna of Mittani saw his action with dismay as mentioned on the statue (l. 42–58). We must bear in mind that Egypt had at least a nominal claim on Palestine and parts of Syria. The cities of Canaan were keen on their independence, a fact that constituted a natural link between Egypt and the Ḫapiru and therefore with Idrimi. Mittani on her part had an interest not to leave the area in one firm hand and opposed of course Egyptian attempts to gain control of the field.[55] The enmity between Barattarna and Idrimi may thus be explained by the former friendship between Idrimi and Egypt. After the conclusion of the vassal treaty between Mittani and Idrimi the latter was able to reign in Alalaḫ for 30 years.

5.5. Political background of Idrimi's biography

The reconstruction of the political background is decisive for the transition from relative to absolute chronology. The growing Egyptian pressure on Canaan is obviously a reflex of the changing politics of Thutmosis III after the death of Queen Ḫatšepsut. Idrimi was sensitive to these changes that came along with the new Egyptian politics and was determined enough to make

[48] Cf. Klengel 1992, 60 n. 95.

[49] This assumption doesn't appear to be far-fetched as Jarimlim was probably much younger than Abban, cf. Collon 1977, 149.

[50] Cf. Zeeb 2001, 101f.

[51] Cf. Gates 1987, 63.

[52] Contra Woolley 1955, 110.

[53] L. 80f. There has been a debate on whether the statue of Idrimi is to be taken as historically relevant (cf. Mayer 1995) or rather as "fictional autobiography" (cf. T. Longman III 1991). The present author is convinced that the genre of the statue and comparable texts allow a historical evaluation even if not every word may be taken at face value.

[54] The text doesn't state explicitly which royal family of which city is meant. Most scholars assume from the words "Aleppo, my ancestral home" that this city was the original home of Idrimi. However, Mayer 1995, 341f infers from the fact that Idrimi returned to "Alalaḫ, my city" (l. 35) rather than to Aleppo that Alalaḫ was Idrimi's birth-place. Both positions require further presuppositions, so that the matter may remain unresolved in this paper.

[55] The seven years of his enmity with Barattarna may represent a symbolic rather than a mathematically exact figure.

things work to his own benefit. With the Egyptian armies backing him, he was able to win his city back, and as Northern Syria was not within the direct reach of Pharaoh, the Egyptian diplomacy must have encouraged him to act as an in-between between Egypt, the Hittites and Mittani. As far as I know, there is only one single reference to Alalaḫ in the Egyptian sources which mentions a "tribute" from Alalaḫ in Thutmosis' 38th year.[56] There is a fair chance that this so-called "tribute" is connected with Idrimi's return to Alalaḫ [57] which means that we are now able to deal with absolute dates.

5.6. Absolute dates for Idrimi's life

I cannot treat the state of the debate on Egyptian absolute chronology,[58] however, the arguments proposed for 1479 as the accession date of Thutmosis III seem very convincing, so I will use this date as reference point from now on. As Idrimi mentions himself that he ruled at Alalaḫ 30 years after his victorious return, we can – provided our reconstruction above is correct – give the following framework:

1479 accession of Thutmosis III. Coregency with Ḫatšepsut.
1457 end of the coregency; change of Egyptian policy to Syria and Palestine, siege of Megiddo.
1448 (ca.) Idrimi's time among the Ḫapiru
1441 Idrimi's return to Alalaḫ, beginning of level IV
(1435(ca.) vassal treaty with Barattarna[59])
1411 (ca.) death of Idrimi.

5.7. The *mašiktu* and its implications

This reconstruction implies that the *mašiktu* – as an event within Idrimi's life-time – must have occurred in the 15th century B.C.E. We now have the task to examine the various possibilities more closely. As far as the present author can see, four interpretations have been proposed.[60]

The most recent proposal has been brought forward by W.H. VAN SOLDT.[61] He argues that the Cypriote Bichrome ware is not found after the destruction of Megiddo in 1456, and that level IV "may have started around this time" (111). As he attributes the palace of level IV to Idrimi's son Niqmepa, he supposes that Idrimi's return took place in 1486 and adds 7 years for the stay in Canaan which would then date the *mašiktu* in about 1493. In a further step he parallels this date with GASCHE'S date of 1499 for Muršili's raid and attributes therefore the *mašiktu* to the same event that caused the fall of Babylon. If VAN SOLDT is right in identifying Muršili's campaign with the *mašiktu*, any other chronology than GASCHE'S ultra-short proposal would be out of discussion – at least if we reject his reconstruction of the events in favour of the one given above.

There are, however, serious arguments against this conclusion:

- First of all, it is not sound methodology to combine the two approaches by VAN SOLDT and the one constructed above, as they proceed from different assumptions, especially as to the founder of the level IV palace. Consequently it would result in a circular argument if we were to date Idrimi as early as VAN SOLDT does, by that means considering the *mašiktu* an early event and then propose a lower chronology based on the fact that our own approach dates Idrimi much later.
- A second argument that needs to be discussed is VAN SOLDT'S reconstruction of the political situation, especially the role of the enmity with Mittani, a point that he mentions himself (112). His explanation – "a period of Hittite influence in the region, which may have been the cause of Idrimi's problems with Parattarna" (112) – doesn't seem very plausible, let alone the question whether it is probable that the latter may be dated to such an early date. Furthermore,

[56] Urk IV, 719, l. 17ff.

[57] Idrimi returned "by ship" which probably was sponsored by Egyptian support. The "tribute" could be a payment in return for this service.

[58] Cf. above n. 18.

[59] The statue dates the "seven years of enmity" after Idrimi's return. It seems equally possible that they are identical with his time in Canaan or overlapped both (cf. VAN SOLDT 2000, 110). In the two latter cases the absolute date of 1435 is, of course, wrong.

[60] We do not take into account the proposal by KÜHNE 1982, 211 who attributes the event to Thutmosis I as any date before 1500 seems incompatible both with the biographical data for Idrimi as with the archaeological remains from Alalaḫ (see below).

[61] VAN SOLDT 2000, 111f.

Emar would not have been a good place to flee from Muršili's attack as this campaign continued down the Euphrates to Babylon.

- A third *caveat* is the fact that VAN SOLDT starts with equating the siege of Megiddo with the beginning of level IV on the basis of the Bichrome ware. It should be noted that the end of the Cypriote wares does only provide a *terminus non ante* for the beginning of level IV, but no definite synchronism, in other terms, even if one were inclined to accept VAN SOLDT's presuppositions, the alleged date for the death of Idrimi might be a decade or so later than 1456 so that *mašiktu* and fall of Babylon need not necessarily be as close together as proposed.

A second proposal has been worked out by MAYER[62] a few years ago. According to him, the *mašiktu* is the result of a Hittite attack under Tudḫaliya I. For this proposal, MAYER calls our attention both to a year date at Ekalte/Tall Munbāqa[63] and to the historical introduction of the Talmi-šarruma treaty, in which a later retrospective is given of a destruction of Aleppo by Tudḫaliya. Further, he argues that for such an attack after the Muršili campaign – which we need to place within the 15th century – there is only one probable political situation: the reign of the so-called peace-queen Ḥatšepsut, being the period between 1479 and 1457.

- The main problem with this argument is the fact that for the time being there is no possibility to give a precise date for Tudḫaliya. Hittitologists generally give a date later than the mid-15th century[64] and cite a possible synchronism with Idrimi's successor Niqmepa.[65] As there exists a further synchronism that parallels Idrimi with Zidanta II,[66] MAYER's argument remains to be re-evaluated by further sources.[67]
- A second point may be asked: Attributing the *mašiktu* to a Hittite attack easily explains the later hostility between Idrimi and the Hittites (Idr. l. 64–78) but it can't be seen what role Mittani played in the event.
- Remains the Talmi-šarruma treaty:[68] From a later perspective it is argued that a king of Aleppo first was in peace with Ḫatti, then concluded a treaty with Mittani as well, which caused Tudḫaliya to destroy both and to lay Aleppo in ruins (*iqqur*). However, not taking the chronological argument into account, there is no mention on the statue that there was a former treaty between Aleppo and Ḫatti. It is therefore generally assumed[69] that this destruction of Aleppo was after Idrimi's time. WILHELM[70] opts for a "Schwächephase des M.-Reiches <Mittani, F.Z.> ... die mit den Eroberungen Thutmosis' III zusammenhängen dürfte". With no further evidence neither for a second destruction of Aleppo nor for a probable date for Tudḫaliya it seems wise to leave the matter aside and not to put too much historical weight on it.[71]

Another possibility should not be forgotten. It is still possible that the *mašiktu* is the outcome of an evolution that is not mentioned elsewhere, as e.g. an internal uprising in Aleppo comparable to the one in Irride (10.02). In this case we can not expect to obtain further information.

The *vox communis*[72] holds Barattarna responsible for the *mašiktu*. This would explain the hostility between Idrimi and Barattarna as mentioned on the statue; on the other hand we must again ask whether Emar as the place of asylum was not under the influence of Mittani at the time in question. Still one can argue that Idrimi's statement that he was "a servant of the citizens of Emar" (Idr. l. 12) might reflect exactly this kind of non-suzerain state under the hegemony of Mittani.

---

62 MAYER 1995.

63 Munb. 80,32. Note that WILCKE 1992, 124f reads 1 KAM.MA instead of ^{m}*Tu*.

64 Cf. KLENGEL 1998, 110.

65 The Hittite king is not mentioned by name, but cf. CTH 41 + 131.

66 Cf. KLENGEL 1998, 95f.

67 The more so, as the dating of the Munbāqa texts is still a matter of discussion. Some scholars date them significantly later than Mayer does (cf. e.g. WILCKE 1992) which is a crucial threat to Mayer's argument.

68 CTA 75.

69 Cf. KLENGEL 1998, 114.

70 Cf. WILHELM 1993/97, 291.

71 Given the fact that Muršili fell to a *damnatio memoriae* it appears possible that the historical introduction of KBo I 6 mixes several events: The political situation under Idrimi (treaty with Mittani) and the earlier destruction of Aleppo by Muršili were simply seen together and ascribed to Tudḫaliya. In this case there would be no valid conclusion to the *mašiktu* allowed.

72 Cf. KLENGEL 1981, 237.

Not naming the *mašiktu* by its real character would then be a rhetorical device motivated by the wish not to put the foregoing actions of the partner into a bad light, once an agreement was finally reached.

The discussion shows that the absolute dating of the event and its evaluation are not dependent on the identity of the causing factor of the *mašiktu*. We may still rely on the conclusions reached above: The *mašiktu* took place between about 1457 (change of Egyptian policy to Syria and Palestine) or shortly before (reign of Ḥatšepsut) and 1448 (alleged date for Idrimi becoming a Ḫapiru). This rules out VAN SOLDT's equation with the Babylon raid, whereas MAYER's proposal rests on too many additional pillars to be a final solution. On the other hand it remains possible that the Hittites were responsible for the *mašiktu* as a flight to Emar would then get the family out of the aggressor's reach. A destruction of Aleppo by Barattarna seems not impossible nor is an internal uprising or a similar event we do not know about.

Getting back to the events of Idrimi's life. After the *mašiktu* and his time as refugee in Emar he became SA.GAZ. If we accept the idea that this act brought him into a positive relationship to Egypt and is to be dated about 1448 then there is a possible reconstruction of the political background: Idrimi took advantage of Thutmosis' 8th campaign in his 33rd year (1446).[73] He deserted from the sphere of influence of Mittani to support the Egyptians. This action brought him into hostility to Barattarna who could not tolerate such an action. The Egyptians, on their part, accepted Idrimi as a welcome ally. His duty was to keep the area unsafe and to needle-pick Barattarna. After a certain time the Egyptians decided that Idrimi was more useful as a steady partner and enabled him to establish himself at Alalaḫ (1441), obviously this time to serve as a glacis against the Hittites (Idr. l. 64–78). However, Idrimi again changed sides and made his vassal treaty with Barattarna again.

5.8. Archaeological Aspects

The discussion presented above enabled us to embed the history of Alalaḫ as shown by textual sources, namely the statue of Idrimi, into a framework of absolute dates. The results reached so far are, however, not very decisive for the matter of Ancient Near Eastern Chronology. Still, we found an absolute date of about 1440 for the beginning of level IV, so that we have to proceed now to evaluate levels V and VI. As these produced almost no textual sources we have to rely on archaeological evidence. The main arguments are:

- Both levels are archaeologically coherent, there is no significant change whatsoever between.[74]
- The division into levels and sub-levels is based on architectural remains and pottery-sequences.
- Towards the end of level VI the defence walls were considerably reinforced.[75]
- Imported Cypriote ware ("Monochrome and Bichrome ware") has been found (level VIB–VB).[76]
- During level VIB we face the transition from MB II to LB I.[77]

The latter point is most important for absolute dating of the fall of Babylon. Comparisons with other find-spots, especially Tell eḍ-Ḍab^{c}a show beyond doubt that the end of the Middle Bronze Age[78] is to be connected to the Palestinian campaigns of Aḫmose after the latter's 11th year, in other terms: level VI continues for a not too short time period after a *terminus non ante* that must be dated after 1539, perhaps as late as 1528.[79] This conclusion raises the question if there is an event that may be connected with the end of level VI. It should be remembered that there is a significant reworking of the fortification of the city towards the end of level VI, but no destruction attested. It would seem therefore that the end of level VI can reasonably be attributed to the Muršili campaign. To invest in the security of their city was certainly a sensible thing to do for the inhabitants as the Muršili campaign was a

[73] Cf. KLENGEL 1992, 92–94.

[74] Cf. GATES 1987, 63 and GATES 2000, 78.

[75] Cf. GATES 1982, 6f.

[76] Cf. GATES 1987, 62–64.

[77] Cf. GATES 1987, 71.

[78] Such shifts are generally not radical changes but there may be a certain time of co-existence between older and younger forms (cf. WARBURTON 2000, 48). We are dealing here with the first signs of the existence of the new period.

[79] If one accepts an ultra-low chronology of the 18th dynasty as e.g. DEVER 1992, 16 does.

foreseeable event – especially if Muršili had indeed sworn "to revenge the blood of Ḫattušili" by campaigning in the Aleppo area. In any case the preparation of this campaign did not go unnoticed by the Alalaḫians. If we accept this argument then level VI is more or less[80] identical with the reign of Ḫattušili and should not have lasted longer than about forty years,[81] of which ten to no more than thirty years after the *terminus post quem* just mentioned. This would mean that the fall of Babylon has to be dated in absolute terms not earlier than 1529 and not later than 1498, so that both the "Short chronology" and the "Ultra-short chronology" are just possible while a date in between is more probable as neither the latest nor the earliest possible date for Aḫmose are the most convincing. The same is true for the assumption that the beginning of the Late Bronze Age should be perfectly identical with the change from level VIA to VIB.

There is another argument: The imported Cypriote wares found at Alalaḫ from level VIB on until level V can be connected with an undisturbed sequence at Tell eḍ-Ḍabᶜa reaching from the end of the 12th dynasty down to Thutmosis III. Bichrome Cypriote pottery is found there (and in other find-spots as e.g. Megiddo and recently Kinet Höyuk[82]) from strata D/2 to C/3 which confirms our point.

Excursus 1: Tall Munbāqa and chronology

The long-awaited publication of the texts from Tall Munbāqa by W. Mayer[83] may reveal a further connection between Syria, Egypt and Ḫatti. The evidence from Tall Munbāqa allows the conclusion that this archive was in use for about 60 years and came to an end by a destruction. This event is attributed by Mayer[84] to the Syrian campaign by Thutmosis III in 1446 with the beginning of the respective stratum at Munbāqa, which means that the Hittite campaign to Babylon must be dated at about 1507.[85] At first sight this would fit perfectly into an "ultra-short chronology" but the chronological classification that Mayer offers has not gone unchallenged by other scholars.[86] If one is inclined to date the Munbāqa texts later than Mayer does, this argument is void. The matter cannot be discussed at length in this paper as any reassessment of the question needs a broader comparison of the archive of Munbāqa with the archives of Emar and Alalaḫ IV with respect to typology, script and grammar, which cannot be presented here. For our purposes it may suffice that if Mayer is right there is a strong option for an ultra-short chronology with 1507 as the date for the fall of Babylon.

Excursus 2: The latest debate on chronology

In the year 2002 two brief notes[87] appeared in NABU and Akkadica respectively that are of interest for this matter, even though both authors don't mention Alalaḫ. C. Michel stresses the fact that the Mari Eponym Chronicle mentions a solar eclipse in the year after Šamši-Addu's birth. She evaluates the possible eclipses, taking dendrochronology into account and concludes that the eponymy of Puzur-Ištar is to be dated in 1833. With this result she argues that a middle chronology is still the best solution, however, it ought to be reduced by about 15 years. The obvious question what consequences an option for another solar eclipse – especially the one of 1764 – would mean to the problem has been raised immediately in a sharp reply by D. Warburton. He criticises Michel's method of dealing with the astronomical data as highly "subjective",[88] the more so, as her result doesn't fit with the dendrochronological material. Both, astronomy and dendrochronology, converge according to Warburton with an ultra-short chronology (113).

[80] Allowing a few years of difference both at the beginning (time elapsed between Ḫattušili's accession and destruction of level VII) and at the end of Ḫattušili's reign (time between his death and Muršili's campaign to Aleppo and Babylon).

[81] Gates 1987, 65 gives level VIA "not more than a decade or so of occupation", implicitly correcting her former statement (Gates 1982, 6), that level VIA and VIB "lasted a similar length of time".

[82] Cf. Gates 2000, 87f.

[83] Mayer 2001.

[84] Mayer 2001, 18.

[85] Mayer 2001, 18f argues with the social history as reconstructed from the texts: After the Hittite destruction of Aleppo the area suffered a time of pauperization that explains according to Mayer the social background (land sales to private persons) of the earlier time of Munbāqa.

[86] See e.g. Wilcke 1992 and most recently Sallaberger 2001, 495 (published 2003).

[87] Michel 2002 and Warburton 2002.

[88] Warburton 2002, 110.

Michel called her position a "slight change" to the Middle chronology while Warburton (114) names it a "revolution" as it implies "the abandonment of the very pillar upon which the 'Middle Chronology' was founded", namely the Venus tablets. With the assumption that the Mari Eponym Chronicle makes indeed a mention of the eclipse of 1764 we would have to reduce the date of the death of Šamši-Addu to about 1692[89] which necessarily reduces the respective date for the fall of Babylon to 1507.[90]

Excursus 3: Connection between Muršili's raid and Thutmosis I

If we accept the dating of the fall of Aleppo to the year 1507 B.C.E. we might draw a connection between the Hittite raid of the North Syrian area and the campaign by Thutmosis I. Both events would then have occurred within a relatively short period of time. The campaign of Thutmosis I to Syria shortly after the Hittite raid might have been – from the Egyptian point of view – an ideal singular opportunity: Thutmosis I was well aware that the Hittites were busy enough with internal affairs because of the trouble arising after Muršili's return and on the other hand Syria lay more or less defenceless after the previous Hittite attack.[91]

6. Conclusion

The archaeological and written sources from Alalaḫ do not allow a definite solution for the question of an absolute chronology of the 15th and 16th century B.C.E. However, with the assumptions and interpretations presented above, a strong point can be made to rule out any chronology that is longer than the "Short chronology". It suggests an even shorter chronology, even if this further reduction does not necessarily point to Gasche's ultra-short position. Far from being certain, the evidence seems to converge on a date of about 1507 for the fall of Babylon.

[89] Following Veenhof 2000, 139 there is "a margin for only a few years"

[90] It may be more than a mere coincidence that this date fits perfectly into a 8-year-cycle that is commonly mentioned when dealing with the Venus tablets.

[91] This makes the renovation of the fortification walls of a Alalaḫ even more probable. The occurrence of two such defeats in Northern Syria might also be an argument for Mayer's assumption of pauperization (see above n. 85).

Bibliography

ALBRIGHT, W.F.

1942 A Third Revision of the Early Chronology of Western Asia, *BASOR* 88, 28–36.

1957 Further Observations of the Chronology of Alalaḫ, *BASOR* 146, 26–34.

ASTOUR, M.C.

1997 Ḫaššu and Ḫasuwan. A Contribution to North Syrian History and Geography, *UF* 29, 1–66.

BECKMAN, G.

2000 Hittite Chronology, *Akkadica* 119–120, 19–32.

CASPERSON, L.W.

1986 The Lunar Dates of Thutmose III, *JNES* 45, 139–150.

COLLON, D.

1975 *The Seal Impressions from Tell Atchana/Alalakh*, AOAT 27, Neukirchen-Vluyn/Kevelaer.

1977 A New Look at the Chronology of Alalakh Level VII: A Rejoinder, *AnSt* 27, 127–131.

1982 *The Alalakh Cylinder Seals*, BAR.IS 32, Oxford.

DEVER, W.G .

1992 The Chronology of Syria-Palestine in the Second Millennium B.C.E.: A Review of Current Issues, *BASOR* 288, 1–25.

EDER, C.

1995 *Die ägyptischen Motive in der Glyptik des östlichen Mittelmeerraumes zu Anfang des 2. Jts. v. Chr.*, OLA 71, Leuven.

GAÁL, E.

1982 On the Chronology of Alalah Level VII, *AUSB* 22, 3–53.

GASCHE, H. *et al.*

1998a *Dating the Fall of Babylon. A Reappraisal of Second-Millennium Chronology*, MHEM 4, Gent/Chicago.

1998b A Correction to "Dating the Fall of Babylon. A Reappraisal of Second-Millennium Chronology (= MHEM 4), Ghent and Chicago, 1998", *Akkadica* 108, 1–4.

GATES, M.-H.C.

1981 Alalakh Levels VI and V: A Chronological Reassessment, *SMS* 4/2, 1–50.

1987 Alalakh and Chronology again, in: *HML* II, 60–86.

2000 Kinet Höyük (Hatay, Turkey) and MB Levantine Chronology, *Akkadica* 119–120, 77–101.

GURZADYAN, V.G.

2000 On the Astronomical Records and Babylonian Chronology, *Akkadica* 119–120, 177–186.

HESS, R.S.

1988 A Preliminary List of the Published Alalakh Tablets, *UF* 20, 69–87.

HUBER, P.J.

2000 Astronomy and Ancient Chronology, *Akkadica* 119–120, 159–176.

KITCHEN, K.A.

1987 The Basics of Egyptian Chronology in Relation to the Bronze Age, in: *HML* I, 37–55.

KLENGEL, H.

1981 Historischer Kommentar zur Inschrift des Idrimi von Alalaḫ, *UF* 13, 269–278.

KLENGEL, H.

1992 *Syria 3000–300 B.C. A Handbook of Political History*, Berlin.

1998 *Geschichte des hethitischen Reiches*, HdO I/34, Leiden et al.

KLINGER, J.

2000 Zur Geschichte des hethitischen Reiches, *OLZ* 95, 1–13.

KÜHNE, C.

1982 Politische Szenerie und internationale Beziehungen Vorderasiens um die Mitte des 2. Jahrtausends vor Christus (zugleich ein Konzept der Kurzchronologie) mit einer Zeittafel, in: RENGER, J. and NISSEN, H.-J. (eds.): *Mesopotamien und seine Nachbarn. Politische u. kulturelle Wechselbeziehungen im Alten Vorderasien vom 4.–1. Jahrtausend v. Chr.*, BBVO 1/1 (= Compte Rendu de la XXVe Rencontre Assyriologique Internationale Berlin, 3.–7. Juli 1978), 203–264.

LANDSBERGER, B.

1954 Assyrische Königsliste und "Dunkles Zeitalter", *JCS* 8, 31–73; 106–133.

LONGMAN III, T.

1991 *Fictional Akkadian Autobiography*, Winona Lake.

MACHULE, D.

1993/97 Art. "Munbāqa, Tall" B. Archäologisch, in: *RlA* 8, 418f.

MAYER, W.

1993/97 Art. "Munbāqa, Tall" A. Philologisch, in: *RlA* 8, 417.

1995 Die historische Einordnung der "Autobiographie" des Idrimi von Alalaḫ, *UF* 27, 333–350.

2001 *Tall Munbāqa-Ekalte II. Die Texte*, WVDOG 102, Saarbrücken.

MICHEL, C.

2002 Nouvelles données pour la chronologie du IIe millénaire, *NABU* 2002, Nr. 20, 17f.

MILLER, J.L.

2001 Ḫattušili I's Expansion into Northern Syria in Light of the Tikunani Letter, in WILHELM, G. (ed.): *Akten des IV. Internationalen Kongresses für Hethitologie. Würzburg, 4.–8. Oktober 1999*, StBoT 45, Wiesbaden, 410–429.

NA'AMAN, N.

1976 A New Look at the Chronology of Alalakh Level VII, *AnSt* 26, 129–143.

1979 The Chronology of Alalakh Level VII Once Again, *AnSt* 29, 103–113.

NAGEL, W. and EDER, C.

1992 Altsyrien und Ägypten, *DaM* 6, 1–108.

NIEDORF, C.

1998 Die Toponyme der Texte aus Alalaḫ IV, *UF* 30, 515–568.

NIEMEIER, W.-D.

1991 Minoan Artisans Travelling Overseas: The Alalakh Frescoes and the Painted Plaster Floor at Tel Kabri (Western Galilee), *Aegaeum* 7, 189–201.

OLIVA, J. MOMPEÁN

1999/2000 Alalaḫ VII Chronographica. Una revisión del archivo sobre la base de los textos de Yarim-Lim, *AuOr* 17/18, 229–239.

OTTEN, H.

1958 Keilschrifttexte, *MDOG* 91, 73–84.

OTTO, A.

2000 *Die Entstehung und Entwicklung der klassisch-syrischen Glyptik,* UAVA 8, Berlin/New York.

READE, J.

2000 Absolute Dates and Assyrian Calendars, *Akkadica* 119–120, 151–153.

2001 Assyrian King-Lists, the Royal Tombs of Ur and Indus Origins, *JNES* 60, 1–29.

SALLABERGER, W.

2001 Zu einer Urkunde aus Ekalte über die Rückgabe der Hausgötter, *UF* 33, 495–499.

SMITH, S.

1940 Alalakh and Chronology, London.

SOLDT, W.H. VAN

2000 Syrian Chronology in the Old and Early Middle Babylonian Periods, *Akkadica* 119–120, 103–116.

STEINER, G.

1989 Die Dauer einer „Generation" nach den Vorstellungen des Alten Orients, in: *HML* III, 170–195.

1996 Muršili I: Sohn oder Enkel Labarna-Ḫattušilis I?, *UF* 28, 561–618.

VEENHOF, K.R.

2000 Old Assyrian Chronology, *Akkadica* 119–120, 137–150.

VILLARD, P.

1986 Un roi de Mari à Ugarit, *UF* 18, 1986, 387–412.

VON BECKERATH, J.

1997 *Chronologie des Pharaonischen Ägypten. Die Zeitbestimmung der ägyptischen Geschichte von der Vorzeit bis 332 v.Chr.*, MÄS 46, Mainz.

WARBURTON, D.A.

2000 Synchronizing the Chronology of Bronze Age Western Asia with Egypt, *Akkadica* 119–120, 33–76.

2001 *Egypt and the Near East. Politics in the Bronze Age*, CivPrOr IV/1, Neuchâtel/Paris.

2002 Eclipses, Venus-Cycles & Chronology, *Akkadica* 123, 108–114.

WILCKE, C.

1992 AḪ, die "Brüder" von Emar. Untersuchungen zur Schreibtradition am Euphratknie, *AuOr* 10, 115–150.

WILHELM, G.

1993/97 Art. "Mittan(n)i, Mitanni, Maitani" A. Historisch, in: *RlA* 8, 286–296

WISEMAN, D.J.

1953 *The Alalakh Tablets*, OPBIAA 2, London.

WOOLLEY, L.

1953 *Alalakh. An Account of the Excavations at Tell Atchana in the Hatay, 1937–1949*, Reports of the Research Committee of the Society of Antiquaries of London, Oxford 1955.

ZEEB, F.

1991 Tell Leilan und die Gründung des altbabylonischen Alalaḫ, *UF* 23, 401–404.

1998 Die Ortsnamen und geographischen Bezeichnungen der Texte aus Alalaḫ VII, *UF* 30, 829–886.

2001 *Die Palastwirtschaft in Altsyrien nach den spätaltbabylonischen Getreidelieferlisten von Alalaḫ (Schicht VII)*, AOAT 282, Münster.

Abbreviations

Aegaeum — *Aegaeum*, Liège.

Akkadica — *Akkadica*, Gent.

Akkadica 119–120 — *Just in time. Proceedings of the International Colloquium on Ancient Near Eastern Chronology (2nd Millennium BC). Ghent 7–9 July 2000. Akkadica 119–120*, Gent 2000.

AnSt — *Anatolian Studies, London*

AOAT — *Alter Orient und Altes Testament*, Neukirchen-Vluyn/Kevelaer, since 1996: Münster.

AuOr — *Aula Orientalis*, Barcelona.

AUSB — *Annales Universitatis Scientiarum Budapestiensis de Rolando Eötvös Nominatae. Sectio Historica*, Budapest.

BAR.IS — *British Archaeological Reports. International Series*, Oxford.

BASOR — *Bulletin of the American Schools of Oriental Research*, New Haven.

BBVO — *Berliner Beiträge zum Vorderen Orient*, Berlin.

CivANE — Sasson, J.M. (ed.) 1995, *Civilisations of the Ancient Near East*, New York.

CivPrOr — Civilisations du Proche-Orient. Neuchâtel/Paris

DaM — *Damaszener Mitteilungen*, Mainz.

HdO — *Handbuch der Orientalistik*, Leiden et al.

HML — Åström, P. (ed.): *High Middle or Low. Acts of an International Colloquium on Absolute Chronology Held at the University of Gothenburg, 20th–22nd August 1987*, I: SIMA 56 (1987); II: SIMA 57 (1987); III: SIMA 80 (1989). Gothenburg.

JCS — *Journal of Cuneiform Studies*, New Haven.

JNES — *Journal of Near Eastern Studies*, Chicago.

MÄS — *Münchner Ägyptologische Studien*, Mainz.

MDOG — *Mitteilungen der Deutschen Orient-Gesellschaft*, Berlin.

MHEM — *Mesopotamian History and Environment. Monographs*, Gent.

Munb. — Text numbering as in Mayer, W., 2001.

NABU — *Nouvelles Assyriologiques Brèves et Utilitaires*, Paris

OLA — *Orientalia Lovaniensia Analecta*, Leuven.

OLZ — *Orientalistische Literaturzeitung*, Berlin.

OPBIAA — *Occasional Publications of the British Institute for Archaeology at Ankara*, London.

OxfEncANE — Meyers, E.M. (ed.) 1997, *Oxford Encyclopedia of Archaeology in the Near East*, New York/Oxford.

RlA — *Reallexikon der Assyriologie und Vorderasiatischen Archäologie*, Berlin.

SIMA — Studies in Mediterranean Archaeology, Gothenburg.

SMS — *Syro-Mesopotamian Studies*, Malibu.

StBoT — *Studien zu den Boğazköy-Texten*, Wiesbaden.

UAVA — Untersuchungen zur Assyriologie und vorderasiatischen Archäologie, Berlin/New York.

UF — *Ugarit-Forschungen*, Neukirchen-Vluyn/Kevelaer, since 1996: Münster.

WVDOG — *Wissenschaftliche Veröffentlichungen der Deutschen Orient-Gesellschaft*, Berlin.

UNTERSUCHUNGEN DER ZWEIGSTELLE KAIRO DES ÖSTERREICHISCHEN ARCHÄOLOGISCHEN INSTITUTS

Herausgegeben in Verbindung mit der Kommission für Ägypten und Levante der Österreichischen Akademie der Wissenschaften von MANFRED BIETAK

Band I	MANFRED BIETAK, *Tell el-Dab^ca II. Der Fundort im Rahmen einer archäologisch-geographischen Untersuchung über das ägyptische Ostdelta*. Wien 1975.
Band II	LABIB HABACHI, *Tell el-Dab^ca and Qantir I. The Site and its Connection with Avaris and Piramesse*. Aus dem Nachlaß herausgegeben von EVA MARIA ENGEL. Unter Mitarbeit von PETER JÁNOSI und CHRISTA MLINAR. Wien 2001.
Band III	JOACHIM BOESSNECK, *Tell el-Dab^ca III. Die Tierknochenfunde 1966–1969*. Wien 1976.
Band IV	MANFRED BIETAK und ELFRIEDE REISER-HASLAUER, *Das Grab des ^cAnch-Hor, Obersthofmeister der Gottesgemahlin Nitokris* (mit einem Beitrag von ERHART GRAEFE). Wien 1978.
Band V	MANFRED BIETAK und ELFRIEDE REISER-HASLAUER, *Das Grab des ^cAnch-Hor, Obersthofmeister der Gottesgemahlin Nitokris. Teil II* (mit Beiträgen von JOACHIM BOESSNECK, ANGELA VON DEN DRIESCH, JAN QAEGEBEUR, HELGA LIESE-KLEIBER und HELMUT SCHLICHTHERLE). Wien 1982.
Band VI	DIETHELM EIGNER, *Die monumentalen Grabbauten der Spätzeit in der Thebanischen Nekropole* (mit einem Beitrag von JOSEF DORNER). Wien 1984.
Band VII	MANFRED BIETAK, *Tell el-Dab^ca IV. Stratigraphie und Chronologie* (in Vorbereitung).
Band VIII	MANFRED BIETAK, unter Mitarbeit von CHRISTA MLINAR und ANGELA SCHWAB, *Tell el-Dab^ca V. Ein Friedhofsbezirk der Mittleren Bronzezeit mit Totentempel und Siedlungsschichten*. Wien 1991. Denkschriften der Gesamtakademie, Bd. 9.
Band IX	EIKE M. WINKLER und HARALD WILFLING, *Tell el-Dab^ca VI. Anthropologische Untersuchungen an den Skelettresten der Kampagnen 1966–69, 1975–80, 1985*. Wien 1991.
Band X	JOACHIM BOESSNECK und ANGELA VON DEN DRIESCH, *Tell el-Dab^ca VII. Tiere und historische Umwelt im Nordost-Delta im 2. Jahrtausend anhand der Knochenfunde der Ausgrabungen 1975–1986*. Wien 1992.
Band XI	KARL KROMER, *Nezlet Batran. Eine Mastaba aus dem Alten Reich bei Giseh (Ägypten). Österreichische Ausgrabungen 1981–1983*. Wien 1991.
Band XII	MANFRED BIETAK, JOSEF DORNER, HANS EGGER, JOACHIM BOESSNECK und URSULA THANHEISER, *Tell el-Dab^ca VIII. Interdisziplinäre Studien* (in Vorbereitung).
Band XIII	PETER JÁNOSI, *Die Pyramidenanlagen der Königinnen. Untersuchungen zu einem Grabtyp des Alten und Mittleren Reiches*. Wien 1996.
Band XIV	MANFRED BIETAK (Hrg.), *Haus und Palast im Alten Ägypten. Internationales Symposium 8. bis 11. April 1992 in Kairo*. Wien 1996.
Band XV	ERNST CZERNY, *Tell el-Dab^ca IX. Eine Plansiedlung des frühen Mittleren Reiches*. Wien 1999.
Band XVI	PERLA FUSCALDO, *Tell el-Dab^ca X. The Palace District of Avaris, The Pottery of the Hyksos Period and the New Kingdom (Areas H/III and H/VI), Part I. Locus 66*. Wien 2000.
Band XVII	SUSANNA CONSTANZE HEINZ, *Die Feldzugsdarstellungen des Neuen Reiches – Eine Bildanalyse*. Wien 2001.
Band XVIII	MANFRED BIETAK (Ed.), *Archaische Griechische Tempel und Altägypten, Internationales Kolloquium am 28. November 1997 im Institut für Ägyptologie der Universität Wien*. Mit Beiträgen von DIETER ARNOLD, ANTON BAMMER, ELISABETH GEBHARD, GERHARD HAENY, HERMANN KIENAST, NANNO MARINATOS, ERIK ØSTBY und ULRICH SINN, Wien 2001.
Band XIX	BETTINA BADER, *Tell el-Dab^ca XIII. Typologie und Chronologie der Mergel C-Ton Keramik. Materialien zum Binnenhandel des Mittleren Reiches und der zweiten Zwischenzeit*. Wien 2001.
Band XX	MANFRED BIETAK and MARIO SCHWARZ (Eds.), *Krieg und Sieg. Narrative Wanddarstellungen von Altägypten bis ins Mittelalter, Interdisziplinäres Kolloquium, Langenlois, Schloß Haindorf, 29.–30. Juli 1997*.

VERLAG DER ÖSTERREICHISCHEN AKADEMIE DER WISSENSCHAFTEN

Band XXI	Irmgard Hein und Peter Jánosi, *Tell el-Dab^ca XI, Areal A/V, Siedlungsrelikte der späten Hyksoszeit.* Mit Beiträgen von: K. Großschmidt, K. Kopetzky, L.C. Maguire, C. Mlinar, G. Philip, A. Tillmann, U. Thanheiser, E. Winkler†. Wien 2004.
in Druck	David Aston in collaboration with Manfred Bietak, and with the assistance of Bettina Bader, Irene Forstner-Müller and Robert Schiestl, *Tell el-Dab^ca XII. A Corpus of Late Middle Kingdom and Second Intermediate Period Pottery.* Part I. *Introduction and Pottery of the Late Middle Kingdom*; Part II. *Pottery of the Hyksos Period and Conclusions.*
in Druck	Nadia el-Shohoumi, *Der Tod im Leben, eine vergleichende Analyse Altägyptischer und rezenter Ägyptischer Totenbräuche. Eine phänomenologische Studie.*
in Druck	Peter Jánosi, *Giza in der 4. Dynastie. Die Baugeschichte und Belegung einer Nekropole des Alten Reiches, Band I, Die Mastabas der Kernfriedhöfe und die Felsgräber.*

BERICHTE DES ÖSTERREICHISCHEN NATIONALKOMITEES DER UNESCO-AKTION FÜR DIE RETTUNG DER NUBISCHEN ALTERTÜMER

Herausgegeben von der Ägypten und Levante der Österreichischen Akademie der Wissenschaften (Herausgeber ab Band VII: Manfred Bietak)

Band I	Manfred Bietak und Reinhold Engelmayer, *Eine frühdynastische Abri-Siedlung mit Felsbildern aus Sayala – Nubien.* Wien 1963. Österreichische Akademie der Wissenschaften, Phil.-hist. Klasse, Denkschriften, Bd. 82.
Band II	Reinhold Engelmayer, *Die Felsgravierungen im Distrikt Sayala – Nubien. Teil I: Die Schiffsdarstellungen.* Wien 1965. Denkschriften, Bd. 90.
Band III	Manfred Bietak, *Ausgrabungen in Sayala – Nubien 1961–1965. Denkmäler der C-Gruppe und der Pan-Gräber-Kultur* (mit Beiträgen von Kurt Bauer, Karl W. Butzer, Wilherlm Ehgartner und Johann Jungwirth). Wien 1966. Denkschriften, Bd. 92.
Band IV	Karl Kromer, *Römische Weinstuben in Sayala (Unternubien).* Wien 1967. Denkschriften, Bd. 95.
Band V	Manfred Bietak, *Studien zur Chronologie der nubischen C-Gruppe. Ein Beitrag zur Frühgeschichte Unternubiens zwischen 2200 und 1550 v. Chr.* Wien 1968. Denkschriften, Bd. 97.
Band VI	Fathi Afifi Bedawi, *Die römischen Gräberfelder von Sayala Nubien.* Wien 1976s. Denkschriften, Bd. 126.
Band VII	Eugen Strouhal und Johann Jungwirth, *Die anthropologische Untersuchung der C-Gruppen- und Pan-Gräber-Skelette aus Sayala, Ägyptisch-Nubien.* Wien 1984. Denkschriften, Bd. 176.
Band VIII	Manfred Bietak und Mario Schwarz, *Nag^c el-Scheima, eine befestigte christliche Siedlung, und andere christliche Denkmäler in Sayala – Nubien.* Wien 1987. Denkschriften, Bd. 191.
Band IX	Manfred Bietak und Mario Schwarz, *Nag^c el-Scheima. Teil II. Die Grabungsergebnisse aus der Sicht neuerer Forschungen.* Wien 1998. Denkschriften, Bd. 255.

In Vorbereitung:

Eugen Strouhal und Erich Neuwirth, *Die anthropologische Untersuchung der spätrömischen-frühbyzantinischen Skelette aus Sayala, Ägyptisch-Nubien.*

Eugen Strouhal und Erich Neuwirth, *Die anthropologische Untersuchung der christlichen Skelette aus Sayala, Ägyptisch-Nubien.*

CONTRIBUTIONS TO THE CHRONOLOGY OF THE EASTERN MEDITERRANEAN

Edited by MANFRED BIETAK and HERMANN HUNGER

Volume I	MANFRED BIETAK (Ed.), *The Synchronisation of Civilisations in the Eastern Mediterranean in the Second Millenium BC. Proceedings of an International Symposium at Schloß Haindorf, 15th–17th of November 1996 and at the Austrian Academy, Vienna, 11th–12th of May 1998*, Wien 2000.
Volume II	VASSOS KARAGEORGHIS (Ed.), *The White Slip Ware of Late Bronze Age Cyprus. Proceedings of an International Conference organized by the Anastasios G. Leventis Foundation, Nicosia, in Honour of Malcolm Wiener. Nicosia 29th–30th October 1998*, Wien 2001.
Volume III	MANFRED BIETAK (Ed.), *The Middle Bronze Age in the Levant. Proceedings of an International Conference on MB IIA Ceramic Material. Vienna, 24th–26th of January 2001.* Wien 2002.
Volume IV	MANFRED BIETAK (Ed.), *The Synchronisation of Civilisations in the Eastern Mediterranean in the Second Millennium BC. II: Proceedings of the SCIEM 2000 – EuroConference, Haindorf, 2nd of May–7th of May 2001.* Wien 2003.
Volume V	CELIA BERGOFFEN, *The Cypriot Bronze Age pottery from Sir Leonard Woolley's Excavations at Alalakh (Tell Atchana).* Wien 2004.
Volume VI	HERMANN HUNGER and REGINE PRUZSINSZKY (Eds.), *Mesopotamian Dark Age Revisited. Proceedings of an International Conference of SCIEM 2000, Vienna 8th–9th of November 2002.* Wien 2004.
forthcoming	MANFRED BIETAK and ERNST CZERNY (Eds.), *Scarabs of the Second Millennium BC from Egypt, Nubia, Crete, and the Levant: Chronological and Historical Implications.*
forthcoming	MANFRED BIETAK and ERNST CZERNY (Eds.), *The Bronze Age in the Lebanon. Studies on the Archaeology and Chronology of Lebanon, Syria, and Egypt.*
forthcoming	JACQUELINE PHILLIPS, *Aegyptiaca on the Island of Crete in their Chronological Context: A Critical Review.*

VERÖFFENTLICHUNGEN DER KOMMISSION FÜR ÄGYPEN UND LEVANTE DER ÖSTERREICHISCHEN AKADEMIE DER WISSENSCHAFTEN

Begründet von FRITZ SCHACHERMEYR †
Herausgegeben von MANFRED BIETAK

Band 1	GÜNTHER HÖLBL, *Ägyptisches Kulturgut auf den Inseln Malta und Gozo in phönikischer und punischer Zeit.* Wien 1989. Österreichische Akademie der Wissenschaften, Phil.-hist. KLasse, Sitzungsberichte, Bd. 538.
Band 2	ULRICH LUFT, *Die chronologische Fixierung des Mittleren Reiches nach dem Tempelarchiv von Illahun.* Wien 1992. Österreichische Akademie der Wissenschaften, Phil.-hist. KLasse, Sitzungsberichte, Bd. 598.
Band 3	PETER JÁNOSI, *Österreich vor den Pyramiden. Die Grabungen Hermann Junkers im Auftrag der Österreichischen Akademie der Wissenschaften in Wien bei der großen Pyramide in Giza.* Wien 1997. Österreichische Akademie der Wissenschaften, Phil.-hist. KLasse, Sitzungsberichte, Bd. 648.

VERLAG DER ÖSTERREICHISCHEN AKADEMIE DER WISSENSCHAFTEN